Mommy Burnout

Mommy Burnout

*How to Reclaim Your Life and Raise
Healthier Children in the Process*

DR. SHERYL ZIEGLER

DEY ST.
An Imprint of WILLIAM MORROW

HarperCollins books may be purchased for educational, business, or sales promotional use. For information, please email the Special Markets Department at SPsales@harpercollins.com.

FIRST EDITION

Designed by Michelle Crowe

Library of Congress Cataloging-in-Publication Data has been applied for.

ISBN 978-0-06-268368-7

18 19 20 21 22   LSC   10 9 8 7 6 5 4 3 2 1

*For all those who are yet to be parents, including my children,
Isabella, Hazen, and Hudson; may you learn from us
and
For all the mothers who bravely shared their stories with me*

Contents

Introduction

I have worked with children my entire professional life, so you might be wondering how it is that I am writing a book on mothers. Well, it turns out that when you work with children, you have to work with their parents to fully engage. For some therapists that is a challenge—but for me it is my passion. Early in my career, I came to understand that the New York City youth that I was counseling in upstate New York would be going back to the same home they came from after they completed the program. I realized that much of the work that we were doing would have little influence over them when back in the chaos and poverty they were coming from. When I was accepted into a doctoral program in Colorado, I knew I wanted to keep working to help children, but that I also wanted to understand the systems that affect those children—family systems, community systems, and employment systems. While gaining this understanding, I shifted my focus away from just children, to families. And as such, in the past fourteen years I have come to understand the plight of the American mother very well through my work. I have celebrated with, cried with, and mourned with thousands of mothers. I have experienced my own journey of motherhood in richer ways because of this connection to women, all that they endure, and how big they love.

I was born in Harlem, to a teenage immigrant single mother. As a young child, I lived on welfare and food stamps in New York City. I have experienced all levels of disadvantage. I have lived a middle-class life in upstate New York and I have lived an upper-middle-class life. I received higher education after being awarded a full scholarship from the Bill and Melinda Gates Foundation. My experiences have given me the comfort to relate to just about anyone, and I work every day to make good on the promise I made to myself and my scholarship funders: that I would pay forward the gifts I have been bestowed any way I can.

This book is one of my pay-it-forward projects. I have witnessed thousands of mothers in their battle to raise their children well. I have listened to countless women say that they feel they are the only ones going through certain challenges in their parenting or marriages. After hearing these stories for so long, I started feeling like I was carrying around a huge secret. And although much of my job entails keeping secrets, I felt like this was a secret worth sharing. In 1963, Betty Friedan wrote of "the problem that has no name" in her landmark book *The Feminine Mystique*. By 2010, I thought that my work had allowed me to create a set of universal truths about motherhood today. And, by examining these truths and acknowledging them, I wondered if there could be a shift in the motherhood landscape. By giving a name to Friedan's "problem" with no name, at least in the context of my work, could women's health and happiness improve? And ultimately would the lives of children improve? And hence, the problem, for me, became mommy burnout.

Let me rewind for a moment here. Throughout this time, I became a clinical director in a residential treatment center for kids, started a private practice, and tried to get pregnant to start my own family. And, I began to experience what I was observing in women. I couldn't get pregnant. I was commuting an hour each way on a busy highway to a high-stress job, was detached from my friends and family back in New York, and was newly married in Colorado. Just thinking about that time now brings me back to that space of stress, worry, and loneliness.

When a year had passed without getting pregnant, I sought out fertility treatment, resigned my position, went on a yoga retreat, and headed to Hawaii for a vacation with my husband. Lo and behold, I got pregnant with my daughter on that trip. At the time, when people told me, "See, you just needed to relax!" it took all my restraint not to snap at them. What were they talking about? I wanted this baby so badly I would have done just about anything, and they were suggesting that *I was the cause of my infertility*? No, I refused to accept that narrative. I didn't want that story filling up my baggage.

Fast forward to today: I have three children. My second, a son, was conceived in Costa Rica, and my third, another son, I didn't have to leave the country for! The third child was the only one I didn't have to "try hard" to get. With all of the knowledge I have gained from working with women, from tirelessly researching the impact of stress and from seeking out my own treatment and support, I have come to terms with the fact that stress did play a role in my ability to bring my babies into the world. That was a tough realization, because all I had ever wanted was to be a mother. But now I see that I was enveloped by stress, and thought I could power through it to get what I wanted. Now I know better.

I felt the urgency to write this book just about the time that I had my second child and my world turned upside down. All of a sudden, I felt like everything went into fast forward. What was a lovely, manageable life for my husband Steve and me, with one child and my beloved dog, living in a funky loft, turned into having to move into a "real" house and juggling more than ever. My kids were two years and three months apart, and I felt like I had two babies at home. I was potty training and nursing at the same time. And the feeling of being overwhelmed at home was combined with an increased level of visibility in my work. I started getting media requests to do news interviews in my area, and essentially became a go-to therapist for all child-related stories. While this was exciting, it was also exhausting. When you go on TV, you want to look your best. I still had baby weight to lose. I had to do my hair. I had to look relaxed and refreshed. None of which I felt at the time!

When I returned from maternity leave eleven weeks later, I found going to work much easier than being at home. I was now a mama of two and of course more evolved and enlightened—I had more to give my clients. I took in people's stories and viewed them through my new perspective. I began to see patterns of guilt, shame, regret, and doubt in mothers. I saw the experiences of motherhood in a deeper way than before, and was personally far more connected to the depth of their struggles. We were in the same place, and I could relate to my patients. This made me a better therapist.

I think the change in my life also made my work with children far more emotionally profound. I had a strong empathy pouring out of me for young patients. I struggled to hear their stories of being bullied, or of going through their parents' divorces, or of trauma and abuse. I needed to regain my center so that I could continue to best treat them. And eventually, giving support to their mothers became a way I could do just that. By naming the symphony of issues that made mothers feel stressed, isolated, depressed, and like failures "mommy burnout," and by working to provide a plan to help lift mothers out of this cycle, I could affect the lives of children in a broad way. I have transitioned through the stage of being a therapist and not being a mother to being a therapist who is now also a mother, and it has been through this transition that I have uncovered how serious burnout can be in motherhood.

This book has been seven years in the making. It is amazing to me how long it has taken, but in those years I have spoken to more women and men than I could ever count. And every time I got the same reaction: "You have to hurry up and write this book." I hope that I have done all those people justice, and that through reading real stories from real women and pairing that with my own experience and lots of research, you will learn and grow—and fight the mommy burnout.

I have learned and gotten more out of this project than I can describe. I learned about the profound impact of stress on our brains and bodies, and maybe most of all I learned that no matter who you are, how much money is in your bank account, where you live, and whether or not you work outside of the home, we all have a lot more in common than we think.

Mommy Burnout

Chapter 1

Why Am I So Overwhelmed?

What Mommy Burnout Looks Like

Sound Familiar?

- You have trouble falling asleep, or staying asleep.

- You lack energy throughout the day.

- You beat yourself up for parenting decisions and choices that you make.

- You reach for junk food too often, or go whole days without eating a real meal because you are just too busy.

- You wonder if you look forward to your glass or two of wine at night just a little too much.

- You pop painkillers daily because your head is pounding, your back aches, or your neck is in spasm.

- You get sick whenever the kids get sick, but for longer, and more severely.

- You have little to no interest in sex.

- You dodge your friends' phone calls, and just text instead because you don't have the energy for a conversation.

- You can't remember the last time you did something just for yourself.

- You feel like you're in a bad mood, or snap at your kids often.

- You double book, forget appointments, and overschedule yourself and your kids.

- Once in a while, you just sit alone and cry because you feel over-whelmed.

- You are tired ALL THE TIME.

If this looks like your life, this book was written for you. You are most likely suffering from mommy burnout.

Stacy was forty-four years old and married with three-year-old twin daughters when we started working together. She had struggled with fertility issues and finally gave birth to her girls when she was forty-one years old. When we met, Stacy had been married to her husband for seven years. Stacy had a college degree and had a successful career in graphic design before she resigned to raise her children full-time. Her husband worked and traveled often as a software salesperson.

Stacy initially called me to get "tips and strategies for raising toddler twins." It didn't take long for me to realize that something else was going on with her. Stacy was one of the first moms who came to see me for mommy burnout, although, at that time, I hadn't yet uncovered this condition. As I learned more and more about Stacy's day-to-day struggles—mainly, persistent feelings of being overwhelmed, exhaustion regardless of how much she slept, moodiness that made her feel out of control and guilty, and resentment toward her kids and husband—I realized that Stacy's mothering experience was far from unique. I was hearing similar stories from other clients as well.

From Stacy's story and the countless moms I have since spoken to—in my office, after parenting presentations I have given, or even while chatting with my friends—I have come to realize just how serious mommy burnout can be. Like Stacy, when most moms first come to see me, they have no idea that they have a real problem. They just feel overwhelmed. Or they assume that with a few new parenting strategies in their back pocket, their days will run more smoothly. Mommy burnout sneaks up on moms over time. Aside from being one of my first mommy burnout clients, Stacy's story is also significant because of how bad things got for her. By the time she sought out help, her mommy burnout had bled into all areas of her life.

Thirteen years ago Stacy blew into my office with snow-soaked sneakers and red-rimmed eyes. It was December, and Denver was freezing. She was late for her first session, so I suspected that once she arrived she'd be out of sorts. I knew only Stacy's basic information from our initial phone conversation: that she had a husband and young twin girls and that she hadn't been feeling like herself for some time. I was prepared to ask her more questions to get a better sense of her situation, as I do with all my clients, but Stacy didn't need any coaxing. She jumped right in.

"I need help," she blurted out as she quickly sloshed across my office and flopped down into a chair. Her eyes were already welling up with tears.

"What's going on?" I asked as I sat down across from her.

"I was rushing out of the house this morning and I couldn't find my boots," she explained. She unzipped her jacket and let it fall off her shoulders onto the chair behind her. "I'm always rushing. It's like I'm allergic to being on time. I don't know what my problem is. I wasn't always such a mess." She looked down for a moment. "Sorry I'm late to our first session."

I'd heard this from many of the women who came to see me. Making an appointment for themselves is a "luxury" since they are already spread so thin. They spend their days getting their kids dressed, fed, and out the door in the morning before they set off on their own errands or to their office. Their afternoons are a flurry of helping their kids with homework, shuttling them to various activities, getting dinner on the table, and getting the kids through their bedtime routines before finishing up their own work and finally collapsing into their beds at night. Those who are married barely have the time or energy to even have a real conversation with (as opposed to barking some orders at) their husbands. I know that by the time these moms make an appointment, they are desperate. They may feel like they have tried it all and nothing is working, their family is falling apart, or their kid is getting into some serious trouble.

As Stacy settled back into her chair, she patted the snowflakes from her short brown hair and began telling me about the drama from that morning. Her three-year-old twin daughters had gotten up early and thought it would be fun to give their dolls a bath. They went into the bathroom, turned on the tub, and bathed all their dolls, including the ones made of yarn. Stacy was startled awake at five thirty by the girls wailing over their ruined toys. "But that wasn't the worst part," she said. "They left the tub on! I almost broke my leg sliding across the bathroom floor."

When I asked where her husband was that morning, she explained that he was traveling for work. Stacy considered him lucky to be away, even if he was working. He got to sleep through the night, have room service deliver a warm breakfast up to him, and have a car service drive him to his meeting that "didn't have Cheerios crunching beneath his feet." Stacy was a little jealous that he got to spend his days talking to other adults. She questioned whether going back to work herself would make her feel like a "normal person" again.

Like many moms who stay at home with their young kids, Stacy described days spent picking up toys, reading the same stories over and over, and bracing herself through tantrums. Her patience was long gone and she had started snapping at her kids when they asked her to play with them. "I'm sure they'll end up in your office in a few years," she said with a sigh.

Before motherhood, Stacy had been a graphic designer. She told me that she had hated working for someone else and was happy to quit before she had the twins, but now she missed being out in the world. She longed for the days when she *did* something with her days, when she created something tangible. She felt like she was getting dumber every week because she really wasn't using her brain. But then she felt guilty about feeling that way because of all she and her husband went through just to have the girls.

Stacy had gotten married in her late thirties and then went through several rounds of fertility treatments before she finally got pregnant. Like many of the moms that I work with, she never expected that getting pregnant would be so difficult. The emotional and financial turmoil that infertility caused her was overwhelming. And like other women in her situation, she assumed that once she finally got pregnant and had her babies, all would be blissful. But what I find is that women who had challenges getting pregnant go through the same roller coaster of emotions following the birth as the moms who got pregnant easily. They can suffer from postpartum depression, they are just as exhausted, and they need breaks, too. The difference that I have observed, however, is that the moms who struggled with fertility can carry more guilt with these common post-baby feelings because they wanted their babies so badly and now feel like they have little right to complain.

I also struggled with fertility issues with my first baby. I knew that after an intense uterine fibroid surgery, I would not be able to conceive easily and that I had a 50 percent chance of miscarriage. It took over a year to get pregnant, and two rounds of interuterine insemination didn't work. I tried herbs, ovulation trackers, acupuncture, meditation, guided imagery, therapy, reducing my workload, headstands—you name it! The stress and grief that I felt that year is something that I will never forget. When I finally did get pregnant, I felt like I didn't have the right to complain about anything because I should just be grateful that I was pregnant, even though I was sick every day for the first nineteen weeks.

As with any new mom, the transition to motherhood was jarring for Stacy. *Sleepless nights. Round-the-clock feedings. Forgetting if she had brushed her teeth that morning.* Stacy's growing pains ultimately surged into full-blown postpartum depression. She took antidepressants for several months, but stopped when she felt that her symptoms were under control. She started sleeping better feeling happier and socializing more—until now.

Stacy recounted a story from the previous week when she hid from her kids. They were running around the house calling for her while she was crying in the shower. She just stood there, letting the water run all over her body, hoping that the twins would entertain themselves so she could get a few minutes of peace. Stacy knew what she was going through wasn't normal. She just didn't understand what the exact issue was. She hadn't taken her medication in about two years, but she had started to wonder if she needed it again. She was snapping at her kids. Rushing around all the time. And, she had started to treat her husband like her third child, which was having a negative effect on their relationship.

Stacy described her husband as a loving, caring man who traveled often for work. This kind of schedule created some tension, as she would get a routine down and then feel like just when she had a rhythm going, he would come back and "mess things up." She knew he was just trying to help and have fun with the girls when he was home, but it made Stacy crazy when he chased them around the house pretending to be a monster at bedtime. She felt like he was just making her job of getting them to sleep impossible. This is a common sentiment among the many mothers that I see whose partners travel frequently for work. They want their significant other around to help, but then when they are around, they feel like they just get in the way. Many of these women get annoyed answering questions about their schedule, where things are, what the kids are and aren't eating that week, and just when their husbands are up to speed, they leave again. It is easier when they are gone.

Stacy explained that she often just felt "off" and joked that she had some kind of delayed version of "baby brain." Since having kids, I can totally relate to this feeling. I've sometimes wondered if there was something wrong with me because I don't always feel rested after a long night's sleep and I sometimes get a serious afternoon lull around three o'clock. Sometimes I've felt like my brain is literally "off track." I've even sent my kids off to school without their lunches, having made them myself only minutes before they walked out the door. This, by the way, would create another errand for me to squeeze into my day, which frazzled me even more and made me late to whatever I had going on that morning. But baby brain isn't the cause of my fatigue and forget-fulness. And it wasn't at the root of Stacy's, either. Stacy's kids were three years old. She was about two years too late for baby brain.

After that first meeting, Stacy and I fell into a rhythm of weekly sessions. It was a bit unusual for me because, for the most part, I meet my mom clients when they bring their kids in for treatment. Especially at that time in my career, I was seeing mainly kids, or kids with their parents. I had only a few individual adult therapy sessions at this point. Stacy was one of my first clients who came to me to get support just for herself. She knew that it wasn't the three-year-old twins that needed to be in therapy, but she didn't understand what was going on with her, either. Stacy chose to see me because she assumed that I would give her some ideas on how to handle issues she was facing with her toddlers, and that would make her feel better. She, like the countless other moms I've seen in my practice, didn't realize that their issues weren't centered around parenting strategies. They need support for themselves.

Once my practice started growing, I realized that I was see-ing parents alone for half of my time. Mom after mom sat down in my office to talk about the same struggles. One mother I met with around this time spent her session comparing her children to stalkers. "Every time I turn around in my house, one of my kids is standing right there waiting for me. I can't get away from them," she said. Another client had recently shared that she had locked her kids out of the house because, in her words, "It was either them or me."

Before I had my own children, it was hard to imagine what would drive moms to these measures. Moms would tell me about putting hot sauce or soap in their kids' mouths for talking back; locking kids in their rooms or the garage because they wouldn't stay put for time-out; leaving kids home alone while they took a drive because they were afraid they would lose it on their children; taking doors off of hinges; aggressively force-feeding picky eaters; threatening to call the police to take kids away for bad behavior; shaming their child on social media by videotaping their meltdowns; and stopping their cars, kicking kids out, and driving away. The list goes on and on. Once I did have kids and my brood became more challenging, I understood how moms could reach this breaking point.

When my older son was five years old, he went through a stage where he would not stay buckled in his booster seat while we were in the car. Without the five-point restraint of a car seat, he could just unbuckle himself whenever he was protesting something or refusing to go somewhere. I found myself on edge in the car with him. I was constantly in a place of trying to decide if I should just drive with him unbuckled and having a full-blown tantrum in the backseat or pull over and try to reason with him. Eventually, I started threatening that I was going to drive to the police station and have the police officer explain to him why seat belts are so important. I'd never imagined that I would one day need to threaten my five-year-old with going to talk to a police officer, but there I was with my five-, seven-, and two-year-olds in the backseat watching my every move. Just like me, the moms I was talking to were loving, well-meaning, and involved with their kids . . . and they were stressed to the max. They had just had it.

Also, these women believed that they were the only ones struggling—something I knew to be untrue. I remember one client, Janie, telling me, "I don't know any other mom who feels this crappy all the time. They all seem so together, so happy and so calm. When someone does admit that her life is overwhelming, she just laughs it off." She smoothed her blond hair behind her ears.

"Have you ever told any of your friends about how *you're* feeling?" I asked her. "Maybe that would open the door for them to tell you what's really going on with them."

"Of course not," she said with wide eyes. "How are you supposed to tell someone else that you daydream about locking yourself in your bedroom alone for the day without sounding like a complete nut?"

I knew all these moms were experiencing the same issue, but at that point, I hadn't put a name to it yet. Mommy burnout was just a collection of stories from the women I met with. It was simply a handful of symptoms driving moms to their beds in the middle of the day, or making them think that frantically racing around their neighborhoods in search of the *unicorn* of all birthday cupcakes for their kid's classroom (gluten-free/dairy-free/sugar-free/peanut-free and still great-tasting) was necessary, or causing them to snap at their well-meaning husbands for riling the kids up at bedtime.

Over the last thirteen years, I have sat through session after session with moms in my own practice, read through countless mommy blogs and articles, and even laughed through a movie about moms behaving "badly" because they needed a break from their day-to-day lives. And in that time, I have come to realize that we are all pushing ourselves to the brink, creating a level of mental and physical exhaustion that often overwhelms us. Thus, a new kind of burnout, "mommy burnout," was born.

Look at Stacy. She was wiped out, physically and emotionally. She questioned the purpose and meaning behind how she spent her days. And although she would never have admitted this to anyone but me (her paid therapist), she resented her kids for snuffing out her freedom. Stacy could no longer come and go as she pleased. She had to negotiate Saturday mornings with her husband so she could work out or go shopping alone at Target. She literally had no time for herself. Grays were always peeking through her hair color, her nails were perpetually chipped and uneven, most of her shirts were stained or worn thin, and she hadn't seen her own doctor for an annual checkup in years. She often talked about the "good old days" when she could go to the bathroom by herself. Stacy loved her children more than anything, but felt guilty because they did not completely fulfill her. Her brain felt like mush and she always felt "on." The only time she felt like she could breathe was when they were napping. She wished she could nap, too, but something always needed to be done. I've heard people who were burned out from their jobs complain about their work and their bosses the exact same way— saying that their jobs didn't fulfill them, that their bosses killed their creativity, that they were slaves to their email at all hours of the day.

When you think about it, many moms function as the COO of their family. Does "If it weren't for me, nothing would get done at my house" sound familiar? You could argue that for moms, their home is their office, metaphorically—for stay-at-home moms *and* moms who work outside of the home. Unlike workers who can quit the jobs they hate, moms, excluding the most dramatic of circumstances, will not leave their kids. As a mom, you can't just go get a new "job." So, what happens next, when you are admittedly suffering from mommy burnout, but trapped?

A few weeks into our sessions, Stacy mentioned missing her friends back home. She had moved to Denver eighteen years ago after falling in love with Colorado during a ski vacation with her then boyfriend. She had grown up with these other girls like they were sisters. There were four of them and they all lived in the same neighborhood. They spent every afternoon together and told each other everything.

With a few questions, I learned that Stacy hadn't seen them in almost two years. These friends still lived around the town where they grew up. But with Stacy's husband's travel schedule, it was just too hard for her to get away. She spoke to them when she could, but it was getting harder and harder to connect. They all had young kids and were all always running around.

Stacy went on to tell me that while she worked at an office, she had great "work friends." They would do happy hours, ski on weekends, and keep up with each other's lives. Once she came up against her fertility issues, though, she began to retreat. She didn't feel comfortable sharing everything she was going through. She told a few coworkers that she was trying to get pregnant, but after several months with nothing but negative pregnancy tests, she stopped talking about it and her friends stopped asking. After the baby shower and the initial newborn baby excitement, they just all drifted apart from one another.

I often see this period as a common transition point. When a woman leaves her job to stay home with her kids, she usually loses touch with friends from the office. It's a significant loss socially, but (in reflection), moms will say that they were too busy and tired to maintain those friendships anyway. It is at about this time that they realize they are in a different stage of life and need new friends—"mommy friends," as I refer to them. I use that term often, because that is the common denominator in which these friendships are established. They may be moms of your kid's friends, a co-room parent, or a neighbor who has the same aged kids as you do. Outside of you both being moms, you may not have much in common, but that's all you really need to form these kinds of friendships. I see some moms shun mommy friends because they feel like they don't have enough in common to have any kind of connection, but, really, connecting over the experience of motherhood is enough. And more than being enough, it really is necessary for their emotional health.

Stacy had met some other moms at the music class that she took her girls to on Tuesday and Thursday mornings, but she didn't feel particularly close with them. She just didn't feel like she clicked with this group of women. They were all nice enough, and she would sometimes join them for an early lunch after class, but the last time she did that was over a month ago. Going out alone at night was challenging, since babysitters are so expensive and her girls would cry the whole time she was away from them. Stacy felt comfortable going out only if her husband could watch the kids, but that was rarely because he was so often away—and, when he was home she felt guilty leaving, because she believed she should be spending time with him. "I feel like I'm chained to my house," she told me.

Stacy was open to making friends and meeting up for a meal or coffee, but it wasn't her priority. And with the twins, she just found social obligations too difficult. It was hard for her to talk with the girls around. They would constantly interrupt her, so she felt it was easier to just not go. While Stacy was telling me this, I could picture the scene: a couple of moms outnumbered by kids, trying to maintain a sense of calm at Starbucks. I understood her struggle, but I also knew that she needed those connections.

As Stacy told me about her friends (or lack thereof), I thought back to a UCLA study that was published in 2000. This study focused on the difference between how men and women react to stress. The researchers found that both sexes experience the initial fight-or-flight-or-freeze response to stressors, and the release of various hormones, including oxytocin. You feel the effects of oxytocin, or the "feel-good" hormone, while breastfeeding and during orgasm, and it also helps to counteract stress. Yes, your body pumps out oxytocin to help you combat stressful situations and, in fact, women reap this benefit even more than men. Let me explain.

The UCLA study noted that women feel the effects of oxytocin more strongly. Estrogen, it seems, heightens the effects, while testosterone dampens them. These researchers also uncovered that this greater appreciation of oxytocin nudges women to take care of their children and reach out for support from other females in times of stress. Scientists refer to this instinct as the "tend and befriend" response. In primitive times, these behaviors kept the females and their kids alive by prompting moms to calm and quiet their children and whisk them away from danger. With a strong female network, they had a group to blend into and other moms to stand with them when threatened. In a 2008 article in *Monitor on Psychology* for the American Psychological Association about the role of oxytocin in stressful situations, social psychologist and lead author on the UCLA study, Shelley E. Taylor, PhD, further explained, "When it is operating during times of low stress, oxytocin physiologically rewards those who maintain good social bonds with feelings of well-being. But when it comes on board during times of high social stress or pain, it may 'lead people to seek out more and better social contacts.'"

In my practice, I have observed that today's moms have fewer close and intimate friendships than in the past, which means that they have few people to reach out to when their toddlers have been hanging on them for the last eight hours straight or their teenager has lost her phone again. They have few if any outlets to calm their stress. Still, you *must* scratch this biological itch. To compensate, I theorize, many moms direct their oxytocin-created urges into "over-tending" to their kids and "under-befriending" with their girlfriends. Women experiencing mommy burnout tend to have imbalanced reactions to their natural stress response.

Stacy had mentioned a few instances when "scary mommy," as she referred to herself during her over-tending moments, emerged. One time, a little boy shoved her daughter on the playground and Stacy started screaming at him. "I probably should have just spoken to his mom, but I couldn't control myself," she explained. "The little boy actually ran away from me." Another time, Stacy learned from her daughters that another little girl from class had hosted a tea party and didn't invite them. Stacy was beside herself wondering what she or her daughters could have done to be excluded. It bothered her so much that she called the mom the next day to find out what happened. "It turns out that we hadn't been excluded," Stacy told me as she spun her wedding band around her finger. "The mom said that her daughter is going through some phase where she makes up stories all the time. There hadn't been any party."

I hear examples of this kind of over-tending daily in my practice—for both very young and older children. One story I hear repeatedly involves parents co-sleeping with their kids. I had one patient who slept on the floor of her twelve-year-old son's room every night. "If she leaves his room in the middle of the night, he wakes up and comes into our bed," the father told me during one session. Variations of this story come up constantly in my office. Nighttime room sharing (by default) with their kids is today's mom's dirty little secret, but so many moms do it. In my practice, one of the top five issues I deal with is getting kids out of their parents' bedrooms and sleeping in their own rooms.

This over-tending does not address the true issues at hand. For example, if your child is older than ten and you're still sleeping in his or her room, there's probably something else going on with your child that you feel bad about. Maybe your child doesn't have many friends. Maybe your child has anxiety. But sleeping on your kid's floor doesn't lead to a long-term solution. Over-tending never does. I understand the need for these quick fixes sometimes, but what starts off as "just a few times" easily turns into weeks and months. And it doesn't make you feel better, either. It doesn't quash your stress; it only exacerbates it.

As Stacy continued to spiral out of control, her girls were pulled into her storm. She would snap at them if they asked for a second story at bedtime. She would paint with them for two minutes before making up an excuse to leave the room. When it was Stacy's turn to bring snacks in for the girls' music class, she forgot. "The other kids gave me the stink eye," she told me. "It was so embarrassing." Stacy's girls began having more tantrums and fighting bedtime.

Stacy's daughters were still young, so they did not understand how their mother's situation was impacting them. But with older kids, they do *get it*. They understand when their friends leave on the bus for a class trip and they are left behind at school because their mom never sent their permission slip back. They feel embarrassed when they show up late to a school event because their mom never read the email. Feeling left out or "different from" is a major source of stress for children. Not to mention the overall feeling of uneasiness in the home.

Snapping at your kids only makes you and your children feel

worse. And while we all do it from time to time, it's important to remember that stress begets stress. Kids who are under persistent stress, like their moms, are more likely to suffer from anxiety, regular tantrums, sleep troubles, and even physical pain, from bellyaches to headaches. As kids buckle under this unspoken pressure, their mom's job gets even harder.

Rushing, which seems to be the baseline speed for moms today, can also create issues. Stacy recounted a story where she was trying to rush the girls out the door so they wouldn't be (too) late for their dentist appointment and her kids just stood still, frozen and staring at her. Stacy didn't consider that her girls felt the negative impact of her rushing just as much as she did. The physical effects of rushing on your body—the racing heart, the jumbled-feeling brain, the shallow breathing—kids also feel. "I'm a shitty mom," Stacy said after we discussed this.

"You're not a shitty mom," I told her. "Just add a few extra minutes onto the time you need to get ready so you can slow down." Moms can usually predict how their child is going to respond to certain situations like getting ready for school in the morning, bath time, bedtime, and sitting down with the family for dinner. To avoid the same upsets every day, see if you can proactively figure out a few solutions to prevent the problems before they begin. I know this might take some time to do (time that you don't *really* have!), but I have seen this make a huge difference in moms' lives and in their kids' lives, too. After Stacy realized how much smoother it was to get the girls out the door when she started getting them ready earlier, she found other times during the day when she could also be proactive, especially around bedtime. As she fell into new routines, and worked with her husband to maintain them when he was home, she felt more in control of her days and felt better about herself as a mom.

As the months wore on, Stacy continued to experience successes and also some setbacks. Therapy is often like that. We have a saying that goes, *it usually gets worse before it gets better.* It's not uncommon to experience dips in your progress as you move forward. Recovery is not always a straight line.

Also, once we start peeling back the layers in therapy and breaking down the walls that you've built to "protect yourself," it feels scary. Therapy can feel good for some time, but then there is usually a period of feeling vulnerable and exposed. Maybe you feel like you should be intimate with your partner, but you don't want to. Or you should be more patient with your kids, but you can't stop snapping at them. It can feel uncomfortable to admit these things, even to your therapist. Many moms feel a lot of shame and so they hold back and retreat, both in therapy and in their lives.

Over our first year working together, Stacy sometimes skipped going to the music classes and returning phone calls from the moms she had met there. She sometimes connected with her old friends on the phone, but not on a regular basis. Her house grew less tidy on the weeks her husband traveled. "What's the point in putting all the toys away every night when these kids are just going to pull them back out in the morning?" She relied on takeout more nights than she was comfortable admitting to feed herself and her family. With her husband out of town and no one around to notice what was happening behind her closed doors, no one knew how much Stacy was struggling.

"I take a two-hour nap every afternoon," she practically whispered to me during one session. "I set the girls up with an iPad in my bedroom and I go to sleep. I just can't get out from under this fatigue." Mommy burnout stems from chronic stress, which impacts you both physically and emotionally and wears you down. You just never get a break; there are no pauses to your discomfort, which is exhausting.

When her husband was in town, Stacy definitely had more energy and motivation. She could see that his travel schedule, though taxing, did make her excited about seeing him return, which was usually Thursday nights. However, during a week that he was in town, her nit-picking escalated into a full-blown fight, admittedly instigated by her. One night, her husband casually asked if she was okay because she had forgotten to pick up the dry cleaning for the third day in a row, and she blew up at him. This was out of character for her, as their relationship before kids had been filled with fun and travel with her "best friend." They hardly ever fought in the early days of their relationship. Stacy had also stopped having sex with her husband. "I fall asleep with one of the kids most nights to avoid him." Her lips drooped downward. "I'm just too tired and stressed out."

If I had a dollar for every time a mom tried to explain away her mommy burnout with the phrase "stressed out," I could stop working. Yes, many moms, and certainly the moms that I see, are stressed out. But it's not just stress that's the problem. It's that you can't ever turn your stress off. Let me explain.

Acute stress, which is the stress that most people think of, is confined to a specific experience and it has an end. Think about an upcoming work project, planning for your daughter's birthday party, or preparing your home for your in-laws to visit. Some of these things might be thrilling, others might be scary, but they are all stressful to some degree. To combat the stress, you'll fall back into one of three buckets of stress responses—fight, flight, or freeze.

If you're a fighter, you will most likely lash out at people, become aggressive, and pick fights. If you are more prone to the "flight" stress response, you will zone out or physically leave the stressful situation. If you "freeze," you will experience a sudden rush of feeling overwhelmed and freeze up, physically and/or emotionally. A cascade of hormones such as adrenaline and cortisol will automatically push you to these stress responses and help you to maintain them. You may notice that your heart rate increases, you get a sudden burst of energy, or you may even vomit. These reactions are your stress response kicking into gear and preparing your body to respond.

Our bodies are designed to handle stress this way to save our lives. And it works. Back when we were running from saber-toothed tigers all the way to dodging a sketchy-looking guy in a dark alley today, the whole purpose of our stress response has been to keep us alive. We even have a system, the parasympathetic nervous system, whose job is to halt the stress response and calm your body when you are no longer in danger. The parasympathetic nervous system helps to slow your heart rate and gets your gut moving normally again.

Yet, when this same stress response is triggered in non-life-threatening situations it can wreak havoc in your body. Your body responds the same way, causing you to become enraged because a red light is taking too long to turn green or to bolt from the room when your toddler starts melting down. In each case, you experience a fight-or-flight-or-freeze response and all the physical costs, even though these frustrations pose no real threat to your life.

What's Your Stress Style?

We all have different stress styles. Some of us fight. Some of us flee. And some of us freeze. And, chances are, your stress style has changed over the years and depending on the circumstances. Most likely, though, you probably have one or two styles that you fall into most often. Answer the questions below to figure out which styles describe you best. Then we'll walk through how to combat each one.

1. **Your toddler is taking forever to get into the car and you have a meeting in ten minutes. You:**

   a. Yell at your toddler and shove him into his car seat.

   b. Walk away and tell your toddler that you're just going to leave without him.

   c. Go through the motions while you are basically checked out. If your child is talking to you, you might be hearing what he is saying (he may even be telling you that he is missing a glove or forgot his lunch in the house), but you just hear noise.

2. **You husband is late coming home from work again and the kids are screaming that they are hungry for dinner. You:**

   a. Snap at your husband and shut down his excuses when he arrives.

   b. Make some mac 'n cheese and sit your kids in front of the TV.

   c. Let your kids fend for themselves and decide not to mention anything to your husband.

3. Your boss emails you that your proposal needs to be done by Friday, but you have a packed week already. You:

    a. Fire off an email with all the reasons why this can't be done in this time frame.

    b. Ignore the email for the rest of the day.

    c. Feel overwhelmed and unsure what to do next. Eventually, you do respond to your boss.

If you had two or more "a" responses, you are a "fighter."

Common "fight" reactions to stress include: You become angry, irritable, and agitated.

Your anti-stress diet can include: Activities that calm your central nervous system down, such as deep breathing, guided imagery, or restorative yoga, as well as confiding in a close friend.

How this style impacts your kids: It models for your kids to act on their already impulsive thoughts and hinders their ability to learn the value of stopping and thinking before acting. They, too, might become reactive in the face of stress.

If you had two or more "b" responses, you "take flight."

Common "flight" reactions to stress include: You become depressed, and isolate yourself. You may check out by checking into social media more than usual, watching television, or putting headphones on to tune out the world around you. Some women physically leave by running out or taking a drive, but more commonly mentally flee their problems.

Your anti-stress diet can include: Activities to wake up your nervous system, such as massage, walking, or jogging outside in nature. You are likely less of a talker when under stress, but you still need to express your feelings. Try journaling as a means to communicate.

How this style impacts your kids: Your kids may struggle to express themselves. They may seem shut down and withdrawn and not able to identify their feelings well. They may also learn poor coping skills in difficult moments.

If you had two or more "c" responses, you "freeze."

Common "freeze" reactions to stress include: In a crisis, you freeze up, feel stuck, or can't seem to move.

Your anti-stress diet can include: Activities that engage both your arms and legs to "rev up" your nervous system. Consider physical activities like running, dancing, or swimming and mindfulness activities like imagery to activate your brain and get you in touch with the present situation.

How this style impacts your kids: Kids of these types of moms may not know what to do when stress arises. They will simply stare at you when you ask them to do things or shut down and won't answer questions. They won't fight and they won't leave; they will just stare and be unresponsive.

Stacy's stressors—new babies, sleepless nights, her husband's travel, lots of running around for errands with the kids—were acute. In time, her tension persisted beyond each incident until she was always stressed. "I feel like there's no end in sight," she would say to me. Stacy's baseline stress levels had inched themselves up to a point where even during normal, everyday situations when she wasn't in "danger," she would respond. This is when her mommy burnout took hold.

With mommy burnout, tension persists beyond the initial stressful event until you're just frazzled. Chronic stress is typically associated with extreme events that are ongoing, like spousal abuse, caring for a sick family member, or living in extreme poverty. What I've learned with my clients is that they are experiencing the same persistent tension. And like their chronic stress counterparts, their bodies are also wearing down.

Several months into our sessions, Stacy went a few weeks missing appointments. "Just found my car keys, won't be there, will be too late" she emailed me one morning. "I'm so sorry," she confessed to my voicemail another day. "I forgot about our session." The next time I saw her, I asked her about this.

"I just couldn't keep anything straight in my head," she told me. She recounted a story of paying for some groceries a few weeks before and then walking out and driving home with the bags still at the store. Another morning, she had glared at her husband for eating the last two slices of bread for breakfast. In response, he pulled a bag of English muffins out of the fridge, placed them on the counter, and went off to work without saying another word to her.

Stacy carried every frustrating situation around with her, accumulating and building on them every day until she was buried. When you're chronically stressed, your brain suffers. Your hippocampus will shrink and not function as well, which may also lead to memory problems, difficulty learning new things, and even more poor stress control. Your prefrontal cortex may also get smaller and become underactive. Has your judgment become questionable? Do you have trouble calming yourself down? This could be why.

Leaving your cortisol switch "on" also flips your amygdala into overdrive, which is like keeping your finger firmly pushed down on the fight-or-flight-or-freeze button in your brain. Like Stacy, you may feel anxious, on edge, and hypervigilant, even when there is no threat to your safety.

Acute Stress to Chronic Stress in Moms Can Evolve from:

- Headache to chronic migraine
- Stomachache to IBS
- Overeating to obesity
- Eating comfort foods to bingeing alone
- Flirting to having an affair
- Irritability to rage
- Verbal aggression to physical aggression
- Infrequent sex to no sex
- Declining some social events to avoiding all social events
- Masking details of your life to overtly lying

- Spending limited time with friends to only connecting through technology

- A few bad nights of sleep to insomnia

- Finding daily life demanding to finding it overwhelming

- Sadness to depression

- Worry to anxiety

- Forgetfulness to memory impairment

In the fall, Stacy's kids started preschool. Like many kids on their first day, one of Stacy's twins got upset when it was time for her mom to leave. She wailed and clung to her thigh. "Don't leave me, Mommy!" her daughter screamed. Stacy had mixed emotions about her daughters starting school. She was heartbroken to see her child so upset, but she was ready to have some time to herself. I considered Stacy's mixed emotions progress, as only a few months earlier, she would have been numb to this whole situation.

But when Stacy came to see me later that morning, she was upset. "I've been swallowed up whole by motherhood. I'm nothing like the woman I was before I had kids. I used to get dressed up, put on a little makeup, go out with friends, have fun. I *used* to have sex," she sniffled. "I never thought my life would be like this. I miss the old me. I've lost my whole identity to my kids. I'll do anything to just feel happy again." Stacy needed to find a way out of her mommy burnout, for her own sake and the sake of her kids and her husband.

This was a turning point for Stacy. She was now seeing what needed to change in her life. She recognized that she needed to make time for herself if she was going to get better. Not only did she get the much-needed break by having the girls in preschool three half days a week, but she needed to discover how to take care of herself during those mornings alone. Stacy and I spent some time brainstorming activities that she could do while the girls were in school that would ease her stress and feed her energy. She ultimately decided to meet one of her mommy friends from music class for coffee once a month to talk out whatever issues they were both facing with their kids at that time. She joined a spin class once a week that gave her an opportunity to physically work off her extra stress, and she even started a volunteer graphic design project at her kids' preschool. She realized how much she had missed her creative work and interacting with other adults on these kinds of projects.

Over the next several years, I worked to fully identify mommy burnout, to help distinguish it from simply feeling stressed and other emotional issues. I now use an informal set of criteria that I've created that's grounded in the Maslach Burnout Inventory (MBI), a system used to measure employee burnout. I have revised and added criteria to the MBI based on my own experience with moms and their families. When I'm sitting face-to-face with a mom who's telling me about how stressed out she is or the baby brain she's experiencing with her eight- and ten-year-old kids, I'm listening for her level of emotional and physical exhaustion, resentment toward her children and spouse, feelings of failure, whether she still has hobbies and passions of her own, and whether she can ever turn her stress off.

As I mentioned earlier in this chapter, recovery isn't always a straight line. Though you will be moving forward in your recovery,

Do You Have Mommy Burnout?

Here are questions I would ask a client to discern whether she has mommy burnout and, if so, to what degree. Choose the answer that most sounds like you:

1. **After a few hours away from your home, you are pulling into your neighborhood and you know that your kids are home. You:**

   a. Feel happy to go home and see your kids. When you step inside, you greet everyone with hugs and ask about their day.

   b. Pull over to check your phone one more time to see if there are any texts, calls, or emails that you can respond to before going home. You take a deep breath before stepping into your house and try to remain calm as you greet your kids.

   c. Take the long way home. A sense of dread fills you as you approach your house. You know that once you open that door, you will be flooded with homework that you have to help with, a dinner that must be made, and lots of wrangling to get your kids to bed.

2. **When you wake up in the morning, you:**

   a. Feel rested and even energetic.

   b. Hit snooze a few times and wish you could get one more hour of sleep.

   c. Plan when you can sneak back into bed and take a nap.

3. When you get a call from the school that your child just vomited:

   a. Your first reaction is to drop everything and go pick her up. You wonder if you should call the doctor immediately.

   b. You ask the school nurse if she can keep your kid there for a little while longer so you can finish what you were doing. You need just a little more time before you're back on mommy duty.

   c. You get annoyed at your child for ruining your day. You think, *Why couldn't she just wait until the end of the day to get sick?*

4. You bump into another mom whose kid just made some elite sports team. You:

   a. Feel happy for them and think, *They really deserve it. They worked hard.*

   b. Feel happy for them, but also worry that your kid's not progressing enough.

   c. Feel like a failure and think that you should have sent your kid to an extra sports camp last summer.

5. When you reflect on your stress, would you say that you:

   a. Occasionally feel stressed, but taking a few deep breaths or going for a walk usually helps.

   b. Often feel stressed, reaching for a glass of wine or diving into social media to calm you.

   c. Always feel stressed and nothing helps.

6. Think about your hobbies and how you spend your time. Would you say that you:

    a. Do activities that you love (like tennis or jogging) and feel lucky that you get to do them with your friends.

    b. Try to keep up with your hobbies, but sometimes you just have no time.

    c. Think, *who has time for that stuff?*

Results

- If you answered "a" to four or more of these questions, then you are managing your stress well and I wouldn't diagnose mommy burnout.

- If you answered "b" to four or more of these questions, then you are riding along the low-to-moderate range of mommy burnout. It would be a good idea to get a handle on your stress now.

- If you answered "c" to four or more of these questions, then you may be experiencing the more severe side of mommy burnout and might want to get help or find ways to alleviate your stress before you experience permanent effects.

you may still experience some dips along the way. Some old feelings may resurface, but this doesn't mean that all your progress has been wasted. After weeks of making progress and starting to feel some glimpses of the "old Stacy" return, I immediately understood that she had encountered a dip in her progress when Stacy came into my office questioning whether she should go back on medication, return to work, or plan a weekend away by herself. I asked her what had prompted these questions.

Stacy had been folding laundry in the basement the week before while her girls were in their room playing. She could hear them giggling and laughing, and was relieved that they could finally occupy themselves while she got some stuff done around the house.

Then she heard a thud. And screaming. "The bad kind," she explained. "When you know that something is wrong." One of the girls had fallen off their bed while they were playing. "Mommy! Help me! Help me!" her daughter called out to her. She could hear the tiny patter of the other girl's feet across the floor. Instead of immediately running up the stairs to her daughter, Stacy folded another few pieces of laundry as she felt her energy drain from her body. Finally, she trudged up the stairs and could only think to herself, *Mommy needs help, too.*

I knew that Stacy *could* get through her mommy burnout, that she would fully recover. She had already made so much progress and was seeing things change in her life. Her energy levels were slowly rising and her moods were evening out. She was taking better care of herself and communicating more with her husband. She just needed more time to work on bigger-picture issues like building a support network of friends she could lean on and making meaning of her life within this new stage of womanhood. This dip in her progress simply meant that we had more work to do.

Identify Your Mommy Burnout and Ease Your Sense of Being Overwhelmed

Identify your stress style. Are you primarily a fighter, a fleer, or a freezer? When you know your stress style, you can better identify when you're stressed and when to act to alleviate it. Your physical health and sanity relies on keeping single stressful events from turning into chronic stress.

Be proactive to prevent stress before it starts. Whether you need to run, meditate, or take a painting class, know what works for you. And, more importantly, do what works consistently.

Compartmentalize your life. Create boundaries. Although your home life may bleed into your work time and vice versa, set time boundaries for yourself so you're not doing everything at the same time, all the time. This means you may take an hour at your desk to schedule upcoming appointments for yourself and your kids before turning your attention back to work. At home, you may designate an hour or two for work after dinner, before spending time with your family. If you're an at-home mom, designate "mommy time" to break up your days.

Manage your time. Rushing around all the time only increases your tension (and your kids' stress!). Plan proactively. If you know you need to walk out the door at eight thirty in the morning, start getting your kids ready to leave thirty minutes earlier than you might think necessary. You may be surprised to learn that by so doing, you have a few extra free hours a week. Use that time for yourself.

Get some perspective. The way we perceive everyday frustrations has a lot to do with how we manage our stress. Are you someone who often blames others for stressful situations? Do you make excuses as to why you're not happy? The next time you feel your stress rising, take note of how you are looking at the situation and see if you can reframe it in a more positive light. Strive to find the positives in any given situation. Studies indicate that optimists manage stress better.

Take steps to manage aspects of your life that bring you down. Many people feel trapped in their current situations, but you probably have more control over your life than you think. Take a good look at *where* you work, *where* you live, *how much* money you *make* or *spend*, *what* you eat, and *how* you parent your kids—chances are good that some of these circumstances can be tweaked to make a difference to your everyday experience.

Add nature into your daily life. Take a walk outside, go for an outdoor swim, ride your bike, or read a book in a park. Nature is inherently calming.

Tend, but don't over-tend, to your kids. It's good to be there for your kids, but know when to step away. Let your children try to work out their problems on their own and then offer help only if they still need it.

Connect with other women. This is one of the most important things you can do. As we learned from the UCLA study, your body craves female friendship when you are tense. The more you deny yourself these bonds, the worse your mommy burnout will become. Find women you can talk to, vent to, and laugh with.

BONUS EXERCISE

Connecting with your kids is actually a great way to recharge your energy. Take a few minutes to brainstorm some activities you can do with each of your kids alone, so this will be one-on-one time for you and each child. One idea to get you started is to involve your child in something you enjoy doing (opposed to what your kid wants to do), such as gardening or knitting or even cooking a favorite meal. Another idea is having your child read a book to you.

Chapter 2

Didn't I Used to Have Friends?

The Connection Between Mommy Burnout and Isolation

Sound Familiar?

Moms that I see usually don't realize how important friends, of all kinds and degrees of closeness, are to their health and stability. In addition, they aren't aware of the unhealthy ways they seek out connection. Skim through this list and see if any of these sound like you. Do you:

- Get frustrated when your spouse gets bored with your conversations about your argument with your sister, or what outfit you should wear to a dinner party over the weekend?

- Peruse Facebook and social media for several hours every day (even if that's split up throughout the day) to "catch up" on what's going on in your friends' lives?

- Share way too much personal information—like a fight you had with your boss, that you are a little short on money that month, and even your frustration that your spouse doesn't help out enough around the house—with your children?

- Feel like you need therapy just to be heard, or continue to go to your therapist because it feels good to talk for an hour—even if you believe the treatment is no longer valuable?

- Feel like your friends don't "get you" anymore?

- Talk a lot about characters in your favorite television shows and what's going on in "their lives"?

- Believe that everyone else's marriage, children, and financial situation are better than yours, so you stop talking about these topics in an honest way?

- Not initiate sex because you no longer feel any intimacy with your husband?

- Just send links to articles or videos to your friends instead of actually talking to them, in the hopes that they will understand how you are feeling?

- Find that you no longer have any real friends beyond casual acquaintances?

Amy was thirty-four years old and married with two kids, an eight-year-old daughter and ten-year-old son, when we met. Amy had her first child at twenty-four. She'd finished two years of college, but then decided it wasn't for her and never graduated. She had worked as an office administrator by day while her then boyfriend finished up school to become an engineer, but left work soon after she had her first child. She had been married twelve years by the time I saw her.

Amy initially came to see me with her daughter, who was having trouble keeping friends and making new ones. She was getting left out at school and was no longer invited on playdates on the weekends. At the height of her frustration with her daughter's social isolation, Amy started making appointments to see me alone. I ended up seeing her daughter every week in the afternoon and Amy weekly in the mornings for about a year. It was during these sessions that we realized that Amy had "friend issues" of her own. Without any close confidantes nearby, Amy felt lonely and isolated most of the time.

Not having close friends to confide in is one of the biggest drivers of mommy burnout. As with Amy, the lack of close friends pushes moms to find other ways—which are often unhealthy—to fill their emotional void. These failed strategies often make moms feel even worse and perpetuate their feelings of isolation. But it doesn't stop with them. Moms are doing their best with the tools they have, but without positive models to teach them how to forge healthy friendships, their kids suffer as well.

I must admit that when Amy would come to see me, I would look forward to her stories. She's hysterically funny and very endearing. She also has one of those loud, booming voices that carries through walls. I would hurry her back to my office because I knew that the people in the office next to mine would likely hear her talking in the hallway, such is the level of feeling she puts into her stories and even her greeting when she sees me.

One day when the office was especially busy, Amy came in for an afternoon appointment. A steady hum of muted conversations from the waiting area and people walking in front of the closed door to my office created a background of white noise for our session. Only occasionally could we hear brief moments of laughter or a raised voice from a client or therapist in another office.

Piercing through the white noise of the whole office suite, though, was Amy divulging (quite loudly) her innermost feelings about her husband and sex. "I still love him. I think he's beautiful and so smart. But the heat is gone," she said. "At least for me. I have a set of excuses that I rotate to get around having sex when he approaches me. Isn't that sad?" At one point, Amy even compared her husband to a good-looking roommate. She explained that they used to have a great sex life, but now the thought of sleeping with him made her stomach turn.

But before Amy started talking (loudly) to me about her sex life in our sessions, she spent our time together discussing her daughter's issues at school. Her eight-year-old had spent the whole first half of the school year without a single playdate. At school, classmates would reject her at recess, and she had not been invited to a single birthday party that year, either. She also kept fighting with the few friends she did have. Amy was concerned that she would soon be completely alone if she didn't learn to get along with the other girls. "How is this possible?" Amy said in that first session, her words ricocheting around the whole practice. "Kids have friends." She turned to her daughter sitting in the chair next to her. "I don't understand. What happened to your friends?"

Eventually, Amy came to see me by herself. The issue with her daughter was pushing her over the edge. She lay awake at night thinking about the situation and suffered with knots in her stomach during the day. "Who else do you talk to about what's been going on with your daughter?" I asked her during one of our first private appointments. "Who are *your* close friends?"

The first person who came to mind for Amy was her husband. But, by Amy's account, "He can only focus on these conversations for three minutes—*maybe*—before he tells me that she will be fine, it will all work itself out, and that I need to stop worrying." She really didn't know who else she could confide in and vent to. She clearly wasn't going to unload to the moms of the girls who were being mean to her daughter. Amy did mention two or three friends whom she would meet for coffee some mornings, but she didn't want to share this with them. "I'm sure in the half hour that we have together, they don't want to hear about my pain-in-the-ass daughter and her problems," she said.

I had heard variations of this excuse before. It's not uncommon for moms to feel uncomfortable talking about their (perceived) failures, insecurities, and lack of confidence with friends. For many moms, their "friends" are the other moms they chitchat with on the sidelines of their son's soccer game or neighborhood women they have a glass of wine with every few months. The conversations in these situations are light and easygoing. These kinds of friendships are great. They are necessary. But so are *real* confidantes. And so many of the mothers I've met with don't have them—at least not close by. I also find that when the issues revolve mainly around something that a woman's child is dealing with, they are a lot less likely to be shared. So, things like having no friends, failing grades, a learning disability, or an anxiety disorder are not topics of discussion that are freely shared among casual friends.

A 2011 study in *Social Networks* found that we have fewer intimate relationships than we used to. In an interview with *Live Science* about this study that same year, lead author Matthew Brashears, PhD, explained, ". . . we should be less concerned about social isolation, or lacking any social contact, and more concerned about social poverty, or not having adequate support." It's not that women don't have friends, but really that they don't have many friends that they feel they can confide in. And those that they can confide in don't often live nearby. It's not like Amy didn't have any other women in her life, just not any close by with whom she felt comfortable sharing her most vulnerable thoughts and feelings.

I could certainly relate to that feeling. I moved to Denver leaving behind a great group of childhood friends. We even had a name for ourselves in high school, the Awesome 7. Many of these women are still my best friends, so I didn't initially feel compelled to get close to the new moms when I moved and became a mother. I was slow to be vulnerable with them and share my true feelings because I already had people I did that with. But with time, I started to feel lonely. It took time and a fair amount of effort to drag myself out to a "girls' night" when I was tired or a lunch during the workday, but it has paid off. These new friends haven't replaced my old connections, but they are meaningful to me because I know that they are near me when I really need them and we share in each other's daily lives.

I have often wondered if having fewer people to share our most personal problems with negatively impacts the mothers who come to me. There had to be some connection between these moms' lack of close friendships and their feelings of being overwhelmed. Experience has taught me that it isn't the quantity of friends that matters but the quality of friends. And it's the quality of friends in each of our buckets—from work friends, to neighbors, to mommy friends, to best friends—that actually matters. Having someone to talk to at work about challenges with your job helps prevent workplace burnout. Having a neighbor whom you can ask for an egg or share a glass of wine with on the porch on a sunny afternoon is also important. Being able to ask a mommy friend to pick up your child at school because you are running late alleviates a lot of stress. And having a best friend whom you can tell that you want to run away because you are so overwhelmed is vital to your emotional health. All these levels of friendship are important.

Many of the women I see at my office grew up among close friends. They just drifted apart from many of them as the years went on. I completely understand how easy it can be to put your husband, career, and children before your friendships. But as a therapist, I also know the impact this can have on your own well-being.

Amy was no different. She had two best friends as a young girl. They were inseparable all the way through high school. The only significant fight she remembers among them was over a boy, but that blew over quickly. She had yet another group of close friends during her time in college, and then again when she started working. She spent her twenties going to museums, dinners, and clubs.

"Sounds like you had a full social life when you were younger," I said. "And plenty of girlfriends to talk to and hang out with. So, where are these women now?"

"I used to have lots of fun," she said. "My life now is nothing like it used to be. But, you know how it is." Amy leaned back in her chair. "After you get married, your girlfriends scatter. And then after the babies come, you're pretty much holed up in your house just raising your kids."

A 2015 study published in *Human Nature* found that to maintain friendships, women need to talk to each other, and often. It's this consistent connection that seals the bond between women. But without sustaining your friendships or forging new ones, you slowly lose the skills that help you connect easily with others. Many moms have admitted that even when they are in conversation with friends, their minds are elsewhere. One client told me that while her friend was telling her about how her son had broken two fingers playing basketball, she was running through her to-do list in her head. "This other mom was practically crying to me and all I could think about was that I only had fifteen minutes left to make it to the dry cleaners before they closed." Listening to your friends, it seems, takes time that you feel you can't spare.

A few years ago, I started craving the sensation of chewing ice. I would crunch through my days, probably annoying anyone within ten feet of me. I would also discuss my ice chewing with various people who would ask me what was in the red Solo cup that I carried around everywhere. What I noticed—over my crunching—was that everyone had an opinion or some advice about my new compulsion. "Check your thyroid," one friend told me. Another advised me that my ice chewing was a sign of sexual frustration. I eventually went in for my annual physical and discovered that I had become anemic and that my iron deficiency was the cause of my ice cravings. It's called pagophagia and falls under a group of disorders where you crave non-foods like paper, chalk, and, in my case—specifically as a result of my low iron—ice. All I needed to do was take an iron supplement to break my craving.

Aside from learning this weird fact about iron deficiency and ice, I also realized something from my various conversations about the topic. Not one girlfriend *asked* me if the cravings got worse as my days wore on. No one wondered aloud whether something triggered this craving. I didn't get a single question about how all my chewing was impacting me socially or emotionally. No one asked me about *me*. But every single person I spoke to jumped into *solving* the "problem."

Men often adopt this "fix it" communication style because they are wired that way. It's instinctual for them. But when women talk, they often want to be heard, not given solutions. Like many moms, Amy looked to her husband to listen to her deepest feelings, but she never got that satisfaction from these conversations. "Invite the other girls here and have them play together," he would tell her. When Amy's husband didn't support her speaking to the parents of other kids, or hovering over her daughter, she deduced that he didn't worry about these emotional issues—and as a man he just didn't get it. But deep down, she wanted him to "get it." She wanted his support. She sometimes felt like he just wasn't on her side, leaving her to manage their kids all by herself.

A lot of the time, women are dissatisfied and frustrated with this kind of (typically male) conversation where they are told what to do before they have even finished their story. They want more connection. But in today's world of limited time and emotional bandwidth, I observe (and experienced with my own ice-crunching issue) that women are also adopting this more traditionally male-oriented style. They don't sit back and listen as often. Instead, they jump in quickly to give advice so they can get back to what they need to focus on.

The flip side of listening is being able to ask someone to listen to you. One of my favorite books is *Lean In,* which talks about the gender gap in leadership roles. Throughout her book, Sheryl Sandberg urges women to sit at the table, keep their hands raised, and find their voice. She is nudging women in business to make their opinions and needs known. Based on my experience with my clients, I have come to think that women need to do the same in their personal relationships. In my field, we have another saying along the same lines: "You have to lean in to the discomfort."

Just like in the business world, many women hesitate to be assertive with their friends when they need help because they fear the social consequences. "I don't want to come off as overbearing or bossy," clients tell me. They rehash stories about women who are "too chatty" and how they are snubbed or talked about behind their backs. Social fears keep moms quiet and apart. But, if you have reached the point where you are seriously considering leaving your kids alone in the house so you can take a drive or locking them in their bedrooms, you *need* to reach out to a friend—whether it's your best friend who lives in a different time zone across the country or the mom you occasionally have coffee with after you drop your kids off at school. And you need to know how to express to your friend that you really need to be listened to. And when you want advice you should ask for it. Whatever it is you are needing—a night out, a shoulder to cry on, reassurance it's not just you feeling like the world is falling down around you—telling your friend what you need up front helps you to get that need met.

I had one client who would text her best friend during the day a simple message like, "Need to talk. When are you free?" This gave her friend a chance to carve out time to give her the undivided attention that she needed. Another client would start off her conversations with, "I just need to vent, so don't tell me what to do until I'm done talking." Both these tactics were well received and, in fact, inspired their friends to do the same.

When I brought up the idea of asking other women to just lend an ear with Amy, she was resistant. "Why can't I just talk about this stuff with you?" she said. "You're a good listener and you give good advice. Why do I need to involve these other women?" I often think to myself, *if my clients had just one best friend, my practice might be cut in half.* Although I'm sure some of my clients see me as a friend, the reality is that therapy is not friendship. Therapy is inherently more one-sided and goal-oriented than friendship.

Amy did eventually warm to the idea of leaning on some of the women around her. One afternoon, she had to go to a doctor's

How to Ask Your Friends to Listen When You Need to Talk

Listening seems to be a skill that many people don't make time to practice anymore. Whether you feel too rushed, too overwhelmed (to listen to someone else's problems), or too tired, the fact is that—even with the best of intentions—you and your friends may not be really hearing one another. On the rare occasion that you do talk to a friend or family member about something that is bothering you, you may be met with opinions and advice that you didn't ask for and loaded questions, but no real support or empathy.

When you are frustrated and just need to vent or share, consider the following tips for helping your friends understand what you need, so that you can get it:

Be positive. People often speak in "negatives." They let others know what they *don't* want. For example, you might tell your child *not* to cross the street or your husband *not* to leave his socks on the floor. But, really, it's more effective to tell people what you *do* want them to do. The brain processes affirmative statements better than negative directions, so this approach is more likely to deliver positive results.

When you need your friend to listen to your problem and not fix it, consider saying something like, "I would like to give you a call later to just download. It would really help me out if you could just listen to me." This way, your friend will understand that she is not expected to come up with a solution. Can you imagine how good it would feel if someone said that to you? Pressure's off!

Be complimentary. Provide context or a compliment around what you are asking for. People, in general, want to please those around them. If you set your friend up with a genuine compliment, she will want to live up to your praise.

For example, if you'd like your friend to simply listen to you, consider saying something like, "You're a great listener and that's what I need right now, so I thought of you." This kind of statement lets your friend know what you want and makes her feel good at the same time.

Be a good listener yourself. And finally, if you want your friends to listen to you, you must also listen to them. If you're not sure if your friend is looking for advice or just an open ear, ask her. In doing so, you'll attract the behavior that you offer to others.

If you're not sure that you're on the right track with your listening or other friendship skills, ask a friend for feedback. Choose someone whose opinion you trust and ask if she thinks you are being a good friend. Be aware that going this route means that you must be open to all feedback, positive or negative. Remember, these skills aren't just for you. When you practice friendship skills for yourself, you are also modeling these same skills for your kids, which will make it easier for them to build healthy and satisfying friendships of their own.

appointment and didn't think her kids would sit through it. She mentioned this to her neighbor, who told her that the kids could stay at her house while Amy was gone. This neighbor was even happy to offer them dinner.

"That's a great first step!" I said. "How did it go?"

Amy thought for a moment. "I should have felt relieved, right? Well, instead I felt ashamed. Like I couldn't handle my own situation and now this other mom knew it, too." Amy was glad she didn't have to reschedule her appointment and that she got an hour to herself (at the doctor's office!), but now she felt like she needed to avoid this neighbor.

Amy was having what researcher and writer Brené Brown, PhD, would call a vulnerability hangover. We've all experienced this at some point, when we shared something personal with someone or exposed ourselves in some way and then felt shame or regret. I remember an incident where this happened to me. I was chaperoning a school trip with one other mom whom I knew only in passing. We got to chatting on the bus ride and I felt comfortable with her. When we got to the rest stop, I said with a chuckle, "I'll have to let all the kids go to the bathroom before me. It takes forever for me to finish peeing these days." The other mom laughed with me, but I was instantly mortified. I thought, *TMI alert!* I kept my emotional distance from this woman for the rest of the day. I was concerned that Amy was now going to do the same thing.

In time, and without forging any real connections with other women, Amy looked elsewhere. She spent a lot of her time zoning out online. She pored over pictures and posts on social media. And wondered why her life and her kids were not as great as those of her online "friends."

Because she wasn't intimately connected with her Facebook friends, she never got the backstory about the (probable) drama behind these perfect pictures. Amy would show me pictures from Facebook and point out that the kids were always in groups of friends. "*These* kids look happy and well-behaved," she would say. Like other moms I treat, this sense of failure only made her try harder, and feel worse.

Amy threw herself into helping her daughter socially and keeping her son focused on achievement at the highest level, or as she put it, "setting her kids on the right path," and in the process, her perceived success or failure as a mom became dependent upon her children's success or failure in any given activity. Basically, any activity that she read would lead to smart, well-rounded children, she enrolled them in. Her kids have learned to play multiple instruments, have black belts in karate, can code at a college level, run their own dog-walking business, and are accomplished artists—just to name a few of their skills. Amy ran herself ragged driving them to multiple classes and practices every afternoon. She needed an Excel spreadsheet of their activities, competitions, and lessons to keep everything straight. She also started volunteering to help in her daughter's class once a week and made sure that she went on every class trip. When her daughter was in Girl Scouts the year before, she was the troop leader. She also volunteered to coordinate the holiday party and fall food drive. "I figure I can poke my head into her classroom and check in on her while I'm at the school," she told me.

Over-scheduling or getting overly involved in your kid's activities is a common over-tending symptom. And as we saw in chapter one, over-tending doesn't empower your child. Children need to feel they can accomplish things on their own. I had another client, Susan, who would volunteer for everything from manning the ticket booth sales at her daughter's theater performances, to organizing the volunteers who would bring the food and drinks for the party after each performance, to helping backstage with costume changes.

Then, one day her daughter broke down during a session. "You're always helping everyone else, but you aren't there to support me. You didn't even see me perform the lead on opening night. You were too busy helping someone else backstage. What about me?"

Susan sat silently while her daughter continued to rant. After the session, and in private, Susan admitted to me that she was relieved about what her daughter had said. "I didn't want her to feel like I was happy that she was upset. But now I can stop running around like a maniac. In my mind, I was doing all of that for her but now I realize I can do less and she would be happier."

Because Amy didn't confide in any of the other moms she knew about what was going on with her kids (and she clearly wasn't going to take her husband's opinion into account because she felt like he didn't really understand the issues anyway), she had no perspective on whether her daughter's social issues were normal. She also didn't have any sort of gauge on just how much work parenting can be. As a result, her parenting irritations ballooned. She would start screaming if she had to ask her kids more than once to come to the dinner table or get ready for bed. She started threatening them that she would throw out any clothes they left on their bedroom floor. She took them out of the private school for the gifted and talented they were attending and home-schooled them for two years, but gave up because she was "sick of them not doing their work, lying about completed assignments, and complaining all the time during their homework." Amy significantly underestimated how many times throughout the day a parent teaches, corrects, and guides her children. Her experience of parenting was now a tremendous letdown and a lot more work than she ever imagined. "My husband and I are decent people. Why are my kids such animals?" Amy said during one session.

Amy's mommy burnout eventually bled into every part of her life. She freaked out at the checkout girl at the mall one afternoon for taking too long with the person in line in front of her. She was always running back to a store because she had forgotten to buy something she needed and only ever ate half of her meals, always while standing up at the kitchen counter. She could barely even choke down her favorite lasagna dinner. Most food just looked unappealing to her. Amy also started sharing her frustrations about her daughter with her now ten-year-old son, which only confused him and made him pull away from her and more into himself. She napped during the day and secluded herself away from her family on the weekends. In sessions with me, Amy popped Tums for her constant heartburn and drank coffee to stay awake while we spoke.

When things seemed especially stressful for Amy, I asked her again about those girlfriends from when she was younger. It turned out that when she was experiencing the most difficulty, she avoided these friends. She stuck to quick texts because she knew if she spoke to them on the phone, they would know that something was wrong and she just didn't want to admit to them how lost she felt as a mom. She told me about how one morning, she was meeting with her small group of friends who live nearby for coffee and only one of them noticed that Amy wasn't very engaged in the conversation and asked if anything was wrong. Amy just said she was tired, which kicked off a discussion among everyone else about how tired they were. Amy was relieved to have the focus taken off of herself, but she also felt a tinge of sadness that she didn't feel like she could really share what was going on in her life with anyone.

In time, Amy's stress spilled over to her daughter. Her daughter was refusing to do anything around the house and was also struggling to manage her own anger. Being told to do almost anything resulted in her screaming, yelling, slamming doors, and pounding her fists. "No wonder you don't have friends!" Amy shouted at her daughter one night in anger. She immediately regretted it, but there was no way to take it back.

Even at Amy's daughter's young age, she knew that something wasn't right. "She just never stops," the daughter complained to me about her mom during one session. "So, I feel like I can't stop. I go to school all day, then I come home and do tons of homework, then I have to practice the flute, eat dinner, take a shower, and read before bed. I never have time to even hang out with friends on the weekends or after school. I don't know how I could even have friends. I'm always busy!"

When I asked her how things were going with the other girls at school, she looked down at her lap.

"It's not that I don't want to have friends," she said with tears in her eyes. "I just don't know what I'm doing wrong. I don't know why they don't like me."

What Amy didn't realize is that part of parenting is teaching your children about friendship. Your kids notice how you interact with others. They learn to identify when someone is their friend, how to make a friend and keep a friend, from you. Amy's daughter *never* saw her mother with friends. She rarely saw her mom on the phone with friends, or having people over for dinner. Her daughter wanted friendships of her own and was even able to articulate that she didn't need a lot of them. She would say to me, "I just want one or two friends that I can do stuff with and who like the same things that I do." It was probably no coincidence that Amy's daughter wanted a similar friendship style to what Amy had once had—just a small group of close friends.

Be certain that your kids will notice if you aren't connecting with other parents at the bake sale or on the sidelines of their soccer games. They will see you hiding behind your phone. They will notice that you are "too busy" to stop and say hi to your neighbor. Like Amy's daughter, your kids may model your relationship style, which will continue to shape their lives for years to come.

Also, remember that, especially with young children, your social calendar directly impacts your children's. I had a tween client, Jenny, who told me that she wished her mother drank coffee. When I pressed her for what she meant by this, she explained that the other girls' moms all drank coffee and hung out together during drop-off. And that the daughters of those moms were also friends. "If my mom drank coffee," she explained, "then she would be friends with those moms. And I would be friends with those girls."

Amy's daughter also didn't have the advantage of palling around with the kids of her mom's friends because Amy was lacking in these relationships. While the other girls in her class had playdates and their moms hung out and talked, Amy's daughter studied and practiced her instruments while Amy zoned out on social media.

Teaching Your Kids About Friendship

Parenting includes teaching your kids about friendship. If you are shy or have been "too busy" to keep up with your friends, here are some friendship tips that will benefit both you and your kids.

Get to know the parents of your kids' friends. If you see that your kids are gravitating toward certain friends, get to know their parents. Model friendship skills with these parents, such as good listening and how to make and keep plans.

Be friendly. You don't have to become best friends with every person who crosses your path. Just being friendly will teach your kids basic friendship skills. Smile at people on the street. Make eye contact with your waitress. Share a quick story with the person ringing up your groceries. Even small children pick up on these social cues.

Make sure your kids know when you are spending time with your friends. Tell your kids when you'll be meeting Susie from down the block for lunch while they are at school or that you are talking to your friend on the phone when they interrupt your conversation. Showing your kids that you make and protect time with friends will help them place more value on their own friendships.

Nurture your friendships. Send your friends birthday cards. Invite them over for holiday dinners. Make sure you show your kids how to make their own friends feel special.

Explain the difference between "likes" online and in-person relationships. As more and more social interaction takes place online, it's important to highlight the importance of face-to-face friendships to your children.

Then, one day Amy strolled into the office with a big smile on her face.

"You look happy today," I commented.

Amy swallowed and then said in her booming voice, "I've met someone." Her eyes were shining and her smile was huge.

I had a feeling Amy might be stepping into a bit of trouble, since I knew she hadn't been too keen on forging any new bonds with other women. "What exactly do you mean?" I asked her.

"He's actually a guy I used to know before I got married. We never dated, but there was always something there between us," she told me. "We reconnected online and started talking about old times."

By Amy's account, their initial conversations started out as light and flirty, but eventually grew into more intimate con-versations. Amy was sneaking out of the house to call him and looked forward to his calls and texts throughout the day. When she didn't hear from him, she would miss him. "I get butterflies when I see his name flash on my phone."

Although I was surprised when she shared this news with me, I wasn't totally shocked by it. I know that women are tempted to go outside of their marriage when they feel lonely. Amy was feeling unsuccessful as a mother and generally disconnected from her spouse. She was avoiding any real emotional connection with her friends, but that didn't mean that she didn't still want that con-nection. As her stress escalated, this emotional need only became stronger.

This man was in the middle of a divorce and was also feeling lonely. In each other, they found someone to confide in and lean on. There was also the initial surge of meeting someone new, and in turn, presenting yourself in a new light. This man didn't know Amy as a wife and mother who was snapping at everyone and hiding out in her room. She could be exciting again. And, for the moments she spoke to him, free.

Eventually, the two made plans to meet up for dinner. The week before they were to meet, they were texting more frequently to make arrangements, and Amy's husband happened to see a message come in from this other man while she was getting the kids ready for bed. The two had a huge fight that evening and Amy promptly cancelled her plans. They barely spoke for weeks after this incident.

Looking back to the UCLA study again, it was clear to me that without friends in whom she felt she could confide, Amy's stress just kept escalating. She was never able to fulfill her natural "be-friend" urges, which created even more stress. She first looked to her husband to fulfill this role, but as we discussed earlier (and will do so in more detail in chapter six), her husband was not going to fill that emotional void. Amy then thought the other man was her answer. But what she didn't fully appreciate was that she was lonely, not romantically, but in being a mother at this stage in her life.

Though Amy continued to see me to work on how she got to this point and her newfound interest in building stronger connections with others, she still resisted reaching out to other women. At one point, she did call one of her childhood friends and unloaded what she had been going through, but that was only one time. Amy needed more consistent connection to ease her stress. Her stress levels continued to rise and, one night, she reached her breaking point.

It was time for her daughter to get ready for dance class and she didn't want to go. "The minutes were ticking down," Amy told me in a hushed voice. "And I didn't want to be late." When shouting at her daughter didn't work, Amy flew into a rage, squeezing both of her daughter's shoulders and screaming in her face. "I can't fucking deal with this right now, just get your goddamn clothes on!" As Amy stood there shaking her daughter, her husband ran up the stairs and yelled, "Amy, what are you doing? Get your hands off of her!" In my office, Amy closed her eyes for a moment and rubbed her temples. She took a deep breath in and exhaled. "When I saw the shock on my husband's face, I snapped out of my rage and realized I had gone too far." Amy explained to me that her husband looked at her as if she were a monster and that her daughter was terrified of her. "I've probably scarred her for life."

When I asked Amy whom she had told about this incident, I knew the answer before she responded.

Amy didn't feel like she could tell anyone else about this incident. She was terrified about what people were going to think about her. She assumed that the few moms she did meet up with occasionally would stop talking to her altogether now. Amy sharing this story with me was vulnerable enough for her. She even feared what I would think of her. Keeping secrets like this is truly bad for your health, though. It's not just hiding the information that is stressful, but also that we keep thinking about the fact that we are hiding information. This kind of thinking sends your stress levels up.

"Clearly you want what's best for you daughter," I said. "I can see how hard you're working, how many things you have brought into her life to make things better for her. And I know it's frustrating when you feel like it's all for nothing."

Amy nodded her head through her sobs.

"But this really is something that you could talk to a close friend about. I know that you think you're the only mom who has screamed and frightened your child, but you're not. And unless you talk to someone, besides me and your husband, it's going to be very hard for you to realize that you're not the only one and forgive yourself."

So, what was holding Amy back from telling her friends what was going on in her life? What propelled her to this point? What's keeping you from sharing the reality of your mothering experience with friends? It's not that you're too busy. Or that your friends are too busy for you (two excuses that I hear daily). Dr. Brené Brown, the same woman who coined the term "vulnerability hangover," has given two popular TED Talks. In 2010 her talk was titled *The Power of Vulnerability*, and in 2012 she presented *"Listening to Shame."* In these talks, Dr. Brown presented research on these subjects.

"For women," she said in her 2012 presentation, "shame is do it all, do it perfectly and never let them see you sweat . . . Shame, for women, is this web of unobtainable, conflicting, competing expectations about who we're supposed to be. And it's a strait-jacket." I agree completely that moms are ashamed of not fitting into this unattainable picture of perfection. And I know it keeps us apart. We don't want anyone to know that our Facebook high-lights are just that, that our bodies are run down, and our confi-dence in our own mothering ability is practically nil.

But there is a way through it. Dr. Brown also explains that to combat shame, you must let people see who you are. You must be vulnerable. If you're like most moms who believe that they are the only one struggling, then the idea of letting someone know that your life and your family are not perfect—that you feel anxious and tired and depressed and angry—can be terrifying. But it's also the only way to experience the complete joy of friendship. You must tell your truth. You must give other moms the oppor-tunity to say, "I feel that way, too."

It took some time for Amy's husband to fully trust her. They are still together and continue to work on their emotional intimacy and forgiveness. Although Amy cut off all communication with that other man, she still thinks about him. "We did have some-thing." Amy ran the charm on her necklace back and forth over the chain as she sat across from me in my office. "We did have a connection. When you have that kind of emotional bond, it's hard to just turn it off."

Amy was also eventually able to get away for a weekend and spend time with her girlfriends from childhood. She shared with them what had happened with her daughter and was surprised by their understanding and that they had their own stories to share about tough issues with their kids. When she got back from her trip, she began meeting up with her local friends for coffee more regularly.

As for her daughter, she eventually agreed to connect again with a neighbor friend who did not attend her school. They had been best buddies when they were younger, but grew apart toward the end of first grade. By reaching out to this girl, she was able to practice (in a way) being a friend, and that gave her confidence to connect with some other girls at school who shared similar interests, including chess and violin.

"I overheard some moms talking at the school the other day," Amy said to me one afternoon, grinning. "And I think one of them has mommy burnout, too. She sounded like me. She also hides from her kids and fights with her husband all the time about nothing."

Is Your Friend Suffering from Mommy Burnout?

Watch out for these signals that your friend might be burned out:

- She stops returning calls.
- She becomes short with you on the phone or her texting style changes.
- She seems more tired than normal.
- She is complaining more than usual.

- You notice something outside of her normal behavior—a quiet mom becoming talkative, or an open mom becoming closed off.

- You can't identify one specific stressor as the root of her exhaustion, anxiety, and persistent forgetfulness or the duration of these symptoms.

Now, let's say that you have identified that your friend is suffering from mommy burnout. How do you approach her?

I get how difficult this is for most people. Most of us don't like to push or pry. The best way to approach your friend is with non-judgment and openness, love, care, and concern. Women generally respond well to this. Call them and say something like, "I've been worried about you," or "I've been thinking about you." If you are too uncomfortable calling, send a text or email rather than staying silent to give her "space."

If the person clearly does not want to share, check in again a few days later. Sometimes it takes a few times for someone to believe that you care and have time for her, so don't give up. If she does give you a little bit of info, decide whether it's appropriate to share something personal about yourself. Sharing can make others feel more comfortable sharing with you. Also, if you can genuinely relate to her issue, let her know that you understand.

"I guess it would be nice to have a close group of girlfriends like I did when I was younger," she admitted. "It's just that making new friends and asking other moms out for lunch or coffee makes me feel like I'm trying to date these women." Amy smirked. "And we know how well it works out when I try to date someone."

"Why don't you try reaching out to one of the moms you sometimes meet for coffee and ask her to do something together, just the two of you. Maybe you can meet for a walk in a park or go to lunch alone. This might help you build a closer relationship."

"I guess that wouldn't be so bad." Amy shrugged her shoulders. "It would be nice to have a friend close by who I could really talk to."

Find Your Friends

Find activities or interests that you have in common. Are you both in the same tennis league? Do you attend the same school functions? Do you live down the block from each other? Finding shared interests will provide conversation starters.

Ask someone to join you when you do something for yourself. Ask another mom to join you on your walk or jog, when you are running to the mall, or while you are going to a reading at a local bookstore.

Remember, the other mom probably feels just as uncomfortable as you. Most people want to be social and to be included. Introducing yourself to someone new at an event will take a lot of pressure off her.

Invest the time. Yes, you are tired, have a to-do list that reaches beyond infinity, and your child is clutching at your thigh as you try to leave the house. But go and meet with your friends.

Be present. Go into your lunch date (or whatever you have planned) with the intention that you will be engaged and present. If you think that something important may come up (such as a child needing to be picked up from school), set your phone to a special ringer for that call. This way, you can leave your phone in your bag and keep an ear open for that specific ring.

Know that friendships are a two-way street. Be open to both sharing and listening. Some of us are good at only one of these things, but both are necessary to form intimate bonds.

FRIENDSHIP CHALLENGE

In the next week, pick up the phone and call a woman from your past, a woman you've had a falling-out with, and a woman you've only recently met. (I know you will be tempted to text or email, but call them.) With one of these women, schedule a time to meet up in person.

Chapter 3

I Know My Mom Is Just Trying to Help

The Difficulties of Creating a Support Network

Sound Familiar?

When you are in the throes of mommy burnout, it's not always easy to see that you need additional support. Here are a few signs that you need to build stronger connections with your family and/or your community:

- You always feel like you have to be in two places at once.

- You feel like a chauffeur.

- You resent having to pay at least $50 for child care every time you want to leave the house without your kids.

- You avoid or sidestep questions from your kids about big "life" stuff.

- You lie to your kids about your fractured relationships with family members.

- You resent your kids for bothering you with too many questions when you are all home together.

- You wake up anxious that you will be late for your morning meeting because your kids will slow you down.

- You threaten to take away privileges from your children, more for the avoidance of things you don't want to do—such as reading at bedtime or playing games.

Linda was thirty-nine years old and married with three kids. When I first met her, she had a five-and-a-half-year-old son who had significant medical challenges, an eleven-year-old son, and thirteen-year-old daughter. Linda and her husband met in college and had been married for fifteen years. Her husband was an architect. She worked part-time (only a few hours a week) in a bakery close to her house.

Linda initially brought her family in to see me because she knew that her youngest child's medical challenges were stressful for everyone and she wanted to make sure that the family was communicating well and that the kids were each understanding their family situation. Although the strain of taking care of her son's extensive medical needs wore on her, Linda struggled with her larger support network. Her mother didn't know how to help her, and Linda found it hard to relate to her friends given the way of life she was leading due to her son's condition.

Linda's struggles were intense, but not uncommon. Yes, her son's issues taxed her own physical and emotional energy, but the bigger issue came when her support network started to dissolve. Especially when there is a strain between a mom and her own mother/mother-in-law, the mom can feel even more alone and incapable in her mothering. Linda did her best to go it alone, but, really, raising a family takes a village.

Linda is that rare breed of woman who is truly secure in who she is. She has no concern about what others think of her. "I know I don't wear the most fashionable outfits," Linda said in her sweet, quiet voice during one session as she straightened her too-big handmade sweater over her slender shoulders. "But I love designing and sewing my own clothes. And I like showing them off, even if they aren't perfect." Linda also made her own lopsided jewelry and crocheted handbags, which she wore proudly.

In addition to her clothing and jewelry making, Linda was very active in her local community. She ran the PTA Speaker Series. She participated in a scrapbooking club in the spring and a knitting circle in the winter. She volunteered at her town's holiday festival and at school events. Whenever there was a need for a fundraising event—whether for new sports uniforms or to help a family in crisis—Linda would organize volunteers to help. Linda had many friends nearby and a very close friend who lived across the country.

As if all of this was not enough to fill Linda's days, she loved being involved in her kids' activities. She would stand next to the cheerleaders at her son's football games and cheer him on too. She was an assistant coach for her daughter's soccer team. She would run up and down the sidelines in her homemade shirt, with her long, raven-colored hair trailing behind her while shouting, "You're doing great, girls!" And every night after dinner, she and her husband would take a family walk with the kids in the park.

If Linda was ever running late at work, her mother would take the kids to their games or practices, which was fine, because she always went too. Her parents lived in the same town and took her kids for a sleepover most Saturday nights. The whole family got together for dinner every Sunday. Before I met her, the biggest gripe between Linda and her mom was over Linda's use of text messaging. Linda's mom would get peeved that Linda never called anymore, she only texted. Linda would get frustrated trying to explain that she was just trying to save time.

When Linda tells me these stories of her life before I knew her, my jaw always falls open. For years, Linda's days were filled with friends, fun activities, and joy. She was energized. And she had support at every turn. Linda was clearly well-woven into the fabric of her community. This is not the woman I met.

Five years before I met Linda, her youngest child was born with a rare genetic disorder. Doctors explained to Linda and her husband that their lives would likely be complicated by long hospital stays and that their young son might not live to see his teenage years. Linda's life suddenly turned from being a busy (sometimes too busy) mother of two to a stressed mother of three who spent months at a time in the hospital. Her phone's address book quickly filled with doctors' phone numbers and her house functioned as a revolving door of therapists. Linda's relationship with her community shifted too.

When Linda's family first came home from the hospital several months after her new son was born, friends and neighbors brought them dinner once a week and inspirational cards filled their mailbox. "Isn't this so nice of everyone?" Linda said to her husband. "So thoughtful." Linda had grown particularly close to one woman who lived down the block. The woman had told her that she would always be there if Linda needed to talk, so she took her up on her offer and invited the woman over for coffee every few weeks. At first, Linda focused her conversations on how lucky they were to still have their baby, since he was so sick when he was born. But a few months into their conversations, she admitted, "It's exhausting. We have doctor's appointments every week and some of them we need to fly to. Then, we also have his care at home and his therapies." Linda told her, "I don't even know if I'm coming or going most days."

Her friend didn't understand her experience, really. She questioned why Linda felt the need to "fly all over" when they had perfectly good doctors nearby. She also hinted that Linda was creating a lot of extra stress for herself that wasn't necessary. Linda's eyes welled up as she sat across the table from her friend. She struggled to keep her thoughts to herself. *She doesn't get my life. No one gets my life.* After that conversation, Linda kept her relationships with this friend and others light and superficial. She talked about things like recipes and her other kids' activities, while her emotional wall grew higher.

Linda's other friends from the neighborhood stopped by when they could, but the conversations were filled with pauses and sighs. She would notice her friends' eyes lingering on her baby's medical supplies while they sat in the kitchen. On the playground, these friends' kids would ask her children what was wrong with their brother. "I would never let our kids say that to someone," Linda cried to her husband. "I would teach them how to act around children with special needs and their siblings."

Linda's mother took an ever-growing role in the family, ferrying the other kids to their activities and making sure that Linda had some time for herself. Being around so often, though, Linda's mom felt comfortable airing her opinions about Linda's life, from the tidiness (or lack of) of her house, to what she gave the kids for dinner, to how often her husband worked late. "James is *still* at the office?" she would say with raised eyebrows and disapproving eyes.

Relationships between adult women and their mothers grow even more complicated with motherhood. Grandparents can be sources of great wisdom and opinions. But these opinions tend to be rejected by moms who are trying to figure things out for themselves, often wanting to do things differently from the way they were raised. The baggage of how a woman experienced her own childhood can interfere with her ability to take advice from her own mother, no matter how good the advice is. Older mothers and mothers-in-law seem to approach opinion sharing in a variety of ways. They either hold it all in until they can't any longer and then unload it all at once or they make passive-aggressive types of comments regularly. In the best-case scenario, they reserve judgment and are there to be supportive in whatever way is helpful. I have found that these relationships are complex and varied, and in instances where there is a special needs child involved, grandparents may feel the need to comment even more because there are so many more moving parts to raising these kids. Overall, these comments don't always provide the support that the grandparent intended.

Even with my own mother, I struggle to take her well-meaning advice. I remember when my kids were younger and they wouldn't stay seated at the dinner table. My mother suggested that I seat the kids at a kids-sized table, instead. And, of course, I rejected that advice. However, weeks later, a feeding specialist who was working with one of my sons made the same suggestion and it worked like a charm.

Even with her mom's help, Linda never wanted her other kids to feel like she had forgotten about them now that the baby required so much attention. She went to as many practices and games as she could, but her time was no longer her own. She had to keep up with the baby's grueling feeding and medicine schedule, and monitor him always. Linda felt the tug between her two older

Do You Know a Mom of a Child with Special Needs?

The number of children with disabilities—be it physical, emotional, or intellectual—is significant. According to the National Center for Educational Statistics, "In 2014-15, the number of children and youth ages 3-21 receiving special education services was 6.6 million, or about 13 percent of all public-school students…" These kids require a lot of additional care and support. And, in turn, so do their moms and other family members. As a family therapist, I know only too well that when one person in a family is struggling, the family unit as a whole struggles.

If you are not the mother of a child with special needs, it's likely that you know one. And it's also likely that you want to help and stay connected to your friend, but have no idea what to say or what to do.

Here are some ideas:

Offer comic relief. These moms typically welcome a coffee break, a personal chat, or getting out of the house to do something fun and that has nothing to do with their situation at home.

You don't have to know what to say. Don't feel like you need to have answers or the right thing to say. Just go ahead and tell your friend that you don't know what to say but that you are there to listen and that you care. And then do just that.

Ask questions. Sometimes people are afraid to ask questions, but questions are much more welcome than advice or avoidance.

Do something special. Send an actual card in the mail. Tuck a gift card to a nail salon or local bookstore inside to encourage your friend to take care of herself, too.

Offer respite. Insist on coming over to help so that your friend can shower, nap, run an errand, or go out on a date with her spouse.

Be there for the long haul. Caregiver moms' circumstances don't often change, so be there for her and stay there.

children and her baby just as many mothers do when they add more children to their family. However, given the more rigorous demands of her youngest, she felt especially guilty "neglecting" (as she sometimes referred to it) her other children and all that they had going on in their lives. After a year of all of this, Linda was tired of dragging herself through her days, so she stopped all her volunteer activities. She went to games and practices only sporadically and left the PTA. She stayed at the bakery, but only for a few hours two afternoons a week. She considered this work time her break. "I just have no energy or time left," Linda would tell me years later. "I'm completely spent."

One afternoon, Linda's mom came over unexpectedly to pick up her youngest after he came home from preschool and told Linda that she would get the other kids from school and take them to their practices that afternoon. "Take a nap, do some laundry, or take a shower," her mother had said. "Enjoy an afternoon for yourself." She also said that she would get the kids washed up and give them dinner before bringing them back home.

Linda quickly ran through the afternoon's schedule. Her mother would get her youngest down for his nap, then get the other two from school and take them over to the municipal fields for their football and soccer practices. Afterward, they would all go back to her place, have dinner, and wash up before going out for ice cream and finally returning home. *That's six full hours to myself,* Linda thought. *I can do anything!* Linda mentally planned to make a Target run, go to the gym, and take a bath. She kissed her son on the forehead, thanked her mom, and turned back to the kitchen as they drove away.

Despite the packed afternoon that Linda had just envisioned, the first thing she did was pour herself a glass of red wine, even though it was twelve thirty in the afternoon. She took the bottle over to the living room, lay down on the couch, and flipped on some horrible talk show with two women screaming at each other over some guy who was dating them at the same time. Linda barely heard what they were saying. She just watched the images flash on the screen and enjoyed the warmth from the wine spreading over her body. Linda had finished two glasses of wine and was just dozing off when the front door sprung open and her older son came barreling through.

"Mom! Mom! Where are my shin guards?" he yelled.

Linda bolted up from the couch and accidentally kicked the bottle of wine onto her hardwood floor. "What was that noise?" her son asked as he ran into the living room waving one shin guard. Linda just stood there, speechless, as her mother appeared behind him, looking at her with pinched lips and narrow eyes. She turned her grandson's shoulders around and walked him back out the front door, assuring him that she had the other shin guard.

"I don't know what that was on the floor," she heard her mother saying as she closed the front door. "Maybe your mom spilled some juice."

Shortly after her youngest son, who was now five and a half, was discharged from yet another two-month hospital stay, Linda and her husband brought the whole family in to see me. "We've been in the hospital since February," Linda explained to me. "It's not uncommon for us to watch the seasons change outside the hospital windows during long stays with our son. This time, though, his doctors suggested that we . . . umm . . ." Linda looked at her husband. "Wait, what was I saying?" I noticed bags under her eyes.

"We just want to make sure that the kids are processing all of this and that they know we are still here for them," he told me. Linda's older son and daughter were now eleven and thirteen, so they were starting to fully understand the extent of their brother's issues.

I noticed that Linda's husband was especially focused on his work. He assumed that his greatest contribution to the family (since he could not control the health of his child) was to establish a secure career where he earned enough money to support his family and maintain health insurance. The older kids were quiet and didn't talk much about what was going on with their younger brother unless they were prompted with questions from me. When they were prompted, they admitted they lived in a constant state of fear that their brother might die. In my experience working with families with a child who has significant needs, I found this family to be rather typical. The father often dives into work to protect his family. Siblings worry, but often keep those worries to themselves. And the mom, by default, is left to give care to the child who needs the most.

Linda then explained that she wanted to make sure she was "doing everything she could for all of her kids." But when her husband complimented her on her patience and dedication to their youngest, Linda only looked away and said, "I just do what any mom would. Of course I'll find the best doctors for him, no matter where they are. And sit through back-to-back therapy sessions. But I just always feel like it's never enough."

My thoughts after this first session were that Linda sounded tired, and that she had been through a lot over the last few years. *Any mother in her shoes would feel overwhelmed.* However, many moms—even those with typically developing children—will often deflect praise around their mothering because they feel like they can be doing more. *If they only knew what I wasn't doing,* moms will say to themselves.

After a few months seeing the family together, I was pleased to see how well the kids were communicating with each other and with their parents. Linda's husband said he felt less stressed, was more productive at work, and was feeling hopeful again about the family's future. As we had discussed, the family members were carving out more time for themselves alone and together as a family. The dad expressed more trust in his son's medical team, which gave him more mental energy to put toward work. And all the siblings were practicing the communication strategies that we worked on in our sessions, such as sharing their own problems (no matter how small) and feeling like these problems were also important. Everyone seemed to be moving forward—except for Linda. She would still yawn through our sessions, lose track of her thoughts, and constantly refer to her "master list" of to-do items that appeared to grow by two entries every time she crossed one off. Since they came to me as a family unit, I felt comfortable telling them that they were at a place where they only needed to make an appointment as they felt necessary.

A few weeks passed before I heard from Linda again. She wanted to come in by herself this time. I assumed that she just needed time and space to vent and share her worries about her youngest child. I was wrong.

"My mother is driving me crazy," Linda said when she sat down.

My head jerked back involuntarily. Before I could even get a question out, Linda kept talking.

"I know my mom is just trying to help, but she's doing too much. She buys the kids presents every time she sees them. She gives them fast food and ice cream when they go over there. And she has no bedtime for them when they sleep at her place. They are always a wreck the next day, and this happens every weekend."

I nodded my head and remained silent.

"I also can't tell if my mom is being a bitch or just asking general questions." Linda explained that her mom would often ask her if she's taking care of herself or if she had eaten that day. "Does she think I look like shit? Does she think I'm getting fat? Or too thin? I can't tell what she means, but I am pretty sure it's not good." Linda's mom was around so much that it felt like she had become another member of their immediate family. "Still," Linda said leaning back in her chair, "having her around *is* helpful. I can nap. She takes the kids to their practices and games. She even starts dinner for me some nights." Linda knew that she needed the help, but she resented that there was a cost attached. She constantly weighed whether it was worth it to accept her mother's help or if she should just suffer through her day on her own.

Research has found that support from parents can sometimes create even more tension in families. I find that many young mothers today view reaching out to the older generation for advice and help as a vulnerable trap that will only open the door for their mother or other close family member to intrude on their life.

My mother-in-law, for example, often emails me parenting articles. And while I know that some of my friends would take this as an insult from their mothers-in-law, I have grown to realize that this really is her way of trying to be engaged in our family and helpful to me.

As Linda was talking, I thought of another client I knew whose mom lived in another state. The woman told me, "I have a good relationship with my mom when she's at her own home, but when she flies in from Florida, it's like my world turns upside-down." My client would clean her whole house, plan for every meal for the length of her mom's stay, buy the foods that her mom liked to snack on, and spend "all of her free time" with her. "I can't get anything done when she's around. Even after the kids go to bed, she wants to watch television with me and talk more, but that's when I usually do the dishes, put away the toys and homework, fold a load of wash, and then finish up work." If she mentioned that she had emails to send out, her mom would shake her head and say, "You work too much." My client was sure that her mother kept an inventory of negative observations about her life when she came to visit her and then shared them with her friends in Florida when she got back home. "But, then again, I do the same thing with my friends," my client told me. "It's just so much easier to text my mother the highlights from my day rather than have her in my house with me."

In 2012, the Clark University Poll of Emerging Adults found that 55 percent of adults between the ages of eighteen and twenty-nine kept in touch with their parents daily or almost every day, either with phone calls, texts, email, or in-person visits. Social trends like young adults extending their schooling and staying single longer support this level of contact. And, of course, the boom of texting, and Skype have made keeping in touch easy.

And that's great. But my experience with clients, both moms and grandmothers, is that even with their texts and phone calls, they are not connecting on an intimate level. The grandmothers I see complain that they never talk to their kids anymore. "I swear," one client told me, "if I hadn't learned how to text, I wouldn't have any contact with my kids." And for today's moms, the time and energy it takes to maintain an intimate relationship with their own mother strains them.

On top of Linda's fatigue and cramped schedule, she also harbored resentments from her younger years, deep feelings she couldn't share. Linda had been close with her mom growing up, but there was always a level of tension between them. Linda's parents were from Italy and very conservative. She felt like she never had a voice. If she did exactly what her mom wanted—dressed how her mom wanted her to dress, dated who her mom wanted her to date, believed what her mom wanted her to believe—then they got along and her mom loved her, Linda explained to me. If she tried to be herself, Linda felt like her mom was disappointed.

As the weeks wore on, Linda's stress levels continued to climb. She would sit slouched over in her chair and report that though she didn't have trouble falling asleep, she would wake up in the middle of the night with her to-do list running through her head. "I've been awake since two thirty this morning," she once told me during an afternoon session. "I've been daydreaming about crawling back into bed for hours." Linda was short with her kids and started pulling away from her husband. She saw him as someone who helped with the kids—he would help make dinner some nights, check their homework before bed, and clean up after dinner—but she no longer saw him as a partner in life. Linda started drinking a glass of wine with dinner every night to "take the edge off." Burned-out moms are more vulnerable to excessive drinking as a way to escape their lives, and I wanted Linda to know that there were other ways to manage her ongoing stress. I suggested that instead of the wine, she use that time for a creative outlet, since she enjoyed making her own clothes and jewelry.

A few months into our private sessions, Linda's youngest came down with the flu and was admitted to the hospital. For four days, he was hooked up to an IV and monitors that beeped every time his heart rate dipped too low. Linda and her husband took turns holding their son's tiny hand at his bedside while the other one napped in a chair in the corner of the room. Linda's mom shuttled the other kids back and forth every afternoon from their school to the hospital and then to her house to sleep at night. While in the hospital, Linda's sleep was constantly interrupted.

Linda came in for a session three days into this hospital stay. Her eyes were red and her face was pale. "My kids want to know where their brother will go if he dies." Linda wiped a tear from her cheek.

All kids will, at some point, start asking questions around sickness and death. I find that moms who don't readily have these answers for themselves will find these conversations uncomfortable and stressful. Regardless of their religious beliefs, I always urge my clients to take some time to answer these kinds of larger life questions for themselves before attempting to answer them for their kids. It's okay to tell your child that you're not sure about these answers. But keep in mind that you will have to give them an answer at some point.

A comprehensive review paper published in *ISRN* in 2012 found that people who are more religious/spiritual are healthier emotionally than people who are not. And my goal was to help

Strengthen Your Spirituality...
Because It Will Ground You

When it comes to mommy burnout, having a spiritual practice (in whatever form feels comfortable to you) will help you in both good and bad times. Here are a few ideas to consider.

Establish a steady meditation practice. There are many ways to meditate—from chanting different mantras and words to sitting silently while focusing on your breath to meditative walking—and they all have value. Carving out this time to be alone and silent and to quiet your mind is extremely beneficial, especially if you are feeling stressed or anxious.

Create your own weekly ritual for yourself and for your family. This can be attending museum outings, musical performances, or a class or even meeting another family for brunch every Sunday. Look for opportunities to learn about different viewpoints and expand your knowledge base. If you can move these experiences into family discussions, even better.

Set a goal for how you will give back or donate as a family. Together with your kids, choose a local food bank, animal shelter, or homeless shelter where you can donate money or volunteer. Giving feels good and will help bolster your emotional energy.

Start a book club in your own family. Each week, let a different family member choose an age-appropriate book for everyone to read. Then, plan a meeting to discuss the book. You can boost the spiritual nature of this exercise by choosing books that focus on different life experiences and life lessons.

Linda feel emotionally healthier. I would never suggest religion as a treatment plan, but I did believe that some sort of spiritual practice might bring her some comfort. "Think about these questions," I told her. "What can you experience by yourself and as a family that will lead to deeper conversations about big-picture issues like values, spirituality, the world around you, and even love and loss? Is there a community that would make you feel safe and comforted? What can you do on your own or as a family that connects you to others on a regular basis and leads to deeper relationships?"

Linda leaned forward in her chair.

"You don't have to answer these questions now," I told her. "But think about them."

I have spoken to my kids a lot about what happens when someone dies. My kids have drawn out their vision of "heaven" and they have comforting feelings about this place. When our dog passed away, we were all heartbroken, but my children didn't fall apart over this loss because they believed that their dog was living on in a happy place.

Linda folded her arms across her stomach. "I guess, right now, I just want to have an answer for my kids." Keeping this in mind, I wanted to create strategies for Linda to employ when speaking about the toughest issues of life with her children—illness, death, and God.

Thankfully, Linda's son recovered. When he was released from the hospital and they were all settled back at home, Linda noticed how lonely she felt. "Remember when our friends would bring over dinners for us when we came home from the hospital?" she asked her husband over a meal of cereal and chocolate chip cook-

How to Tackle Your Kids' Spiritual/Life Questions

Answering these kinds of bigger life questions for your kids can be stressful, especially if you haven't given these kinds of questions much thought yourself. Many moms also struggle with how to answer such questions in a way (and with language) that their kids will understand.

Use language that you are comfortable with. You can say "the afterlife" or "heaven," for example, and refer to God as "the universe." You want to feel comfortable yourself while answering your child, so use whatever language/terms feel most natural to you.

Use your child's imagination to help answer some of his or her questions. When your kids want to know where their cat went when he passed away, ask them to draw a picture of a comforting and loving place and then draw the cat within the picture. This way, your child can relate to a specific place that is comfortable and happy.

Share that you believe in "something bigger than us." It's okay if you don't have a name or any more description to offer your children. This does not tie you to any one religion, but it does create a foundation for future conversations when someone close gets sick or passes away.

ies. Her friends from the neighborhood did call, and even invite her to lunch, but just the thought of suffering through more awkward conversations gave her a headache, so she declined.

Linda's mother also pulled back on her support with the kids.

I would find out months later that her mother felt like every time she tried to help, Linda would yell at her. She wanted to help Linda and missed her grandkids, but she just didn't know what to do. One afternoon, Linda's mother commented about the laundry still being in the basket from the day before. When she offered to put the laundry away herself, Linda felt like her mom was just being critical and told her that she didn't need any of her mother's help anymore. Linda felt the loss of her mom's support, but also enjoyed the space. At least for a while.

Linda scrambled to find babysitters to take her two other kids to their practices and after-school classes when she was busy with her youngest. For every activity that she missed, Linda would zone out in front of the television. Linda felt like she just couldn't win. She always felt like she had to choose which kid got to have her attention—her sick child or one of her healthy kids. She also felt like she had damaged her two older kids because they did get less of her time, but she didn't know what else to do. She couldn't change her family, so she tried to just not think about it.

When her children would periodically come in to see me, they would tell me that their mom didn't have time or energy for them anymore. "She's always talking to a doctor on the phone, running errands, or zoning out in front of the television," they told me. She forgot about the yearly audition for the school talent show (she and her daughter had always prepared together) and she started showing up late for pickups. I noticed that the kids were also growing increasingly short with each other. We spent more and more of our time together resolving conflicts between them that had started outside of our sessions.

Linda was aware of what was happening in her family, but she didn't have the energy to push back. In fact, she had come to a place where she started to resent her kids for all that they needed from her. "They're like these energy drains," she told me. She quickly followed up with, "But I really do love my kids. I shouldn't have said that about them." Linda felt like a cook, chauffeur, maid, bank, and slave to her kids—and not in the funny, joking way that moms often refer to themselves. She *really* felt this way.

And, the children missed their grandmother. "Why doesn't Nonna come to our practices anymore?" her kids would ask her. "Why aren't we spending the night at her house this weekend?" Linda didn't know what to say, so she avoided their questions. After a few minutes of Linda ignoring them, the kids would go back to their rooms and slam their bedroom doors. One time, Linda's daughter even accused her of doing something to keep her grandmother away. "It's your fault!" she screamed at Linda and then stormed out of the room.

I had worked with another client who stopped talking to her mother-in-law. Her ten-year-old daughter, who was upset by the family fracture, would tell me that her mom would send back the presents her grandmother sent to her. She would cry when her mom wouldn't let her call her grandmother. She felt embarrassed that she was alone at Grandparents Day at school and when, unlike her friends, her grandmother was not at her birthday parties. "Grandmas bake cookies with you and teach you how to sew and are always nice. I miss having my grandma around," she told me. This ten-year-old made a plan of finding her grandmother once she became an adult. That is, if she was still alive.

Things reached a new low when Linda started going back to bed after her kids got on the school bus in the morning. She barely left the house except for her son's doctor's appointments. She rarely had enough energy to shower, and she became accustomed to the persistent charge of anxiety that coursed through her body. She would snap at anyone and suffered from stomach cramps.

She became unpredictable for her children. Some days she would get up before the kids, prepare their lunches, make them

How to Bridge the Gap with Your Mom (and Mother-in-Law)

This older generation may make you want to pull your hair out, but they can also be a tremendous source of comfort and help. Here are a few ways to set aside your differences and still maintain your sanity:

Appreciate what they can give and don't dwell on what they cannot. Focus on their strengths.

Agree to disagree. You don't have to agree on everything to get along.

Tackle old relationship issues. Address old grudges before they blow up again and threaten your valuable connection.

Learn to compromise. You can have more than one holiday tradition and your kids can stay up a little later when grandparents come to visit. The benefits of a close connection outweigh the costs.

Connect on your commonalities. Scrapbook together, cook or shop together. Focus on the joys you share.

Create two-way conversations. Your parents need to share their feelings also. Ask your mom about menopause, being an empty nester, retirement, losing a close friend, or how it felt to sell your childhood home.

breakfast, and seem like the mom they had grown up with. Other days, she would sleep in knowing that her oldest would help with lunches and pour the breakfast cereal. Linda felt out of control and hated who she was becoming. "I need help," she would sob in front of me. "I just can't get out from under this stress."

It's been long known in the field of psychology that strong community ties serve as a boon to your emotional and physical well-being. Since the late 1800s, studies have linked weak social ties to almost every disease, from tuberculosis to schizophrenia to alcoholism. Suicide was one of the first issues studied in relation to community ties. With greater opportunities for women to receive higher education and accept high-demand jobs, they often resort to keeping "in touch" via text messaging only, easily letting go of most close ties.

When Linda lost her community, she no longer had that sense of belonging, and this made her especially vulnerable to mommy burnout. She lost the opportunity to "befriend" other women and to relieve her stress, and so it festered.

One day, Linda received a call from the school that her seventh-grade son had been caught smoking pot. Linda said that she would come pick him up right away, and then slammed the phone down on the counter. She sat down and tried to stop her head from spinning from the shock and self-doubt. *What will I do? What should I say to him? How did this happen? How long has he been doing this? Who is he hanging around with? Who else knows?*

Linda was afraid to call her husband. She knew that he would fly off the handle and she didn't want to deal with her son and her husband at the same time. She stared at her phone for a minute. "I went to call my mom, but I knew she would blame me," she explained. She then thought to call her friend from down the street, but it had been so long since they had spoken about anything significant. Linda took a deep breath. "I thought of calling my best friend across the country, but I was just too ashamed. I also hadn't been very good at staying in touch with her." Tears slid down Linda's cheeks. "I used to have so many people in my life that were there for me. My life was filled with friends. But now, I'm completely alone."

When Linda recounted the story to me, it became very clear that much of her stress was being driven by the fact that she no longer had the support network that she once enjoyed. I stressed to her how important it was to rebuild this network around herself so she didn't feel like she had to "do it all alone" all the time. I suggested that she start by mending the relationship with her friend down the block from her. I knew that mending the relationship with her mom would eventually happen, but it would just take longer. And it would be helpful for her to have support from a girlfriend while she was working on the relationship with her mom. Through our discussion, Linda realized that even though she found this friend's comments about "flying all over for her son's care" to be insensitive, she did understand that no one was going to fully comprehend her life because they just didn't live it. However, this woman did show up for her and offer her support. And that's what's important in your support network.

Mommy Burnout Prescription Plan

How to Build Your Village or Just Join One

Assign friends to each area of your life, such as your work husband and school committee partner. Your community can be made up of different people across all the areas of your life. For example, you might have a neighbor whom you would trust to take your kids to school if you couldn't for some reason, but probably wouldn't tell your deepest secret.

Trust others and loosen up on your control. Your parents might not feed your kids exactly what you would, but it still may be worth it to let them babysit so you and your husband can have a date night alone.

Stop and say hello to your neighbors instead of running straight into your house. Look to the people who are already close by and in your world. Take small steps toward connecting with them.

If you notice that there's another woman who is usually at the gym when you are, ask if you can meet up there. This is good motivation to go to the gym and can make your workouts more fun while you possibly build a new friendship.

Join a local book club, knitting circle, tennis club, exercise class, photography class, or any other group that you find interesting. Follow your passions and interests to your new communities.

Talk to the people in your daily life. Whether it's your doorman, your landscaper, the checkout clerk at the grocery store, or the owners of the local bakery, take time to get to know all the people you see every day.

Create a leadership role for yourself. Whether you become an HOA board member or your neighborhood watch captain, start or lead something that you are passionate about because it focuses your energy on something positive and gives you a little bit of purpose.

BONUS EXERCISE

Find the moms in your area who have kids who are older than yours and connect with them, considering them mommy mentors. Ask them your questions about different schools, activities, teachers, coaches, leagues—whatever you want to know. They are great resources and a great foundation for the village you are building for yourself.

Chapter 4

How Many "Likes" Did I Get Today?

The Social Media Mommy Trap

Sound Familiar?

If you can identify with at least three items on this list, consider changing the way you view or use social media.

- You mindlessly scroll through posts and lose track of time. You don't even process what you're looking at.

- You choose connecting over social media over meeting friends in person.

- You incessantly check your phone after you post something for "likes" and comments.

- You feel lonelier, more depressed, or angry after scrolling through your feed.

- Your kids tell you that you are on your phone too much.

- You have your phone on the table next to you when you meet someone for lunch or coffee.

- You check your social media before your feet hit the floor in the morning.

- At any given time, you are looking for that "postable" moment.

- You spend more time than you'd like to admit crafting captions for your photos.

- You scroll through other people's profiles to find out where they are or if they have been tagged by someone else, because you are sure you have been excluded.

- You fall asleep scrolling through your phone.

Michelle was twenty-nine years old and had a three-year-old son when I met her. She was recently separated from her son's father. They were never married, but they had been together for about a year and a half before breaking up. Hers was not a planned pregnancy. Michelle worked in marketing and sales, and her ex worked at the same company in a similar role.

Issues with her three-year-old son initially prompted her to come see me. He was becoming harder and harder to handle (both for her and the teachers at his school) and was even getting violent with her. These kinds of issues—child is getting into trouble at school or acting uncontrollable at home—drive many moms to me. By the time I met Michelle, I knew more about mommy burnout. And I knew there was more going on with her than just her son's behavior. It didn't take long for me to see that her Internet use had gotten out of control and was impacting her relationship with her son.

Social media has many benefits. It keeps us connected to old friends and family members who live far away. It's kind of an efficiency tool, socially speaking. You can broadcast your message to many people and avoid having to call or text each person individually when you have news. But this ease also comes at a price. These kinds of broadcast messages don't lend themselves to deeper conversations and emotional connections. Moms turn to the Internet to connect. But, really, it's just feeding their feelings of loneliness.

I still remember the day that Michelle and I realized we had something in common from our childhoods—*All My Children*. We laughed so hard that we were doubled over in our chairs. Our mothers had both been obsessed with this soap opera. Right after lunch, my mom would move to the living room, clutch one of our yellow and orange throw pillows to her chest, and puff on her Newport Menthols as the beautiful characters came to life on-screen. If I was home sick or off for summer vacation, I knew that she was not to be disturbed during "her program." I always assumed my mother learned this from her own Cuban mother, who would watch her *telenovelas*—Latin American soap operas—at night with the same level of dedication.

As soon as the last beat of the *All My Children* closing credits played, my mom was on the phone (sitting in the chair closest to the wall at our kitchen table because the cord didn't reach any farther) with one girlfriend after another so they could rehash the whole episode together. Even I knew what was going on with the show because she would talk about it at dinner. Soap operas were a source of running conversation throughout my childhood—my mother thrived on the scandal and intrigue. We even had the *All My Children* board game.

Now that I'm older and a mother myself, I can see that soap operas were my mom's escape. Michelle's mom did the same thing (sans board game). They both disconnected from their everyday lives of laundry and kids for an hour or two every day. They could become fully absorbed into this other life. With beautiful people and passion and drama.

But Michelle and I only made this connection six months into our sessions. When I first met her, she was seated in my waiting area, scrolling through her phone. I immediately noticed her watery eyes, runny nose, and a packet of tissues on her lap. "Looks like you have that cold that's going around," I commented as we walked back to my office.

Achoo! Michelle's sneeze reminded me of Minnie Mouse's high-pitched squeak. "I guess so," she said. "Something is always going around."

"Yes, I have seen a lot of sick clients lately," I said over my shoulder.

Once we had both settled into my office, Michelle kept her phone in her hand.

"Do you need to keep your phone on? Are you expecting an important call?" I asked her.

Michelle glanced down at her phone. "Work is just really busy right now. They are constantly texting me with questions."

"Well, that must be stressful," I said. "To always be on call for work."

Michelle thought for a moment, flipped her long, curly black hair behind her shoulders, and then laughed a little. "You know, I think it would be more stressful to not hear from the office." Michelle paused. "I sound like such an *adult*. It wasn't that long ago that I was meeting my friends for dinners a few nights a week, letting different guys buy me drinks and flaunting my abs in little crop tops."

Michelle had been dating her boyfriend for six months when she found out that she was pregnant at twenty-four years old.

Against their friends' and families' advice, Michelle and her boy-friend moved in together. Both sets of parents were disappointed that the couple decided not to get married before the baby came. Behind closed doors, both sets of parents also voiced their con-cerns over having a biracial grandchild. Michelle was black and her boyfriend was white. Despite all the bets against their suc-cess, the couple stayed together and prepared for their child. And for a little while, they were happy.

As Michelle told me about her pregnancy, her eyes dimmed. She gained seventy pounds during the pregnancy. As her body continued to grow and swell over the months, Michelle's boy-friend would often leave her home alone so he could continue with his social life. "He would play basketball after work and stay out all night on the weekends," Michelle told me. She felt too em-barrassed to talk to her friends or family about her loneliness. And none of her friends could relate, anyway. They were still en-joying the freedom of their twenties.

Months after their son was born, Michelle and her boyfriend split up and he moved out of their house. As her relationship was combusting, her friends were just finally getting engaged. Deep down, she had a hard time being happy for them. She had grown cynical about men, unable to forgive her ex-boyfriend for break-ing her heart.

At her son's preschool, Michelle was the youngest mom by far and was often confused for his nanny. She had some other mommy friends whom she went out with from time to time, but she never felt like part of their clique. At twenty-nine years old, Michelle was starting over, and raising a child alone. This was not at all the life she had imagined for herself.

Michelle worked long hours. She was too tired to date, though she did want to meet someone and get married one day. She didn't have the time to visit her childhood friends or family who lived three states away. And she was trying to handle a three-year-old who considered her walls his paint easel. At some point, Michelle developed a toxic habit. But that's not why she came to see me.

Her son had been kicked out of preschool. She had to scramble to get him in somewhere else so she could work. He was also impatient and irritable. Michelle told me that her son had recently bit her leg because she quickly responded to a work text while making his breakfast. Michelle was frustrated that her son didn't understand that she was a single mother who had to work.

Michelle was busy, but she did find the time to sneak in some social media scrolling throughout her day. In five-minute installments, Michelle would catch up on the goings-on in her friends' and sisters' lives. She figured this was a good way to keep up with what was going on with everyone, even if she didn't have time to see them or talk on the phone. She wished she had more time. She felt like people thought she had all this free time as a single mom because her son was with his father for half the week. But in reality, when her son wasn't with her, she spent her time catching up on chores and errands because she couldn't do any of that with him around.

A few years ago, my family spent a few days at a lake house for spring break. While we were driving up to the house, I remembered that I had left my phone on the kitchen counter. *What will I do?* I thought to myself. *I don't know anyone's number except for my husband's. What if I get lost somewhere? Or need help?* My heart started pounding just thinking about the calls and text messages I would be swamped with after three days away. And that's when I fully realized how dependent I am on my phone and being able to connect with everyone at any time, in multiple ways.

The reality wasn't so bad. When my husband and I split up with the kids during the day, I would just ask people to borrow their phone so I could call him to check in. It was a little uncomfortable to ask this favor of strangers, but not one person balked. I wasn't stranded or tied to my husband's side for the lack of my cell phone. And, when I got home and checked my messages and texts, I hadn't missed any emergencies.

Not having my phone on that trip was a relief. I felt free. I didn't have to catch that perfect picture or text people back each day about how my trip was going. When we were at the house at night, I would check Facebook on my laptop, but I stayed on for much less time than I would have had I been lying on the couch with my phone.

When I think about my mommy burnout clients, I see them struggling to stay connected with friends and family, even when they have access to their phones. They go online again and again seeking connection and to escape their lives, but long-lasting relief remains out of reach. My feeling about Michelle was that she was struggling to adjust to her "new life," without her boyfriend and raising her son alone for half the time. She was turning to social media for connection and for validation that it was *possible* to raise her son alone. She was looking to find moms who were like her. But when she didn't find these women—young single moms of biracial children—in her own social network, she felt even more isolated. She felt like she had no place to belong.

Over the next few weeks with Michelle, I started to get a clearer picture of her days. In the morning, she would wake up either to her phone's alarm clock or her three-year-old son's heel pressing into her forehead. Before her feet had even touched her bedroom floor, she would check her email, news feed, and Facebook account. "I had to see what I missed while I was sleeping," she joked. Finally, she'd rub the last bit of sleep from her eyes and get out of bed.

While brushing her teeth, Michelle would prop her phone up next to the mirror, just in case someone were to call or text (even though no one ever called or texted at that early hour). Then, she'd slip her phone into the pocket of her bathrobe and mentally prepare for the soon-to-be struggle of getting her son dressed, fed, and out the door.

As the day progressed, she would check her social media anytime her brain was not fully occupied. This is what led to her dropping her phone in the toilet one afternoon. She would also leave her phone out in the console of her car while driving so she could see who texted or called. And of course, she placed her phone on the table at lunch with friends and at business meetings.

On several occasions, Michelle was so focused on her phone that she didn't realize it was her turn to talk during a staff meeting. One time, she got bored while one of her colleagues was updating everyone on her project, so Michelle started scrolling through her Facebook feed and noticed that two of her friends had gone out to dinner without her the previous weekend. She was livid because she hadn't had her son that weekend and could have joined them. She got so wrapped up reading about what a great time they had that she totally missed her boss asking for her update. Michelle's colleague had to kick her under the table to get her attention. Her boss was short with her for the remainder of the meeting.

At home, Michelle was stumbling through endless days of single mom-hood. She would fight with her son to get dressed in the morning. Then, she had to threaten him to get him to finish his breakfast before getting up from the table. At school, she would bribe him so he'd stop hiding behind her legs and go into his classroom. During dinner, she'd yell at her son to eat more than a piece of bread with cream cheese for his meal. Then, she'd plead with him to brush his teeth and put on his pajamas and try to talk him out of calling his father to come get him (he would do the same thing for her when he was at his dad's house). By nine o'clock at night, her eyes were like saucers and her neck ached. Her son was usually still running around in his room at that hour, but she was too spent to deal with him, so she would shut his door and try to ignore him until he scurried into her room and hopped up into her bed to go to sleep. With each moment that her son dominated her attention and energy, Michelle felt her tank dip. *How is this my life?* she would think to herself. However, when her son was finally asleep, she would stroke his cheek and remember the adorable things he said during the day, and there were plenty. She did love her son; she was just overwhelmed with her parenting responsibilities and was sad that there wasn't more time to sit and play or to just be with him.

One month, Michelle decided that a short trip away would be good for them. She thought that skiing might be fun and that her son could blow off some extra energy on the slopes. Michelle spent the two weeks leading up to the trip making their reservations and finding restaurants that she thought her son would like.

It was her first time traveling alone with him. Michelle had to pack for herself and for him, and then realized that he couldn't carry anything himself. She made ten trips—literally—between the car and the house to get everything loaded. An hour into her drive, Michelle realized her jaw was sore from grinding her teeth and that she had passed every car on the road. She eased her foot off the gas, took a deep breath, and tried to focus on the fun that lay ahead.

Once they were at the hotel, Michelle struggled to unload the car by herself and lug everything up to their room. She was so exhausted by the time they got settled that she just wanted to nap. By that night, Michelle's head was pounding. Her son needed help to brush his teeth. He needed help to get his pajamas on. He needed help to blow his nose. Michelle knew that this is just how kids are at this age, but she needed him to just do one thing— anything!—for himself. She was totally wiped out. She couldn't help but think of the pictures that her childless friends would post of their vacations. She recalled seeing images of them reading books on the beach by themselves, drinking cocktails with tiny umbrellas sticking out of them, and getting dressed up for a night out with their boyfriend or fiancé. "Why can't I have that?" Michelle would ask me. "Some days, I don't think I can do this mom thing anymore. At least not by myself."

I occasionally hear these types of statements of desperation and when I do, I know that this mom is at the end of her rope. She is overwhelmed and has put all self-care aside. She's probably not sleeping well and feels ineffective and powerless in her role as a mother.

A month or two into our sessions, Michelle missed a week and then came in with a bad cough. Her voice was raspy. She explained that she was just getting over bronchitis. When I pointed out that she seemed to be getting sick often, she mentioned that over the last year or two, she couldn't seem to stay well for more than a few weeks at a time. Years later, I would make the connection that many of my mommy burnout clients do fight frequent illness—stress weakens our immune systems. But at that time, I simply made a quick mental note.

"I think I did something bad," she told me once we had settled into my office.

I remained silent, but nodded my head, inviting her to continue.

"I bought my son an iPad."

"Okay."

"I know it's horrible for me to say, but he's constantly trying to get me to play or look at him or do something with him. He's just always *on me*. I swear, if he could burrow back into my womb, he would. And he never stops asking questions." Michelle had asked the moms in a Facebook group that she was in how to handle an only child who doesn't entertain himself—and more than one told her that they bought their kids iPads. "One mom posted that she downloads educational videos, like 'Elmo loves the alphabet' type of stuff," she explained.

I nodded my head.

"I thought that was a great idea. I could get a break and he could be learning something. But now he won't let me take it away." Michelle cleared her throat and fished around in her bag for a throat lozenge.

"Tell me more about this group. Do you share your personal information with them? Do they know anything about your situation?"

"It's just a group for single moms. I have no idea who they are, but they are always willing to give advice whenever a member has a question." Michelle paused. "Do you think it was a bad idea to get him the iPad?"

I thought for a moment how to answer. "I do understand that when he's on his iPad you get a break for yourself, but the truth is that it's not a good idea for your son to be online for hours at a time." I explained to her that the iPad can be a useful tool when we set boundaries and limits around it. We get into trouble when we allow kids to spend hours a day online and when we use it to calm our kids down. Kids can become reliant on the iPad for stimulation, and research has shown that children who have ADHD are more likely to develop a compulsion to spend increased time on their screens.

"So, what does he do when you try to take it away?" I asked.

"He screams and flails and has a total fit, which negates the whole reason why I bought it in the first place. I wanted some peace and quiet for myself. It's like he's addicted to it."

"So, what are you doing about this?"

"I don't know. It does keep him calm at dinner and with going to bed. And he's not constantly on me. So, there are a lot of benefits for me . . ." she trailed off.

Michelle isn't the only mom using screens as a portable baby-sitter for their kids. I had one mom who bought a new car so that each of her kids could have their own built-in screen because she was so sick of hearing them fight while she was driving. I had another mom who would keep a "spare" iPad in her car so she could never be without one. "I simply can't go shopping or meet my friends for lunch unless my daughter is glued to that screen," she told me. "It's pretty sad because she'll just shovel her mac 'n cheese into her mouth and drop the noodles everywhere without even realizing it because she's so involved in her show, but it's the only way for me to have any kind of adult conversation during the day and get my errands done." Other moms purchase head-phones for the devices so they "don't have to hear those annoying shows anymore," and will take their kids to lunch by themselves and still give them the iPad or their own phone so they don't have to talk to them.

We are in a culture right now that doesn't value boredom or

downtime, which is what leads to creativity. What parents need to realize is that kids thrive with some structured time, but they need unstructured time as well to become critical thinkers and develop emotional intelligence, which stems from problem-solving. We feel that we need to entertain our kids all our waking hours. But because that's not always achievable, we constantly offer up the iPad to fill their time, and we feel good about it because the kids are playing "educational games."

I've even learned my own lesson here. I am stringent with screen time for my kids, but we did used to have a drop-down screen in our car. I told the kids that the screen worked only on the highway, so they had movies and shows only during longer car rides. And, I began to notice that the kids were cranky whenever we got to our destination, but I didn't make the connection at first. When we got a new car without the screen for the kids, we started talking more and using audio books, and I now find that my kids are more cheerful when we arrive at our destination. It's just an easier transition from the car to our activity without the screens.

"Do you often look to this online group for guidance?" I asked Michelle.

"I guess so. Some of their advice is good. Some of it's not. I don't really have any mom friends to talk to face-to-face. My close friends either don't have kids or they aren't raising a child alone. No one I know would understand."

Michelle is far from the only mom looking online for guidance. A 2015 *Pew Research* study found that mothers are more likely than fathers to find parenting information while they are on social media. Moms are also more likely than dads to get support from their social media network and for parenting-related issues. These are good things, right? Well, up to a point.

The biggest problem here is that when moms go online seeking answers, advice, and guidance about parenting, they often don't know whom they are talking to and they lose context both when they are posting questions and receiving responses. They don't always give the full story when they are setting up a question. And they have no idea what kind of expertise the person responding to them has, beyond also being a parent. All of this can lead to unhelpful information and guidance that overwhelms mommy burnout moms or makes them feel worse. Conflicting advice or trying something that doesn't work makes moms feel even more incompetent.

"It's great that you have a place online where you feel connected and understood. What I think we need to work on is making your virtual world an actual world where you are talking to the moms at the preschool, in the neighborhood, or other places where you can have physical contact about these things." I paused. "What keeps pulling you back online throughout the day?"

"It's kind of like playing the slots at a casino," she said. "I keep checking to see if I've gotten an email, or a text, or if someone has commented on something I posted." Michelle cleared her throat. "You never know if you're going to get a good message, text, or post, but the opportunity pushes you to keep refreshing on your screen."

Michelle's comparison of her cell phone to gambling isn't that far off. As people do with gambling, you get a dopamine rush (or a mini-high) when you get texts and "likes." But it doesn't last very long, so you need more to sustain that good feeling. Your focus turns to getting that "feel-good hit," which pulls your attention out of the present. When it comes to stress and mommy burnout, you are vulnerable to this downside of the Internet and social media, which runs along the lines of addiction. You keep going until you realize you can't stop and your actions are impacting others. Because you are not well connected to others, you are vulnerable to the allure of social media for all things—advice and connection in particular—while burned out, so you are desperately seeking belonging. You may feel embarrassed or ashamed to tell someone what is going on in your life, so you can go on sites and ask strangers questions, or read what others have to say. You don't have to be intimate with anyone and yet can feel (superficially) connected. This impacts others, such as your family, when they are trying to ask for help with homework or need something and you keep saying "one more minute" until they either have a fit to get your attention or just give up.

Another client would stay up until the wee hours of the morning playing video games and texting with friends in different parts of the country because she needed adult interaction. She would chug coffee throughout the day and had several near-miss car accidents because she was dozing at the wheel, all because she felt so deprived of conversation that she was willing to forgo sleep.

A study published in the *CSCW '16 Proceedings of the 19th ACM Conference on Computer-Supported Cooperative Work & Social Computing* found that social networks can serve up feel-good validation and support. Like off-line communications, social networking communication culture has seemingly evolved to deliver what people need, but only on a cursory level. Likewise, Michelle felt validated and supported every time someone "liked" or commented on her posts. One time, she posted the word "sad" and got three private messages asking if she was okay. "If I post that I'm having a rough day, it's nice to see the supportive comments come in," she said. "Though, when I say this to you, it sounds kind of lame." But this was not so uncommon—I remember sitting with a young woman at a baseball game who explained to me that if she were to get a picture of the sunset with her Coors Light in front of the Coors Light sign on the field, she would get five hundred "likes." I was shocked that she was chasing the "likes" instead of the bliss of the moment at the actual game.

After probing this issue, and listening to countless moms tell me about their social media use, I have come to believe that women go to the Internet for whatever they need in that moment—validation, advice, connection, curiosity, to feel better about themselves, and (sometimes) even to feel worse. If you want to feel better, you will undoubtedly find posts of your high school nemesis who has since gained weight, pictures of friends whose kids are in the middle of a tantrum, or even a thread about someone who was never very nice to you getting divorced.

Other times, you may want to stay in a down mood. It's like listening to sappy love songs after a breakup. You just want to sit in that feeling for a while, and social media can give you that experience as well, with posts of people who are carefree and traveling the world, enjoying date nights and advancing in their careers. It's far too easy to be envious of people online.

We all get something out of posting on social media. We wouldn't do it otherwise. And through my work I've come to identify several "posting styles" for social media. Here are a few of my favorites:

- **Attention Seeker:** These people seek validation and attention, posting "pray for me" messages or "I just did the most amazing thing" updates.

Are You Misusing Social Media?

The easiest way to figure out if you are misusing social media is to realize what you are getting from it.

Healthy Uses of Social Media:

- To socialize

- To get opinions/answers/experiences from trusted sources

- To unwind from the day by viewing something funny or relaxing

- To stay informed with news

- To belong to a subcommunity of relatively like-minded members

Unhealthy Uses:

- To procrastinate doing a work project

- To express yourself and get feedback, when you feel no one in your family is listening to you

- To just do "something" to fill your downtime

- To maintain connection with friends, because you no longer call your friends or meet up in person—social media makes you feel like you still know what's going on in your friends' lives

- To have the adult conversation you crave because you spend all day with children

- **Bragger:** These posters want everyone to see how great they are. They boast about their kids' awards and achievements as well as their own successes, such as reaching weight loss goals or getting a promotion. They *only* post accomplishments.
- **Compulsive Non-Essentialist:** These folks post every simple fact of their day, like what they ate for lunch, what they drank at the coffee shop, and the vitamins they took that morning.
- **Promoter:** They are constantly promoting what they sell, their way of life, and the bands they love.
- **Meme and Video Poster:** These people love to share humorous or wacky content.
- **Family Poster:** These folks are focused on posting highlights of their family vacations or latest fun activities.
- **Political Inciter:** These people want everyone to know their political and social worldviews, and they are happy to let people with opposing views know that they're wrong in their comments section.
- **Motivational Poster:** They aim to inspire with their daily feed with quotes, videos, and personal stories of triumph.
- **Advocate:** These people champion for a cause, be it medical, social, educational, or a GoFundMe campaign.
- **Casual Poster:** These folks post randomly and infrequently, usually about something positive.

Social media isn't going anywhere. We're going to keep posting and communicating through this medium. However, it is so easy to go overboard with the amount of time you spend posting and the content of what you are posting. If you can identify why you post (i.e., your posting style), it can help you rein yourself in.

It gives you some perspective. The other side of knowing your posting style is to think about the people who will be reading what you post. Have you ever seen pictures of your friends out to dinner without you? You don't want to create that same feeling for other people.

I know that I've been on the receiving end of posts that didn't make me feel good. We have friends who host a holiday party every year, and my husband and I would always go and have a good time. Then, one year I noticed that we didn't get an invite. I thought it was odd, but assumed that they had decided not to have the party that year. Well, I was wrong. They posted pictures from their party and it made me feel terrible. I even questioned whether I had done something to offend this friend or if maybe my invitation had gotten lost in the mail. I've never asked my friend about it, but I'm definitely reserved around this friend when I see her now.

At Michelle's home, things continued to barrel ahead. She was constantly telling her son to wait while she finished a text. She would put on noise-cancelling headphones and scroll through Facebook when he had a tantrum. While he was glued to *Super Why!* she would binge-watch her favorite show, *Gilmore Girls*.

It was around this time that Michelle and I realized our moms shared the same vice, and that Michelle's vice was the Internet. Like our moms, Michelle would emotionally dive into other people's lives; in her case, she would obsessively try to connect with other adults through her posts and texts. Social media was her own *All My Children,* but the reality version and in real time.

Eventually, Michelle started to notice that in her playroom filled with toys, her son would dart between one toy and the next, easily getting bored. He would also gravitate to the baby toys that she had yet to donate. The bells, lights, and music held his attention. His video games of Thomas the Train were more interesting to him than his real train set.

That summer, Michelle (still sniffling) came in and asked me if I thought her son might have ADHD. I often have parents of toddlers requesting an ADHD evaluation. And the reality is that we don't test for this until a child is seven, because we expect toddlers to be highly active and impulsive. Michelle's son was only four years old, so an evaluation wasn't appropriate. But I did want to understand what prompted this request from her.

Michelle told me that her son would say "Mommy" one hundred times in a row; he'd eat a few bites of dinner, and then get up from the table and wander around; and he was constantly losing things—from socks to shoes to parts of his toys. She assumed this kind of behavior was normal, but it was still driving her crazy. She then told me about one night when they were reading and her phone dinged with a text. She told him to wait just one second so she could see who it was from, and he grabbed her phone from her hands and flung it across the room.

"He is in constant competition with your phone," I told her. "He couldn't take it anymore, but he didn't have the words to communicate this to you, so he just acted on impulse."

"What? That's crazy." Michelle sat back in her chair and adjusted her baby-pink tank top.

"Every time that phone lights up, he loses you. He loses your attention. He doesn't know what 'five minutes' means. Or 'one second.' He's just left sitting there, waiting for you to return to him."

Michelle then put her phone on the table next to her.

There was talk of including Internet addiction in the latest edition of the *Diagnostic and Statistical Manual of Mental Disorders*, the reference book used to classify psychological issues, but the editors decided more research still needed to be done. I would not be surprised if this diagnosis, or at least a classification, shows up in the next volume. In the meantime, I use an informal set of criteria of my own that is based on earlier discussions found in a 2009 *Psychiatry* article titled "Should DSM-V Designate 'Internet Addiction' a Mental Disorder?" as well as ideas around addiction in general, to determine if a mom needs to put down her phone.

Do You Spend Too Much Time Online?

I don't count this by the number of hours you spend online, but by number of times you choose to go online. Do you:

- Go online first thing in the morning?

- Bring your phone to the bathroom? (I can't tell you how many people I know who have dropped their phone in the toilet!)

- Fill *any* open time with Internet use?

What happens when you can't get online? If you were to lose or forget your phone somewhere, would you:

- Obsess about not having it?

- Feel naked, unsettled, anxious?

- Believe you can't function without it?

- Feel irritable or angry? (If you would be simply agitated, followed by the relief of having time without your phone/Internet, you are more likely dependent rather than addicted.)

- Feel like you are missing something that you *need* rather than something that you *want*?

- Do whatever it takes to get your phone back regardless of the negative ramifications?

Do you experience negative repercussions because of your social media use, such as . . .

- Avoidance of your family and friends so you can be online?

- Not being present with family and friends because you are thinking of social media?

- Comparing yourself to others you see online and then feeling bad about your circumstances?

- Setting unrealistic standards for yourself based on what you view online?

- Feeling bad about what your kids aren't achieving compared to other kids online?

- Feeling left out or hurt when you see that your kids were left out of fun events?

For the first time, I gave Michelle homework. I told her to take forty-five minutes and meet a friend for coffee, or in the park. "You need to reengage with the world around you."

Eventually, Michelle messaged an old friend from high school who, surprisingly, lived only a few towns away from her. Her friend had posted a "please send prayers" message, so Michelle suggested they meet up to talk and see if she could be of any support to her.

While they were out, Michelle ended up unloading her own worries on this woman. She talked about how her kid was becoming an Internet zombie because she didn't know how else to control him, how frazzled she always felt, how hurt she still was that her boyfriend had moved out, and how scared she was that she would never meet anyone again. "My son was an 'oops moment,'" she confessed. "And then as soon as he was born, I lost my youth, my body, my vitality, and my appeal. I mean, what single, never-been-married guy is going to be in a relationship with a single mother of a nightmare kid?"

Her friend gave Michelle the dutiful "sad eyes," said she was sure everything would work out, and then unloaded her own story about her sick cat and work frustrations. And then that was it. They sat at the table staring at each other in silence until the waitress brought the check over.

"We had nothing to talk about," Michelle said to me. "So much time has passed. We don't know each other anymore." Michelle also confessed to being mortified that she was that starved for adult conversation and connection that she divulged such intimate information to a woman who hadn't been in her life for years.

I have found that Michelle's experience with her old friend was common. When you meet with old friends, it's like having muscle memory, but emotionally. It's easy to slip back into that old dynamic of sharing what's really going on with you. This is why Michelle divulged so much about her life with this woman so quickly. But she was right; they really didn't know each other anymore.

Months later, Michelle came in for an emergency session. I could barely make out what she was saying through her sobs. Her son, now five years old, had gotten up at six o'clock on Saturday morning, so she couldn't do the work that she had planned to do. She gave him a bowl of Cheerios and his iPad with his head-phones so she could get a few emails out. Five minutes turned into ten and then fifteen, and then an hour. Eventually, her son got bored with his device.

He remembered some kids from his kindergarten class on the playground at school laughing about some words that he didn't understand, like "boobs" and "wee-wees." "Mom! Mom!" he called to Michelle while tugging at her arm. Michelle pulled her arm away and told him to wait. Her son knew how to search on Google from watching his parents find videos for him on You-Tube, so he clicked on the icon, sounded out the letters for *boob,* and typed it in. He clicked on the images and started scrolling through.

"I have no idea how long he had been on there when I looked over at his screen," Michelle said. "*I'm* traumatized by what he was looking at. The pictures were so graphic. I can only imagine what he was thinking."

"What did you do when you saw what he was looking at?" I asked.

"I grabbed the computer away from him, which also ripped the headphone off his head. He got scared and started screaming. I was screaming. The whole scene was a mess." Michelle took a deep breath. She said she asked her son how he learned that word and he told her from the kids on the playground. "Then I asked him why he didn't just ask me." She paused, trying to collect herself. "'I did try to ask you, Mom,' he said to me. 'You told me to wait and then never came back.'"

I hear about this kind of incident often—where kids will get themselves into trouble because their mom is trying to get her own work done. And realistically, moms need to find a way to set boundaries when they are with their children. I suggested to Michelle that she designate "work time" and "son time" when she was at home, and not to blend these activities together. Kids will understand that they must wait for you, if they know that they will get your full attention later.

Tame Your Social Media Usage

Set boundaries around usage for yourself and your kids. Create screen-free zones and times in your house.

Know what to ask online and what's better to ask off-line. Don't post very personal information about yourself or your kids online. Also, if you do ask questions, take the answers as guidance and not gospel.

Remember that your posts are permanent. Just like you teach your kids, don't post anything that you don't want the whole world to see. Remorse does not erase what people have already seen.

Put your phone on silent in social situations. Give the people you are with the gift of your attention.

BONUS EXERCISE:
BE YOUR OWN BEST SELFIE

Do you love taking selfies? Are you constantly snapping your kids doing the *cutest* things?

If you're like most of the moms I see, you are trying to capture these perfect moments to share with others and relive as you look back through them. But you don't need the selfies to get that same hit of excitement or calm, or whatever feeling the photo captured for you.

Find one picture that makes you feel especially good and identify the feeling and positive activity associated with it. Were you feeling calm or excited? Were you laughing? Were your kids elsewhere?

Next, figure out one activity that you can do to re-create this feeling and approximate the activity. For example, let's say that you love a picture of yourself on the beach because it makes you feel calm. Maybe you can schedule a massage, go to an exercise class, or take a walk outside by yourself to capture that same feeling again. I realize it won't feel the same, but it will help. And, as a bonus, while you're doing the activity, you won't be on your phone!

Chapter 5

I Just Want What's Best for My Children

How the Need to Achieve Perfection for Our Kids Adds to Mommy Burnout

Sound Familiar?

Options, options, and more options. It's too easy to fall down the option rabbit hole while chasing after that Best Mom medal. The following are a few signs that it might be time to limit your choices.

- You second-guess all your decisions because you believe something better is always "out there."

- You are constantly overwhelmed with researching the best products, services, schools, etc.

- You realize that instead of deciding between products, you just buy more than you need and end up spending more money than you should.

- You stay up at night worrying about decisions you made earlier in the day.

- You feel like your head starts spinning the moment you need to research any upcoming purchase or decision.

- You feel exhausted after a day of shopping.

- You feel like you get lost in the details when you are comparison shopping—think about the last time you bought a new phone.

Mary was forty-six years old and married, with twin teenage boys. She was thirty years old when she had them. She had been married for nineteen years when I met her. Mary had a degree in nutrition, but never used it because she found taking care of her sons to be too demanding to also work. Her husband was a venture capitalist.

Mary initially brought her sons in to see me. They were getting into trouble at school, bullying the other kids and talking back to their teachers, not to mention completely disregarding anything Mary asked of them at home. She felt as though she had lost complete control over her sons. "I don't know where this is coming from," Mary told me on the phone before their first meeting. "I didn't raise them like this." After one of her sons walked out of a family session with me, Mary and I thought it might make more sense to give her kids a break from the therapy and for her to come in alone. That's when I realized how overwhelmed Mary was . . . with choices.

Like many moms, Mary fell prey to the thousands of options we all face every day because she felt she needed to "find the best" for her kids. These moms dart from store to store to store as they seek out just the right pair of sneakers. They spend hours researching the best camps. And they become paralyzed as their kids grow older and more decisions come into play with regards to schooling and extracurricular activities. They think that more options are better. But what I've found is that more options lead moms to burnout.

When I think back to Mary, I remember a story from my own family. About a year ago, I stopped into one of the local ice cream parlors by my house with my youngest son one sunny afternoon. He must have been about three at the time. This store is known for its wide variety of flavors. In fact, there are so many flavors that the list of options stretches across the whole wall. As my son walked the length of the store in front of the glass partition that displays the various ice creams, his eyes grew bigger and bigger with each step, his smile wider.

There were dark, chocolaty flavors and snow-white vanilla choices laced with various candies and fruit. Sprinkled through-out the lineup behind the glass was a cheerful pink strawberry ice cream, an inviting baby-blue cotton candy, and a cool light-green mint flavor dotted with chocolate chips. Somewhere along the middle of his walk along the flavors, his smile faded. By the time he got to the end, tears were falling down his cheeks. "I don't know which one!" he yelled as he ran back to me. I quickly narrowed his choices to chocolate chip or strawberry, and his eyes brightened again. "Strawberry!" he shouted, and then eagerly dug in.

It's well known that giving small children too many choices distresses them. They get anxious, cry, or yell, and some even freeze. For kids, having too many options is a recipe for disaster. But what about with adults? Mary's story is a great illustration of what happens when we try to weed through these overwhelming numbers of choices alone.

"Hello there, Mary," I said as I walked out to the waiting room of my office. She gave me a little hug. I had been seeing Mary alone for about six months at this point.

"Hi," Mary said with her big, warm smile and her "whisper voice," as I have come to call it. She squeezed my forearm a little as we walked back to my office. "How has your week been?" she asked me in a hushed voice as she leaned her head in closer to mine.

"It's been good," I said. "How has your week been? How is that bathroom remodel coming along?"

Mary stepped into my office and said over her shoulder, "It's on hold. I have ten different paint color options up on the wall and I just can't decide which one to go with. I'll just wait for the vision to come to me." Mary giggled a little as she gracefully sat in her chair. She reached into her bag and pulled out a small paper bag with two muffins inside. "Which one do you want?" Mary held the muffins out to me. "They all looked so good this morning. I couldn't decide on just one." Mary flashed that big, warm smile again.

"Thanks," I said reaching for the apple cinnamon. "I'll eat it during my break later. So, how are the boys doing with your in-laws around this week?"

Mary took a deep breath in. "Well, you know these boys just make everything harder." She took only a quick inhale before rambling into the next sentence. "They refused to say hello to their grandparents when they got to the house. They didn't even look up from their video games when they walked in. I can't tell you how mortified I was." Mary took another quick inhale. "I didn't know what to do. They were ignoring me also. And my in-laws were just standing there looking completely appalled by what was going on in front of them. And . . ."

"Mary," I said calmly.

"Yes." Her eyes focused on me.

"Slow down. Let's take a breath together," I said.

Mary leaned back in her chair and took a deep breath before starting again. "Even my own mother thinks I'm a bad mom," she said. "She's constantly reminding me what a good girl I was when I was younger." Mary threw her arms up into the air. "These boys." Mary pursed her lips. "I can't control them. I don't know what I'm doing wrong."

In the few sessions that I had with the boys they were reserved, quiet, and not very forthcoming. Still, they were respectful to me. They did answer my questions. They acknowledged that they grew up with two loving parents, good friends, and everything they wanted and needed.

"Life is good," one of them told me. "Why do we need to change?" the other one chimed in. The twins considered their pranks funny spoofs and made excuses when I pushed them on the "not so funny" aspects of their behavior. They had no real motivation to change. They considered Mary a pushover and gloated that they knew how to "push her buttons."

They mostly seemed to want to be left alone, which concerned me. The few family therapy sessions we had did not go well. Mary and her husband spent the time basically begging the boys to change, but the boys barely acknowledged them. One of the twins got up and left in the middle of the third session, and I had seen only Mary since.

At home and in their neighborhood, the boys' attitudes and behavior continued to remain the same. They would scream at Mary when she attempted to discipline them and refused to hand their phones over to her at the dinner table. They would shoot at the other kids with their BB guns and toilet-paper people's houses. One time, they crawled up on a neighbor's roof and dropped water balloons on people walking by. *They're just innocent childhood pranks,* Mary would tell herself time and time again.

Then, one afternoon, Mary's friend Jane from the next neighborhood over was jogging by Mary's house when Mary stepped outside to get the mail. Jane stopped her workout and walked over to Mary. "Is everything okay with the boys?" she asked. Her eyes were filled with concern.

"Sure. Why?" Mary flashed her trademark big, warm smile.

"You know that your sons are getting a bad reputation around here."

"I'm sure they don't mean to hurt anyone." Mary stood up a little straighter. "They are just boys being boys."

These issues were not new to Mary. When they were younger, Mary had trouble setting boundaries with them. They painted on the basement carpet, used Mary's glass flower vases as their soccer goal posts when playing in the house, and were often too rough with their cat. "I just don't get boys," Mary told me as she rested her head in her hand. "My husband comes home and they all wrestle together on the living room couch. The pillows go flying. The blankets get all tangled up. Why do they have to be so wild?"

As the boys got older, their pranks grew more dangerous and offensive. And their repercussions more severe. The week before Mary called me, her boys (who had a pretty large following on social media) directed their followers to text a boy that they were bullying at school with obscene pictures. They then posted this boy's cell phone number and even his picture. The boys were suspended for a week and put on probation for the rest of the school year.

Over those first six months of our private sessions, the strain of her boys' antics weighed more and more heavily on Mary. She confessed that she had started buying paper plates and plastic cups because she was too tired to do the dishes. She was also ordering in food and buying frozen meals. She bought her boys more new school uniforms online because she didn't have the energy to keep up with all the laundry and they did need clean clothes for school. Though Mary was struggling on the inside, she continued to flash that big, warm smile to the world.

By mid-September Mary, like many of my moms who had college-bound teens, was knee-deep into the college selection process. "I'm in college selection hell," Mary announced as she sat down in my office. She laid her pashmina over the arm of her chair and started bouncing her knees. The boys didn't want to stay in state for school and they wanted to see all their options. Mary was now spending her days coordinating college tours and booking flights to California, Boston, and New York—and that was just the first wave of visits.

The boys had no clear set of priorities (beyond going to a good party school), so Mary was setting up tours all over the country with all different types of schools. They had no real thoughts on what they might want to study and ignored Mary when she asked them about possible majors. She overheard one of them talking about wanting to be a video game developer with a friend, which sent Mary into a frenzy when she reported this to me during a session. "I'll be spending $65,000 a year so he can continue to play video games for college credit."

According to the National Center for Educational Statistics, there were over three thousand four-year colleges in the United States in the 2012–2013 school year. As Mary waded into her options, she discovered that her sons could go to small liberal arts schools, big universities, public schools, private schools, all-male schools, online schools, art schools, trade schools, and community colleges. Much like my son in the ice cream parlor, Mary's brain could not handle so many options. She was overloaded. She was also over-tending to her boys. Mary was more invested in this decision than her sons were. Although the college decision was ultimately going to be the boys', Mary wanted to make sure they knew all their options.

Over the next several weekends, Mary and her husband would split up, each taking one son and visiting different colleges around the country. While her husband was busy texting her pictures of fun dinners and funny stories from the tours he was taking with their son, Mary and the other son suffered long silences and strained conversations. This happened every weekend, even though they would alternate between the boys. Mary had assumed that she would connect better with her boys as they got older, but now she wondered if she would ever feel like they loved her.

During the week, Mary compiled a spreadsheet of the schools they had visited. She was capturing things like tuition, direct flights, Greek life, the student ratio for the coding/programming major, and other factors that she felt were important. When she tried to get her sons' opinions of the schools, though, they would tell her that they couldn't remember which school was which. "We've seen so many schools. It's hard to keep them all straight," one son told her. "Instead of adding to the list, we should start narrowing down the list," the other twin said. But every time Mary took one school off, she would find three more to add on.

"That's it," Mary said to me halfway through their national college tour. "I am giving up. I hired a college consultant and have handed the whole project over to her. She can arrange the rest of the tours and figure out which schools each kid should apply to." Mary's eyes were tearing up. "There are just too many choices. I can't decide. When I was younger, I had two choices, and both schools were in the state I grew up in. I did fine. I went on to get a master's. I don't understand why college selection has to be such a nightmare." Mary paused. "And the boys don't seem that concerned about where they end up anyway."

How to Stop Option Overwhelm

Today, everywhere we look there are options, options, and more options for everything, from jeans to cell phones. Although it can be fun to have so many choices, it's not good for us, nor is it very productive. Here are some ways to cut down on your option overload.

Write out your list of options. It's easier to compare and contrast when you have all your choices in front of you.

Prioritize what is necessary. Be clear on "wants" versus "needs."

Figure out what time of day you have the most energy. Make your more important decisions when your head is the clearest.

Silence technology for a period each day. Give your brain a rest so you can better focus on possibilities.

Stop multitasking and monotask. When sorting through choices, focus only on that task.

Columbia Business School professor Sheena Iyengar has shown that in many instances, too many options lead us to be unsatisfied with the choices we do make or to bypass making the choice altogether. In one of her studies, researchers looked at 401(k) participation and found that for every ten plans that were added to the choice pool, the number of people who committed to a plan dropped by 1.5 to 2 percent. When it comes to less meaningful products, like jams and chocolates, researchers found the same idea holds true. Many times, more options create more intrigue, but they also make choosing difficult.

Choices, inherently, are not a bad thing. Choices give you a sense of power and control. They allow you to be an individual. And to flex your creativity. But when you are bombarded with too many choices, this revs up your stress engine. The choices are nearly endless, and this flood of information alarms your brain and signals your stress response that it's time to turn on.

Think about the last time you researched for a new purchase. Maybe it was for a new stroller, your toddler's new bed, your middle schooler's basketball shoes, or where to go on a family vacation. Did you "fight" by over-researching your options? Was your response "flight," where you gave up on the process midway through? Or did you "freeze" and not do anything at all? "I'll get to it," you may have told your spouse, while you came up with a dozen other tasks to complete instead. The irony here is that no matter which stress response you fall back on, none of them accomplishes the job. At least not in a timely or stress-free manner.

I went through a similar process just before my daughter, my eldest child, started kindergarten. For those of you who don't know, school choice in Denver is nothing short of insane and creates the perfect vacuum for moms to get sucked up into the "I need to choose 'the best' option for my child" mind-set. We have 207 public schools and 82 private schools. That's almost 300 schools in a 44.7-square-mile radius! We have schools that are pre-K, K-8, ECE-12, Montessori, charter, innovation, uniforms, full day, half day, and extended day. Program choices include all-girls, all-boys, green schools, those with farms, adventure-based, arts focused, farm-to-table lunches, scratch-food lunches, science and technology focused, International Baccalaureate (IB), STEM, STEAM, Highly Gifted and Talented (HGT or GT), and many more including "traditional." Yes, regular school, like the one you and I went to, now has a title beyond simply . . . school.

I toured eight schools, spoke to countless other parents about their school decision, and clocked too many hours researching the special benefits of each possibility, only to end up in one of the principal's offices two months in. I just kept thinking, *I only have this one shot to get it right. She only goes to kindergarten once.* When it was finally time to make our final decision, I flip-flopped on our choice three times before settling on a school for kindergarten, only to change my daughter's school again when she started first grade.

Researchers in the field of "choice" have learned that the more options people have, the greater their expectations rise. And, in step with these expectations comes their sense of responsibility. One popular online shopping site pulls up over 6,000 options for the search "women's sandals." Another site pulls up close to 400,000 diaper options. A popular supermarket's online store has five pages worth of chocolate chip cookies. *Out of all these options, there must be one perfect choice,* you think to yourself. *Surely, one of these selections is my ideal.* This is what Mary was feeling. If the college ended up not being the right fit for her boys, it would be her fault.

Just as Mary's whirlwind college tour was winding down, she

felt her anxiety subsiding. "It's almost over," she would say to me. She was looking forward to going to bed again just thinking about the last prank the boys pulled, instead of their behavior plus this hellish list of choices. She started counting down the days to their final meeting with the college consultant.

When we met after that meeting, Mary recounted what took place:

"You guys have been very busy," the consultant had started. "You have been in sixteen cities from coast to coast over the last eight weekends. You have toured at least one school—sometimes more—in each city. Have you boys narrowed your options down at all?" she asked.

Mary's heart was racing. *This is it,* she thought to herself. *This process will be over as soon as they give her their lists of schools.*

The boys looked at each other and then at Mary, but said nothing.

"Well?" Mary prodded them. She looked at them with her big, warm smile.

One of the twins swallowed hard. "I'm not going to college next year. I've decided to take a gap year instead."

Following the initial shock, with the scant stamina Mary had left, she threw herself into finding "the best" gap-year program for her son. Early on in her research, she saw that many top-tier schools, including Harvard, endorse gap years, and so she thought this could be a way to get her son into a better college. *It just has to be the right program,* she thought.

"You can go to a third-world country or to Europe!" she shouted to her son over her shoulder while she searched online. "You can do artwork, build houses, do military work, be a tourist. You can pretty much do anything and get college credit and maybe even a scholarship." Every day, Mary found new options and presented them to her son. She even stopped answering her phone and meeting her friends for lunch so she could concentrate more on these options. Mary did want the best for her son. But she also wanted to save face. *I can't talk to my friends—who all have plans for their kids—without knowing what both of my boys will be doing next year,* she thought. *I must have a plan.*

Behind her back, Mary's sons started calling her crazy. But they were also getting concerned. They never knew if they were going to be greeted with "nice mom," "I don't care anymore mom," or "angry mom." She no longer made their lunches in the morning, giving them money instead. This was something she had always been opposed to, because she knew they would take the money and go off campus with their friends to buy pizza or fast food. "I just don't have any fight left," she told me. Eventually, the boys became so confused by the changes in their mother that they asked to come back and see me.

"I think this whole gap-year research has thrown her over the edge," one of the boys said to me. "She doesn't talk about anything else anymore."

"I think she's just having a midlife crisis," the other one said.

I have another client who took her "best quest" for her son's piano teacher to a whole new level. She researched and spoke to other parents to gather a list of the best teachers in the area, and then she proceeded to grill them (she called these interrogations interviews) about their own pedigree. "Who did you study under?" "Who have you trained?" "Where have you played?" "What do you require of your students?" She asked question after question, and always found a reason why she needed to interview someone else.

She grew weary of the process, though she kept persisting. When she finally settled on a teacher, she kept questioning her choice and was often openly critical toward this person. In her quest to have "the best" for her child, she didn't realize that she was not only stressing herself out, but her child as well. "Mom spent so much time getting me the best teacher," her son told me in private. "Now, I feel like I have to be the best, too."

Getting to "the best" is a quest that many moms take on, only to run themselves into the ground days/weeks/months later. The problem is that our choices are not about the products or programs themselves, but rather how these things reflect on us as a person and as a mother. *I'll be a bad mom if I don't get the organic mattress for my toddler's bed,* you tell yourself as you pore over every organic mattress option you can find (online and in stores). And then there is the food you feed your kids (must be organic, grown locally, no GMOs and no high-fructose corn syrup). Your water bottles must be BPA-free. And your soaps and detergents must be free of dyes and perfumes. Otherwise, you're a bad mom who doesn't care about her kids. At least, that's what you tell yourself while you're online researching the newest, safest lunch container at midnight.

In addition to how these products reflect on us as people and as mothers, researchers have noted that our search for the best kicks into high gear when we don't have all the options before us. *Maybe something better is still out there,* we tell ourselves. Think about how many times you have fallen victim to online shopping. What you intend to be a quick search for new yoga pants sends you into an hour and a half of yoga pant reviews before you realize that you need to pick your kids up from school—and you have yet to make your purchase. There is always another page to scroll through, another pair that might make your butt look perkier, another site that is running a sale. In a store, there still may be too many options, but at least you have them all together to see at one time.

And that's the point that these researchers found to be so meaningful when it comes to decision-making. In the absence of other choices to compare against, we will most likely hold out hope that a better option exists. We weigh our tangible options against this intangible ideal. When you are looking at a group of options in front of you, you compare them to each other. And you will most likely be more satisfied with your ultimate decision.

Are You Stuck in Your "Best Quest"?

We all want the best for our kids, but at what cost? If your search for "the best" is interfering with your life and your happiness, it may be time to consider a different approach. A suitable option that works for you in your current situation might be a healthier goal.

Here are a few tip-offs that you are stuck in a "best quest":

- You second-guess every decision you make.

- You secretly search online for parenting advice to back up what you just did a few hours earlier.

- You sit at your desk at work and troll through job listings at other companies.

- You researched the top three minivans ad nauseam and still wondered if you made the right choice.

- You spend so long searching for the perfect swim program that you miss the sign-ups for lessons.

- You have one hour to get yourself a new outfit for your upcoming vacation and you become completely overwhelmed by which store you should choose to go into at the mall.

- You stare at the row of car seats at the baby store and your mind goes blank.

- You get stressed out when you need to choose the restaurant when you go out with your partner or friends.

For Mary, the number of programs she had to choose from seemed endless. She thought this could be her son's one last shot to get into a great school. She also felt like she had messed up a lot with her sons and that this was her opportunity to do something right.

Amid the gap-year research madness, Mary paused her research one night to cook the family dinner. Just the night before, her husband had questioned why they were eating frozen pizza two nights in a row. While Mary was at the stove, the boys were throwing a football around the kitchen. Her husband, who happened to be home early from work that evening, was watching television while lying on the couch. "Can you two stop yelling in here? And stop throwing that ball around," Mary hissed over her shoulder as she stirred the bubbling tomato sauce on the stove.

The boys laughed off Mary's frustration and, in response, started whispering loudly to each other as they continued to throw the football back and forth. Mary could feel a headache coming on. Her neck was in spasms, but she continued to ignore them. "Honey, can you set the table?" she called out to her husband.

"I'll be right there," he yelled back without moving a muscle on the couch.

Just as Mary was carrying the pot of sauce from the stove over to the table, one of her sons threw the ball again and it knocked into her hands. Mary dropped the pot and the red sauce splattered all over her white tiles. Her husband came running into the kitchen to see what had fallen.

Mary looked down at the floor and her jaw clenched. She looked up at the son who had thrown the ball and pointed right at him. "Fuck you!" she shouted. "And fuck you! And fuck you!" she continued as she pointed at her other son and then her husband. "I have been busting my ass dealing with your college stuff and trying to find the best gap-year program. I'm working to save your butts, to save your future, and it means nothing to you."

Mary's sons and husband stood frozen, their eyes wide. They looked at each other and then back at Mary without saying a word.

Mary started again. "You know what, boys? I'm out of here. You guys are on your own now." Mary grabbed her car keys from the kitchen counter and stormed out of the house. Without thinking, she drove right over to her friend Jane's house.

When Mary told me the story during our session the following week, at least she could laugh. "Turns out that Jane's dealing with the same shit as me. Her kids' stuff is all over the place, they give Jane attitude anytime she asks anything of them, and her husband basically hides out in his office until it's time to eat." Mary shook her head and smiled. "Jane said I was her hero for walking out like I did."

While Mary was at Jane's, she got an almost steady flow of

text messages from the twins and her husband. "Are you coming home?" one of the boys asked. "Should we leave some dinner out for you?" the other twin messaged. "Do I need to hire a lawyer?" her husband texted with a smiley face. "The best part of this whole story comes at the end, though," Mary told me as she squirmed forward to the edge of her seat. "When I got home, the house was spotless. The boys' lunches were made for the next day. And the next morning, everyone got themselves up and fed. I felt like I had fallen into some kind of alternate universe." Mary flashed her big, warm smile.

Then, Mary cleared her throat and sat back again in her chair. The sparkle in her eyes dimmed. "I don't know what to do with them," she said. "My only job in life is these kids. And I'm failing!" Tears rolled down her cheeks as her voice got louder and louder. "They are messy and full of energy. They climb all over everything and burp for fun. I just can't relate to them, my own kids! There is just so much testosterone in my house. I think I would know how to be a mom to girls. I'm a great aunt to my nieces." Mary wiped the tears from her cheeks. "I resent them for showing me every day just how incompetent I am at being their mother." Mary looked down at her lap. "I resent them for being so difficult that I couldn't have a career while raising them. But the boys were constantly causing grief. No matter what age they were, I always had to be around to bail them out of trouble."

Mary's resentment toward her kids reminded me of a Ted Talk I had heard in 2005 given by psychologist and author Barry Schwartz, titled *The Paradox of Choice.* In his talk, Dr. Schwartz explains that although the proliferation of choice *should* make us freer and happier, in many cases the opposite occurs. There's an opportunity cost to every choice we make, meaning that there is always a choice we did not move forward with. And the more choices we have, the more opportunities we give up when we make a choice. I often succumb to this feeling with weekend activities. No matter where I end up—be it a party, a school function, or a sports game with my kids—I'm sitting there thinking about the other places I could be at that time.

Mary's opportunity cost was that she gave up her career as a nutritionist for her kids. When Mary looked at her sons, she saw lost opportunities to be doing something else that she loved and that she was good at. Remember Stacy with the young twin girls from chapter one? She resented her kids for stealing away her identity and her freedom. Amy, from chapter two, who nearly cheated on her husband because she was so starved for emotional connection, resented her kids for dashing the perfect image she had of how children should act, and for the additional (and unexpected) amount of time she had to spend parenting them. Many mothers suffering from mommy burnout secretly resent their kids for whatever they feel they are giving up being a mom. Instead of admitting their feelings, they pretend these choices don't exist, or don't matter, even as they chase them through their days.

I could see how much Mary was struggling and feeling powerless, and so I reminded her that none of her choices are fixed. Mary's sons were about to leave the house, and so she would soon have time to do things just for her. We took our next few sessions to brainstorm and plan Mary's next steps for her life, which ultimately led to her accepting a part-time position at the university hospital's nutrition department.

Limit Your Options and Your Overwhelm

Know what overwhelms you and what overwhelms your kids. Are your kids into the energy of the mall? Does it drain them? How about you? Know what you and your kids can handle and if what you've got planned is too much, make a different plan.

Limit your choices for your kids and for yourself. Avoid anxiety by homing in on only two or three options. Remember: the more options you have, the greater chance you'll end up with a melt-down on your hands.

Set boundaries. Answer the question, "Will this xxx bring my family joy?" Family time is disappearing because many parents accommodate what each of their children want to do by splitting up on the weekends. Sometimes family time is more important than each family member's individual preferences. Focus on compromise, rather than an "all or nothing" decision.

Shift your mind-set from "the best" to what works for your family. Parents are looking for the best school, the best team, the best *everything*, but that's not always feasible and it creates stress. A little dissatisfaction, at first, is not always a bad thing.

Create emotional boundaries. The people in your life should bring you joy. Friends are nearly as essential as food and water to your life, so have only healthy ones. And remember to focus on quality rather than quantity.

Mommy Burnout Prescription Plan

BONUS EXERCISE

Force yourself to choose from only three options (at most) for any decisions that come up over the next week. Afterward, note how this impacted the amount of time you spent researching and what this did to your overall stress level.

Chapter 6

He Just Doesn't Get It

How Burnout Puts Our Marriages in Jeopardy

Sound familiar?

It's not uncommon for common issues between moms and dads to contribute to the mom's burnout. If any of the following sounds familiar, take a step back and think about how you can reconnect with your partner.

- You are more concerned about how your kids are doing than you are with your husband. Sometimes you even forget to ask him how his day was.

- You mainly argue about the kids and how you each handle things. You can't seem to get on the same page when it comes to parenting.

- You avoid issues that need to be addressed in your relationship. You think talking about these issues will only lead to fighting.

- You want to hug and kiss and cuddle with your spouse, but you are afraid that may lead to sex. You avoid touching your husband or letting him touch you.

Heather was forty-one years old and married, with a five-year-old daughter and two-year-old son. Her husband worked out of the home in technology sales while Heather worked as a surgeon and taught at a medical school. They had been married for eleven years.

This couple originally came to see me because their daughter was getting aggressive at home and school, but it soon became apparent that they had their own issues to work out. They were dealing with untraditional roles in the house and struggling to understand the other's point of view when it came to parenting. While this was mildly stressful for her husband, Heather described it as highly stressful for her. Her experience of their arrangement caused her to lose focus at work, worry throughout the day, and dread coming home.

When mothers already feel stretched too thin, they oftentimes will look to their husbands for support that they are sometimes not able to provide. They just aren't wired the same way women are, and so they perceive and handle stresses differently. They also parent differently. When both partners understand the contribution that the other makes to their kids in his or her own way, couples can thrive and moms won't get sucked down into mommy burnout. But when moms unconsciously expect their husbands to fulfill the role of their girlfriends—which happens a lot—they perpetually find that this need is not met, and so they suffer.

I had been treating Heather and Chris for several months when he told me this story. "It was a few months ago, just before Christmas, and I thought I was doing something *nice* for Heather by offering to take the kids to the mall to get some shopping done," Chris explained during a session with his wife.

"I cannot believe you are telling this story," Heather snapped, shifting her body in the chair next to her husband as she tucked her dark blond hair behind her ears.

"Heather was in another one of her 'stressed-out moods' [he used air quotes here], so I thought it was best to just get everyone out of the house."

I nodded my head and looked back and forth between the two of them.

"Anyway," Chris continued, "you know how long it takes to get two little kids bundled into their winter gear and out the door. And Heather is barking out the shopping list to me while we are wrestling the kids into their puffy jackets and mittens."

"I heard the mudroom door close," Heather cut Chris off. "Then, I heard the car back out and the garage door close and I felt like I could breathe again." The house was finally quiet. As Heather walked by the kitchen table, she noticed the coupons that she wanted Chris to use at the mall. She ran outside with the coupons, figuring she would catch him in the driveway. But when she got out there, she saw the kids in the running car, but Chris wasn't with them. *"What the hell is going on? Where is he?* I thought to myself." Just as she was about to open the car door and ask the kids where Daddy went, she saw him rounding the corner from the backyard and zipping up his pants. "My eyes nearly bulged out of my head," she told me. "'What are you doing?' I asked him."

I looked at Chris. "What were you doing?" I asked.

"I went around to the side of the house and peed in a bush." He fought to hold back his smile.

Heather covered her face with her hands. I bit the inside of my lip and struggled to keep a straight face.

"'What are you doing? Are you crazy? The neighbors could have seen you!'" Chris said in his best imitation of his wife's voice. He started laughing. "She yelled at me! I was so afraid of my wife that I peed outside in thirty-degree weather rather than go back inside my house. And I still got in trouble anyway!"

I remembered back to their first session just a few months ago when these two barely looked at each other. She talked over him when he tried to explain that their daughter was fine. And he rolled his eyes while she went on about how their daughter was *not* fine. I got the impression that they hadn't had an actual conversation with each other in a while.

Heather and Chris met in California thirteen years ago, when she was in medical school and he was working in the tech industry. "We clicked immediately," Heather told me in one of their first sessions. "I was always shy. I like to read and am more low-key. I'm more serious. But Chris is so charming. He is always the 'funny one' in a group and the life of the party. I guess I felt like he taught me to lighten up. We laughed a lot. We went out as much as we could. We were all about having fun."

After Heather graduated, she completed a fellowship and landed a job as a surgeon at a hospital in Denver. As part of her position, she teaches at the medical school and works in the operating room weekly. "This job was literally my dream," she explained. "I had been wanting a job like this since college. And I worked really hard to get it." The couple got engaged shortly after Heather's job offer came through and Chris secured an arrangement whereby he could remain in his job, but work from home in Denver. "My career was set. Chris's career was on track. We were together. I expected us to live happily ever after."

Chris added, "I originally thought it would be so great to work from home. I wouldn't have to get up at the crack of dawn to get to the office. I wouldn't have to get dressed up every day or have people noticing when I got to the office and when I left. I was really looking forward to this change." But the reality of working from home proved more stressful than he anticipated. Chris didn't factor in his social personality. "I missed the face-to-face time with my coworkers during the day, things like going out to lunch with someone from my team or a client," he said. "It's lonely working from home."

Heather, on the other hand, could not have been happier. She soon climbed the ranks in her field and had a team of residents she mentored. She became a sought-after lecturer at the medical school, published several well-received papers, and developed an outstanding reputation as a surgeon with a great bedside manner. "I just love what I do. And I know that I'm good at it. I know that I'm helping people."

As Heather grew more and more competent and content with her work, Chris's happiness with his work situation waned. Still, together they were happy. "We planned to have two kids, close together," Heather said. "My sister and I are only two years apart and we grew up so close." Heather looked over at Chris with tears in her eyes during one of our initial sessions. "What happened to our happy life?"

Early on in our work together, Heather walked me through her "typical day." Her days at the hospital never had a dull moment. She would check in on a few patients, remove a bursting appendix, repair a hernia or some other surgery, and then meet with her residents at the end of the day. She often had to cut this meeting short, which she always felt guilty about, because Chris would start texting her just after five o'clock. "If I could only be two places at once," she told me.

In her car, Heather would buckle her seat belt, pull her jacket closer around her body, and pick up her cell to call Chris at home. "I just sit there staring at the phone for a full sixty seconds, debating whether I should call Chris to let him know that I'm leaving," she explained. Most nights, she would place the phone back down on the seat next to her. "I just need a few minutes to myself on the drive home before walking into the house of chaos," Heather said. Then, she would fish a chocolate bar out of her bag and take two bites before turning the key in her ignition.

As Heather drove home, she'd continue to chomp through her chocolate bar as a sense of dread washed over her body. "I have to mentally prepare myself for what I will soon walk into," she explained. In her mind, she imagined the floor littered with the kids' toys and that at least one of the kids would be screaming about what Chris had made for dinner. She'd give it a 50/50 shot that her five-year-old's homework would be done. As Heather pulled into the driveway, she would check her voicemails and emails one last time, hoping that someone needed her to call or email back. Finally, she would toss the empty chocolate bar wrapper back into her bag, take a deep breath in, and open the car door.

Most nights, Heather would walk into the house and then directly over to the children. Within those fifteen or so feet, she would usually slide, trip, or stumble over a small bouncy ball, toy, or juice puddle on the floor. As she regained her balance or picked up toys, Heather would glare in Chris's direction and mumble a hello to him under her breath.

"My son is usually yelling about how he hates carrots or broccoli or whatever vegetable Chris has given him. But, by that time, I have been up since five in the morning and I can't take his yelling, so I tell him to just leave the food he doesn't want on his plate, which sends Chris storming off to hide in his office," Heather explained.

"We agree on something where the kids are concerned, and then Heather backs down as soon as they cry," Chris jumped in to tell me. "I let the kids choose their vegetable and then they have to eat a few bites. I deal with their crying. I can wait them out. Why can't she?"

Heather rolled her eyes at her husband's last comment and then explained that after her husband stomps out of the kitchen, their daughter pinches, hits, or irritates their son in some way. "Then my son cries again and bats at his sister from his chair." Heather rubbed her temples as she replayed the scene for me. "Then I tell our daughter to go sit in the corner for a time-out, but, of course, she never moves. I have zero energy by this point, so I just slump into my chair and push my food around my plate for a few minutes before I clear the table and wash the dishes."

After dinner, Heather would recheck their daughter's homework even though Chris did it with her earlier that afternoon. She would also refold the laundry that he had folded that day. *He literally can't do anything right,* she'd think to herself. Then, she'd sneak a few cookies from the pantry before heading upstairs.

In our sessions, Chris frequently aired his disapproval of the way Heather would waltz into the house and take over without even saying hello to him. "She barely even looks in my direction when she walks through the door." Chris turned to his wife. "It's like you think I'm a stand-in parent until you—the real parent— grace us with your presence. I don't think you trust me as their father." Chris looked at me. "What kind of wife doesn't even say hello to her husband when she comes home?"

"I don't talk to you because every time I walk in the door from work, you are ready to jump down my throat because I'm late or you pick fights with me over something the kids did that day. You just start bitching the second you see me. And then you run into your office and sulk," Heather snapped back at him. "I realize that you're with the kids all afternoon. But I'm working."

Chris practically jumped up from his chair. "You're working?" He laughed, sarcastically. "You're working? Well, I'm working, too. I'm not the nanny. I have a job, a minor detail that you keep forgetting. And I take off early to deal with the kids or to do errands when you ask so that *you* don't have to be inconvenienced." Chris drew in a breath. "And I can't tell you how annoying it is when you ask me to do something and I take time out of my day to do it and then you go ahead and do it yourself. Why do you do that?"

Heather sat back in her chair. "I do that?"

"All the time!" Chris said. His face was getting red. "It's not like I have a road map for being a dad who works from home. My own dad would leave before I went to school and get home in time for dinner. And that's as much as I saw him. I'm trying my best to be a good dad and a good husband." Chris paused. "I love being able to spend time with the kids. But I do *work* also."

Heather looked down at her lap. "I know you do. I shouldn't have said that."

Chris and Heather's nontraditional family roles are becoming more and more common. Pew Research has found that since 1965, the role of the father within the household has undergone a rather dramatic shift. The study reports that between 1965 and 2015, fathers have more than doubled their time spent doing household chores and nearly tripled the time spent with their children. Women, during this same window of time, have expanded their presence on the job front. The Center for American Progress found that in 2015 numbers continued to follow an upward trend in female breadwinners, with 42 percent of women reported as being the primary or sole breadwinner in their family, meaning that they earned at least half of their family's income. As with any transition, these shifting roles have afforded new opportunities for moms, dads, and their kids, but they also come with a fair amount of friction.

As Heather and Chris continued to volley the significance of their roles back and forth, I thought of another couple that I see. They have what our culture would deem more traditional family roles. She stays home with their baby and he works outside of the house.

Recently, the husband took up an old passion of his—guitar. He practices every night after the baby goes down. "It's amazing," the wife told me. "My husband is in the basement. My daughter is sleeping in her crib. And I get to relax by myself in bed for a few hours before I go to sleep. I read my *Vogue* and catch up on mindless television."

Everything was going great until one night, when the husband had a brilliant new idea for his wife. "Babe," he said as he approached their bedroom during his guitar time one Saturday evening. "I know what you should do."

She looked up at him over her magazine.

"You used to sing. Why don't you sing while I play? This way, we can be together. It'll be great!"

The wife's stomach flipped. *Are you kidding me?* she thought at first and then quickly moved to, *There is no way in hell I am giving up my alone time. He doesn't understand what it's like to have a kid hanging on you all day long. The last thing I want is late-night jam sessions in our basement with my husband hanging all over me.* She was right. He didn't understand. But, then again, how could he?

Chris and Heather have also run up against each other as they both try to defend their parenting experiences. "You don't understand what it's like to be a mother," Heather said to Chris during one of our sessions. "I used to be able to talk to you about anything. But as soon as we had the kids, it was like I started speaking a foreign language to you. That support I used to get from you disappeared. My girlfriends who don't live in the house with us understand my life better than you do." Heather reached for a tissue. "You don't understand how stressed I am."

"Of course I don't totally understand your *mothering experience*," Chris said, incredulously. "I'm a father."

Although I knew that Chris was being facetious toward his wife, he was right. It's no secret that men and women are wired differently. As women, our unique brains and hormones nudge us in certain directions, whether we are under stress, looking for connection, or even choosing a movie to watch on a Friday night. Yet when moms and dads come to my office, they are astounded to hear that the experiences of motherhood and fatherhood are also quite different.

According to a Pew Research report, mothers are more likely to acknowledge their helicopter tendencies with their kids. With the couples I see, this overprotection can often be a point of contention. "She is constantly bringing them to the doctor and hovering over them when they play," fathers will tell me. Wives will then launch into their husband's roughhousing with their kids at bedtime and how their husband never seems to know where anything is in the house. "We have this one drawer that's had only our son's onesies in it since he was born six months ago. And, still, my husband will say he can't find any onesies when he is changing him," one client told me. "It's beyond frustrating that even when he's helping, he doesn't actually help!"

All of these differences, and the many hurdles of modern parenting, create difficult situations and often stress. This is where the fault lines between men and women become most apparent because not only do men and women stress over different things, but they handle stress in completely different ways. Men tend to feel stress in response to events involving *external outcomes* and *performance,* such as getting a promotion, providing for their family, and being able to buy a nice house in a good neighborhood. Women, on the other hand, are more *internally* focused and are wired to be more communicative. We experience stress with relationships as well as safety and protection, especially for ourselves and our children.

As discussed in chapter one, our stress response can also be expressed differently by gender. Men, for the most part, will remain in fight-or-flight-or-freeze mode, whereas women will move into a tend-and-befriend mode. When it comes to stresses with their kids, men focus on making the problem go away, while moms focus on tending to their child. This division creates strife in a marriage or relationship unit, as evidenced by this couple. Heather, for example, wanted to talk about why her daughter was aggressive with other kids. Chris, on the other hand, simply wanted strategies to make her stop behaving this way.

They thought they were having the same conversation with each other, but their goals in their conversations were vastly different. Heather wanted Chris to be like a girlfriend who would dissect her issues from every angle and help her process. Women look to their husbands for support and empathy. But men don't typically communicate this way. Yes, they can be supportive and empathetic; it just shows up differently. Chris could never stand in for Heather's girlfriends.

Chris wanted Heather to stop analyzing the situation and spring into solutions with new strategies. He wanted her to partner with him in action, and he was confused and frustrated by Heather reading his action plans as unsympathetic to her feelings. "I think I'm helping with our daughter," Chris told me, "and then

I see Heather eyeing us from across the room with tight lips and shaking her head. It's like I can't do anything right in our house."

Both Chris and Heather wanted something that the other was not capable of giving them. And that's what they focused on. They needed to identify and embrace each other's parenting differences and talents, but that takes some time. Until then, they were talking, but they were not effectively communicating.

Stress Management Strategies for Moms and Dads

Men and women feel stress because of different things and also experience stress differently. It only makes sense, then, that strategies to manage stress would also be different according to gender. Here is a quick guide to stress management for you and your man.

Moms

- Focus on exercise as a stress-reliever rather than a tummy- or butt-firmer. Find activities where you are moving and joyful, and keep doing them, whether this is a half-hour walk through the park or waiting for everyone to leave the house so you can crank up "Hit Me Baby One More Time" and dance around your house. Just find something you find fun and can make consistent.

- Follow your natural instincts and call your girlfriends to vent, cry, or just talk. Don't expect your husband to fill this role, and don't get mad at him when he can't or tries to problem-solve instead. If that bugs you, he's not your "ventee."

- Stop picking the fries off your kid's plate and sneaking Oreos while the kids are brushing their teeth. Junky food only makes you feel worse. Focus on truly feel-good foods like fruits, vegetables, and nuts. If you need a pick-me-up or a treat, go for the good stuff—like dark chocolate. If it is high quality, you'll enjoy it so much more.

- Power nap for twenty minutes when you feel the stress start to overwhelm you. You'll wake up feeling refreshed and better equipped to handle the issues at hand.

- Set an intention for each day by writing your goal for the day down on a sticky note while you are still in bed and before your feet hit the floor every morning. Stick the note somewhere where you will see it often—like in your purse or on your keys—throughout the day.

- Carve out five minutes every single day before lunchtime to close your eyes, sit in silence, and give your senses a rest.

Dads

- Men tend to handle stress better if they can "do something," so let your partner go for that drive, take that bike ride, or start building the deck when he is frustrated or feeling overwhelmed.

- If your guy is athletic, suggest that he join a sports league to get out his stress and meet new friends.

- Suggest that he bond with the kids by roughhousing or playing before dinner—not at bedtime—so everyone gets to bed on time.

- Encourage him to get eight hours of sleep at night, not to burn the midnight oil falling down the Internet rabbit hole or playing video games to get his stress out.

- Find the humor in your days together by sending each other funny videos or watching your favorite funny movies once a week. Comedic relief can often help lighten the whole family.

- Suggest that he get out into nature. Even better, take a walk outside together.

Over the months, Heather and Chris continued to tangle over their daughter. "How can you *not* think this is a problem?" Heather leaned forward in her chair toward her husband and glared at him. The color in her cheeks was rising. She took a sip from her coffee and looked at me, but I remained silent.

"It's a drawing. I don't understand what the big deal is." Chris sat back in his chair and crossed his arms. He glanced in my direction and then back at his wife. "So maybe she was sad that day, so she drew herself crying."

"Even the clouds are crying!" Heather yelled at him, now starting to cry herself. "And this is the fourth drawing like this she has given to me. She's six years old now and miserable. And you don't see it at all." Heather sniffled. "Yesterday her teacher told me that she often instigates fights between other girls. You know she does that to us, too, because we don't agree on anything." Heather sat back in her chair and smoothed her skirt over her knees.

Now they were both looking at me.

"We used to be best friends," Heather said. "We were in sync about everything. I don't know what happened. I remember when our daughter was only a few weeks old. I was still on maternity leave and was up to my ears in laundry. I had stale baby vomit on my shirt from hours before and she had just had her third blow-out diaper of the day. I just couldn't take it anymore. I laid down on her floor and started bawling. And then Chris comes in and starts laughing."

"I was just trying to lighten the mood," Chris jumped in. "You were so serious and dramatic. I mean, babies poop. It's not like it was a surprise."

"He thinks that I'm too serious with the kids, that I freak out every time they get a scratch or have a runny nose," Heather said, teary-eyed. "But I don't think he's serious enough. I feel like he just doesn't take *anything* seriously. And that the responsibility of keeping the kids safe and healthy rests entirely on my shoulders." Heather's lips pushed out into a pout. "He can't even tell when the kids have a fever."

I often hear this from moms. Their perspective is that their husbands are not as clued into their kids as they are, sometimes to the point that they worry that their husbands just don't care. I had another couple whose eighth-grade daughter came out to them as gay. While the wife was not at all surprised, and wanted to show her daughter love and support, the husband was unsure about his daughter's proclamation.

"How does she know that she's gay at thirteen years old?" he said in one session, looking back and forth between his wife and me. "She's too young to make that decision."

The mom scoffed. "Come on, didn't you see the signs? She never liked to wear dresses. She was always playing outside in the mud and getting dirty. Didn't you notice that she never went through the pink stage? She was never into princesses when she was younger. And, now, she never talks about boys or even celebrities that she has a crush on." The wife shook her head. "I have known this since she was a little kid."

"How could you know this?" the husband asked. "Not every little girl is into princesses. Maybe she just doesn't want to talk to us about boys. How do you *know* this? And more importantly, how does *she* know this? I don't believe that a person really knows something like this until they are older."

A mother's intuition. A mother's gut instincts. This special way that moms know their kids goes by different names. A recent study published in *Nature Neuroscience* may have given some credence to this notion. Researchers found that pregnant women experience a "pruning away" of connections within the area of their brain that processes social interactions. This means that soon-to-be moms are left with less brain volume than their spouses or women who have never been pregnant. Teens go through a similar process as their brains mature and they enter adulthood. The prevalent idea here is that this pruning weeds out the extraneous connections that allow us to readily learn new things while the remaining connections lead us to sharper thinking and more balanced emotions that are more necessary in adulthood. Researchers believe this same kind of pruning could be mother nature's way of helping moms transition into their new role in life. Perhaps this pruning helps moms focus more on their baby, which could be why many moms feel that they are more in tune with their kids than their spouses are.

The following morning, Heather and Chris attended a parent-teacher conference at their daughter's school. Heather had to drive over from the hospital, so they came to the meeting separately. Chris leaned over to give his wife a peck on the cheek when they met in the parking lot, but Heather turned her head. "Let's just get through this meeting," she told him. "I have to get back to work."

Are You Expecting Something from Your Husband That He Can't Give You?

Many moms who are burned out look to their husbands for support. And although it is important to maintain your relationship with your husband, it's equally as important to know what he actually can give to you so that you stop arguing and adding to your burnout.

- You get home from shopping excited to tell your husband all about the fabulous new boots that you just bought on sale and then get disappointed when he's not only not as thrilled as you are, but points out that you have five other pairs of boots already in your closet.

- You come home from work and want to vent about your coworker, but you get frustrated when your husband tells you how to handle the situation. You just wanted him to listen.

- You come home upset about your haircut and your husband agrees, "You're right. I liked it a lot better before."

- You come home bursting to tell your husband that two of your neighbors are having an affair with each other and your husband responds with, "What's for dinner?"

- You are secretly upset with your husband for not noticing that you seem sad.

As soon as everyone was settled into the classroom, their daughter's teacher got started. "Academically, your daughter is doing well. She is reading at the top of her class. She writes her name beautifully. I am very pleased with her academic progress."

Chris smiled and looked over at Heather. Heather leaned forward in her chair toward the teacher.

"However, I do have some emotional concerns," the teacher continued. "She cries at least once a day, she yells at her friends, she tries to eat the other kids' snacks." The teacher paused. "I guess you could say that she's a strong-willed child. But I would love to see her playing nicer with the other kids and learning how to calm herself down a bit more."

Heather's jaw tightened as she remembered the chocolate bars in her purse. There was a little back and forth before Chris thanked the teacher for her time and they both walked out of the room.

"Are you still going to tell me that nothing is going on with our daughter after sitting through that conference?" Heather snapped at Chris as they walked to the parking lot. Tears were rolling down her cheeks. "She's yelling at the other kids. She is crying all the time. She's sneaking food."

Chris looked at Heather, but said nothing.

"What?" she yelled at him. "What do you want to say?"

"She sounds a lot like her mother," Chris said.

Chris and Heather took a week off from our sessions when Heather went on a spa getaway with two girlfriends from her childhood. When they came back to my office, Heather showed up with red eyes and Chris immediately sat down and crossed his arms. I tried to make eye contact with Chris, but he just looked back blankly. I turned to Heather and shifted in my chair. "How was the trip?" I asked her.

"You would think that I would be totally rested after a spa trip." Heather gave me a half smile.

I remained silent as Heather patted at her eyes with a tissue.

"The trip itself was amazing," Heather said. "The whole place smelled of lavender, so you couldn't help but relax. We had massages every day, did yoga in the afternoons, and had great conversations while looking out at the mountains." Heather smiled a little. "It felt really good to reconnect."

"Sounds like it was just what you needed." I smiled back at her.

"But then, on the last day, I had a realization that's been bothering me ever since."

Chris looked down at the floor.

Heather took a deep breath. "We were sitting around, nibbling on homemade trail mix from the spa, sipping on warm chamomile tea, and taking in this beautiful view of the mountaintops. And then one of my friends gets a text from her husband. It was a picture of their son, and she starts showing us all the pictures that he had sent her over the three days. As she's scrolling through the pictures, she starts talking about how she misses her family."

Chris looked up at me.

"Then, my other friend says that she misses her family also. And they start getting into all the little things they miss, like one kid's silly dances, and the other kid's attempt to speak in different accents. They both said they missed their husbands and felt rested and ready to go home."

"What did you say?" I asked her.

"Nothing. I said nothing. They both looked at me to chime in and I just kept stuffing my mouth with the trail mix. I didn't want to say that I was happy. I was able to breathe again," she

replied. "There were no sticky fingers grabbing at me. Or shriek-
ing. Or fighting. There were no to-do lists to complete or lunches
to make. I wasn't nagging Chris over something stupid with the
kids. Do you know how good it feels to only brush your own teeth
at night before getting into bed? Or to sit in a nice restaurant and
relax while you enjoy your meal? It was perfect." Heather paused.

I looked over at Chris and then back to her.

"I realized that I didn't want to go home," Heather said.

Chris took a deep breath, got up, and excused himself to the
restroom.

A mother's burnout clearly impacts multiple facets of her life,
including her marriage. Within their marriages, moms can become emotionally unavailable and resentful, like Heather was
that Chris stayed at home and was able to spend more time with
the kids than she did. "I feel like I'm trying to squeeze in time
with my children and it's just never enough," she told me. Some
women judge their husbands doing anything for themselves, like
going out for a jog or out to lunch for work, as irritating, a personal insult to them.

Moms often feel like they live with their partner underneath
the same roof, yet they and their partner live in two different
worlds. "He just doesn't get me," clients will tell me repeatedly.
"These things just don't bother him the way they bother me."
And, unsurprisingly, most of these burnout moms are not having
sex with their husbands. The thought of even cuddling on the
couch or kissing makes many of these women cringe.

The following week, Chris and Heather were back in my office.
This time, Chris started. "It was bedtime and, of course, Heather
was cuddling up with the kids. I was all the way on the other side

of the bed watching Netflix with my headphones on." He glanced at Heather. "And as usual, the three of them fell asleep together."

"I could have only been sleeping for thirty minutes when I heard Chris whispering my name," Heather then piped in. "I opened my eyes to find him hovering over me and the kids. I was startled, of course. Then, as I'm peeling the kids off me and trying to focus my eyes, he's sweet-talking me to go downstairs with him to have sex." Heather crossed her arms and legs.

Chris sat silently next to her, nodding his head.

"I can't believe that Chris still wants to have sex with everything going on right now. I am worried that our daughter is going to get kicked out of school and that something is wrong with me that I don't miss my family while away. I'm pissed that Chris is ignoring all of this. I'm exhausted from work and the kids. How could he even think about sex?" Heather burst out crying.

"We used to have sex all the time, before the kids took over our bed," Chris said.

Heather covered her face with her hands.

"I'm stressed also. But this situation with us and how we deal with the kids isn't going away overnight. Our problems will still be there after we have sex," Chris explained to me.

"I just don't understand how you can flip a switch on and off like that. I need to talk about our issues and get back on the same page before we have sex again. I can't just turn it on like you can." Heather looked at her husband.

"Well, I need to have sex," Chris said. "I don't understand what's so wrong about that, we talk all the time."

I can't tell you how many moms I know who have stopped having sex with their husbands. Just like co-sleeping with their kids (which many moms use as an excuse to avoid intimacy and sex), sexless marriages are another one of moms' dirty little secrets. Most of my clients don't admit to anyone but me that they haven't slept with their husbands in months.

I have heard countless stories of mothers falling asleep with their kids, going to sleep early, and even going into other rooms to change for fear that their husband will see them naked and want to get frisky. These moms will do anything to avoid a roll

What's Getting Between You and Your Husband in Bed?

- Get your kids out of the bed. Reclaim your bedroom so you and your husband can get intimate again—both physically and emotionally.

- Make time to talk to each other—after you put the kids to bed and before you fall asleep or go back to your work or your email, talk to your spouse.

- Make the effort to be affectionate with your husband (kiss, hold hands, hug).

- Make eye contact with each other and stop multitasking. Don't look at your computer while you're talking to each other.

- Make date night a priority, and try to do it at least once a month.

- Make time for one another while the kids are awake. Don't talk only when you are both exhausted. It's healthy for your kids to see you and your spouse talking and acting as a team.

in the sheets with their husband. The burned-out moms I see are having sex only once or twice a month at best.

Why? They are overtired, still angry about an earlier argument with their husband, too drained from their kids and work to feel sexy, self-conscious about their bodies, or all of the above. It can take a while for women to feel sexy again after having kids. Regardless of what they look like, many moms tell me that they just don't feel attractive anymore. Maybe they haven't gone to the gym in a while. Maybe they haven't had their hair cut in months. They don't want to buy new clothes until they lose those pesky ten pounds. They report having little to no sex drive left. They just don't feel pretty, which makes feeling sexy next to impossible.

Many moms also find it hard to see their bodies as sexual after they have carried a baby, given birth, and breastfed. "My boobs are for my baby," they will tell me. "Not for my husband." These are issues that are difficult to talk about—with a close friend or your husband. After a while, many husbands just get tired of waiting for their wives to initiate sex or be open to it. A silent elephant pops up with them in the bedroom.

Heather and Chris each seemed surprised by the other's desire (or lack of desire) to have sex. Heather was stressed about her daughter and kept looking to her husband for comfort. She wanted to talk through their issues. Chris, on the other hand, wanted to do something about their problem. And to him, sex was a healthy way for them to connect as a couple.

"You know, Heather," I said, "I understand that you need to process what's going on with you, your daughter, and your marriage. In addition to talking to Chris at home and in therapy, you may want to talk to other moms who may be in a similar situation. Women are generally wired to communicate in a process-oriented way. Chris may not be or maybe he has processed all he can right now. If you keep trying to talk to him like he's one of your girlfriends, you are going to remain frustrated," I told her. "You also need to let him be a dad in his own way. He's not going to do everything the way you would. But it doesn't make his way wrong. The more space and trust that you give him, the more relaxed you will feel, the more time you will have and the closer you two will get. Just think of the time you will save by not refolding the laundry," I said with a smile.

I then turned my attention to Chris. "Even though Heather's not going to have those long and supportive conversations with you, you can still talk to each other about strategies to help your daughter. You *can* problem-solve together. And you can use Heather's motherly insights to help you develop a plan to structure and support your daughter. She needs to talk to you, and you need to listen. *And* you need to understand that until Heather feels emotionally connected to you, sex may continue to be difficult for her to desire. But that doesn't mean that you can't still be close physically."

I looked at both of them now. "For starters, you need to get your kids out of your bed. You need to create a space that is just for you two. Your kids, and especially your daughter, have dominated your physical space, your conversations, and your emotional triggers. It's time to reclaim your relationship for just the two of you."

For the first time since we'd been working together, Chris and Heather looked at each other with soft eyes. "That sounds like a good plan," Chris said with a smile.

"I like this plan too," Heather said softly. She then leaned over to give Chris a peck on the cheek. "But I'm still not having sex with you tonight." Chris was able to laugh and felt better knowing that at least they had a plan that they both felt good about working on together.

Cool Down Your Burnout and
Heat Up Your Marriage

Let your husband be a dad in his own way. Assuming he is not harming the kids, let him horseplay and connect with the kids in the way that feels most natural to him.

Make time to talk without the kids. Talk about your days, about your relationship, or even the weather. It matters less what you talk about, just that you talk—and don't wait until the kids go to bed. Model this behavior in front of them.

Remember that the marriage that you model for your children has a lifelong effect on the type of relationship and partner they will seek out as adolescents and beyond. Be mindful of the relationship image you are projecting to your kids. Give each other a peck on the lips. Hold hands. And say, "I love you" to each other in front of your kids.

Let your husband help. Let go of how the T-shirts are folded and the dishwasher is loaded and just accept his help. After all, he is your partner in this life.

Plan date nights for you and your husband. Pay attention to how much alone time you both require to feel reenergized as a couple and then schedule it.

Chapter 7

What the Hell Am I Doing with My Life?

The Working Mom's Dilemma

Sound Familiar?

So many moms believe that the other side of the "work" fence is better. They also think that as soon as they feel stressed, bored, or frustrated, that must mean they should change their work status. Whether you work or not is a decision that stems from your family's needs and values.

Read the following list and decide if your work situation is fueling your mommy burnout.

- You question why you are doing what you do, whether that's staying at home with your kids (which you find unfulfilling) or working outside of the home (which makes you feel guilty that you don't see your kids as often as you'd like to).

- You think that what you do (paid work or staying with your kids) may be not worth the stress it causes or the money you earn.

- You still wonder who you will be when you "grow up" because, even at this age, you don't feel like you are able to achieve what you want in life—whether that's financial success, work recognition, or enjoying the time you spend tending to your children and home.

- You feel time is running out to achieve your dreams and you don't know the next steps to take to accomplish what you want in life, whether that's in your profession or your personal life.

- You feel like you should be working if you are at home with your kids and vice versa.

- You wonder about the purpose of life in general and constantly question if doing something different (either working outside of the home or staying with your kids) will bring you closer to clarity around your purpose.

- You secretly have something you want to do in life—like maybe start your own company, travel to different countries, or run a marathon—but it feels too big to accomplish.

Tracy was forty-three years old and married, with three kids. Her daughter was seven years old and her two sons were ages five and three. Tracy and her husband were both divorce attorneys and had built up one of the most successful divorce practices in the area. As lawyers and business owners, they both worked round the clock, making themselves available for clients, attorneys they were handling cases with, and their own employees. To stay at the top of their industry, they both felt they needed to focus on and dedicate their time to their business.

Tracy first came to see me with her daughter, Jenna. She asked that I test her daughter for a possible learning disability because Tracy was getting reports from school that Jenna was losing her concentration in class and making careless errors in her work that seemed inconsistent with her abilities. When the test results came back that Jenna didn't have any specific learning challenges, Tracy asked if she could see me instead. It turns out that Tracy's work schedule was sucking up all her family time and she was struggling to fit everything she needed to do (including seeing her kids) into her days.

The *to work or not to work* dilemma plagues many moms and fuels their mommy burnout, whether they work outside of the home or not. Many career moms struggle with work boundaries (how can they not, when our culture expects 24/7 workdays?). At-home moms, on the other hand, struggle with their purpose and often come to me asking, *Is picking up after my kids and shuttling them around really all that I'm here to do?* Tracy's story was interesting because she experienced both being a mom who worked outside of the house and being an at-home mom in a relatively short time frame.

Another interesting thing about Tracy was her special knack for storytelling. Her tales were so rich in detail and her style was so engaging that you felt like you were living the experience with her. She'd even use different voices when recounting back-and-forth conversations. I noticed this special talent early on in one of our sessions, as she told me a story from her previous week.

"It was early afternoon and I paused from the bread crumbs and spices on the counter in front of me to watch the snow falling in my mother's backyard," Tracy started. She pushed up the sleeves on her cashmere sweater and moved to the edge of her chair. She went on to explain that the play set she had bought her mom for when her kids go to her house after school was already covered. Tracy inhaled deeply and then exhaled. "I breathed in the flavors of turkey, gravy, and fresh cranberry sauce, smiled, and then returned to seasoning the stuffing."

Tracy crossed one leg over the other. "Can you make room in

the oven for this stuffing? It's ready to go in," she had called over to her sister, who was in town with her own family from New Jersey for the holiday.

"I think these sweet potatoes can come out. Let me just get them on a warmer and I'll take the stuffing from you." Tracy slipped into a lower voice when depicting her sister.

Tracy's mom was in the dining room, setting the table with her special "Thanksgiving dishes," each featuring a different color turkey dancing in the center. The husbands and kids were in the living room watching television and playing Monopoly. Jazz music filled the house with a relaxing soundtrack.

Ring, ring, ring. Tracy grimaced in my office just remembering her phone ringing that morning.

"That's a really annoying ring," her sister had said. "Why don't you change it?"

"It's my work phone. The annoying ring sets the tone for whatever annoying conversation I'm about to have," she told her.

"Someone is calling you from work on Thanksgiving?"

"People called me from work while I was in labor." Tracy made herself a mimosa, sat down at the kitchen table, and motioned for her sister to join her.

"At least you get to talk to adults during the day." Tracy then described her sister making her own mimosa, and taking a long sip.

Tracy laughed remembering that comment. "Adults? They act more like entitled adolescents," she told her sister. "You're lucky you don't have to deal with clients who don't think twice about calling you on Thanksgiving."

"Oh, I don't know. It would be kind of nice getting dressed in real clothes every day and actually using my brain."

"You're lucky that you get to wear yoga pants all day if you want to and paint with your kids. You haven't missed a single moment with them. I missed Jenna losing her first tooth and Brandon riding his bike for the first time. I can never get those moments back." In my office, Tracy shook her head.

"Yeah, but there's a lot of other moments during the day that make me want to run from the house screaming that you bypass altogether because you're at work. Your life isn't so bad."

Tracy paused from the story for a moment to take a breath and resettled. She sat up straighter in her chair and pitched her voice higher to signal her mother speaking. "Not you guys too. All the teachers at my school sit in the lounge and talk about how they can't win, whether they work or not. I don't understand your generation."

"What do you mean?" Tracy asked her mom.

"My generation fought so that you guys could have these options. If you want to work, work. If you want to stay home with your kids, then do that. At least you have choices. But you're still not happy," her mom said.

I first noticed Tracy's tension over work the first time I met her. While I was testing Jenna, I noticed that Tracy came with her laptop and phone in hand. Only minutes into the testing, she asked me how long she could step out for before she had to come back for Jenna. She seemed in a hurry to get back to her phone calls, emails, and whatever she had been working on in the waiting room.

I see a good number of parents who bring their child in to see me for therapy or an evaluation along with their "mobile office." I notice their laptops in their bags and can hear them making work calls from their cell phones outside my office. I understand the need to work, and so I usually just make a mental note of this.

Do they seem casual and relaxed around their desire to get back to work or do they hold a lot of tension around being away from their office? I felt that Tracy carried quite a bit of tension around being away from her office.

Two weeks later, Tracy came in to go through the results of Jenna's tests.

"It doesn't look like Jenna has any learning disabilities," I told her. "She's a bright child, scoring in the ninetieth percentile as compared to other students her age. I wonder if she's bored at school. That can sometimes look like being tuned out. Perhaps you can talk to the teacher about challenging her more." I went on to highlight areas where Jenna scored particularly well that the teacher could use as a starting place to get her excited and engaged about learning again.

"Well, I'm glad that she's so bright. I always thought she was doing okay in school. These reports from her teachers didn't really make sense to me," Tracy said while twisting her wedding band around her finger. "Maybe I'm the one with the problem. Maybe I'm the one who needs help." Tracy's cheeks reddened.

"Tell me what you mean." While I had only met Tracy once, I could tell that she was under a lot of stress with managing her kids, her business, and client issues. From my experience, moms like this—who have a lot of competing priorities to manage every day—don't typically enter therapy unless there is some kind of urgency or crisis, like their kid getting suspended from school or using drugs. I saw Tracy taking this step forward for herself, without there being an acute crisis, as a positive sign that she wanted change before her struggles got any worse.

"I feel like my work has taken over my whole life," she started. Tracy would get up every morning at five o'clock to read and respond to emails and prepare for any upcoming hearings. She would then shower and get dressed before waking her kids at seven. She had a half hour to get the three of them downstairs before the nanny came to take over. She and her husband would be at their office by eight and would not get home until seven. Tracy would pick the kids up from her mom's house on her way home from work, the family would have dinner together, and then she and her husband would put the kids to bed. Business calls and emails often interfered with dinner, and Tracy and her husband would go into their separate home offices to finish more work after the kids were asleep.

"I have zero time for my kids, let alone myself or anything else," she told me. "I can't even focus on them for the two hours I'm with them at dinner and bedtime. I rush them through everything so I can get back to work. I sometimes don't get to spend weekends with them because I have cases that I'm working on. What's the point?" Tracy paused. "Why did I have kids if I can't spend any time with them?"

Tracy's fatigue, angst, and guilt were not unique to her. A *Pew Research Study* from 2013 found that 56 percent of working moms struggle to balance their work and their home life (50 percent of dads reported feeling the same strain). This same report found that while men favor jobs with high earning potential, women are more likely to seek out jobs that allow them flexibility. Forty percent of working mothers report feeling rushed most of the time. And most adults also lean toward mothers working part-time as the ideal situation for children.

Because Tracy and her husband owned their own firm, they set up that partnership for the ability to be their own bosses and have a flexible life. They had anticipated that by this point in their careers, the associates in their firm would be doing most of the litigations and settlements and they would just be figureheads bringing in business based upon the established reputation of their work. They imagined they would have the time to put into coaching teams, volunteering at school, and getting away on weekends and holidays, which was what they both looked forward to. Instead, Tracy would sign up for volunteer roles at the school and then be racing around like crazy to fulfill them. She was never able to get her daughter to Girl Scout meetings on time, no matter how carefully she had planned to leave work early. On weekends, her husband coached their son's soccer team, which he enjoyed, but it was draining given how challenging it is to coach five-year-olds. On any given night, both Tracy and her husband were ready to collapse.

What all of this tells me is that we are still trying to capture that elusive balance. The super-mom myth is alive and well, and propelling moms from chronic stress into mommy burnout. Workplace culture needs to shift to accommodate parents, including legitimately promoting flexible work schedules and a workplace culture that values time off to recharge. At home, I think more needs to be done to support one another so that home can actually feel like a resting place. In the previous chapter, we saw a marriage of untraditional roles unfold and the juggle that Heather and Chris were trying to master with respect to parenting. The same kind of close examination needs to occur when both mom and dad work outside of the home.

Working moms often feel like they need to choose between their job and their kids. I had one client who had a limited and fixed number of sick and vacation days for the year. When her son broke his arm and needed to see a specialist, she scheduled the appointment four days after his accident so they could go on a Saturday morning. She couldn't afford to miss work because she feared losing her job would put her at risk for losing the health care benefits that would pay for medical care. She felt lucky that the doctor even had Saturday hours. I had another client with one child who was a highly ranked tennis player and the other, an accomplished track and field star. She not only had to choose which match or meet she would attend, but also which was important enough to miss work to attend. She would have to take off at two thirty twice a week if she wanted to see half their games. Her kids told her it was okay if she didn't see them play every week, but she didn't feel good about it. She wanted her kids to be her priority, but she spent more time with her computer and her coworkers at her office. Neither of these moms ever approached their husbands to take off from their work and be with their kids in the mom's place because they didn't want to burden their husbands. These moms assumed that they would just be able to figure it out and get everything done on their own.

In my own household, both my husband and I are entrepreneurs. We set our own hours and can work around commitments with our children. If I must be at the office, I know that my husband can typically cover for me if something unexpected pops up. Though my kids (and the school and the babysitter and their coaches) always reach out to me first, my husband and I are fairly balanced in our parenting and household responsibilities. We made the decision years ago to forgo some of the amenities of corporate jobs, such as health benefits, a stable income, and paid vacations, to create the flexibility and home life we wanted.

But what about moms and dads who don't have this kind of flexibility? How can single moms and moms who work for a company that is not so flexible slow down? If you fall into this category, I know you are faced with these tough situations sometimes on a weekly basis. Do you cringe at the idea of buying a cake for your child's birthday rather than baking it yourself?

Do you want to be class parent and volunteer for class trips? If you have to work over spending time with your kids sometimes, does the guilt stay with you for days? I tell my clients to find the value in each of their decisions so that when they look at their upcoming week or month, they understand the balance they are creating in total for that time period. This helps alleviate the angst over every single *work versus kids* dilemma that you are faced with. Each and every decision does not have to gnaw at you, and you aren't keeping one big tally sheet that shows your score as a mother. Also, every project—including the garage sale you just decided to organize, the activities you are planning for your daughter's upcoming slumber party, and all the redecorating you're brainstorming—does not need to happen all in the same weekend.

Many working mothers also fear that they are hurting their children in some way by not being home with them all the time. Studies show that although a family's socioeconomic status and structure play a role in how children fare with working mothers, overall there is no significant impact on kids when a mother works outside the home. This guilt that so many working mothers carry with them can thus be released. I have had many teenage clients whose fathers worked a lot while their mothers stayed home with them, and their affection toward each parent was the same. These kids didn't get caught up in the number of hours their dad spent with them versus their mom. They remembered the memories they shared together. I also tell my clients that, in the end, you must simply do what works for you and your family. Each family has their own financial goals, personal goals, and overall values.

Find Your Balance

Even though moms have more opportunities in the workforce today, many continue to feel the crunch of conflicting responsibilities. Here are some ways to smooth out your days.

- If you are married, divvy up the child-care and household responsibilities. You don't have to do everything on your own. Although it is true that many dads are taking on more responsibilities in the home, for the most part, moms still carry the majority of the load when it comes to housework and child care.

- Find the value in how you spend the time you do have. If cutting back on some volunteer work with the PTA gives you back some time to spend with your kids or even just by yourself, that might be worth it.

- Delegate some of your household responsibilities. Even three-year-olds can take their plate and cup from the table to the sink.

- Set achievable goals for yourself. If you're not realistically going to go to the gym at 5:00 a.m., put in a full day of work, go food shopping on your way home, and then cook dinner for the family then don't beat yourself up. Set yourself up for success and create one goal a day that is achievable and feel good about accomplishing it.

As they were growing up, Tracy's mother always told her daughters that they could do and be whatever they wanted, whether they chose to stay home with their kids or build a career outside of the home. She stressed that they should follow whichever path felt most fulfilling to them. Even as a young girl, Tracy's sister had always looked forward to having kids and staying home with them. She told her bosses that she would not be returning to work just weeks after she had her first child. Tracy, though, had always wanted to be a lawyer. She and her husband opened their own firm shortly after they got married, and it quickly became the most successful divorce practice in their area.

What Tracy never factored into her dream was the amount of time it takes to run a successful business. She also never considered the sacrifices she would have to make once they had a family. "I feel like my nanny and my mother are raising my kids and I just come home at night to eat dinner with them and tuck them into bed," Tracy told me during one session. "If my mom wasn't a secretary at the local elementary school, I would be totally screwed. She takes my kids every afternoon after the nanny leaves. My husband and I make good money, but having a nanny for three kids for eight hours a day, five or six days a week, is crazy expensive."

Around the time that Tracy started seeing me, her mom had begun cancelling once or twice a month and Tracy was having to ask the nanny to stay late. As Tracy tallied the family's expenses at the end of the month, she wondered if working was even financially worthwhile. "Between taxes, our expenses, and paying the nanny for extra hours every week, there is a lot of money flowing out of our bank account," she told me. "I feel like I'm funding this woman's European vacations when I can barely get away for the weekend."

I shared with Tracy that I wondered if her mother was desiring some of her own time. I often hear from involved grandparents who come to see me that while they are happy to help their own child and see their grandkids, these kinds of arrangements can start to feel like a part-time job to them and more responsibility than they want at that time in their life. Tracy brushed her bangs back off her forehead and thought about what I had said for a moment.

"How did you envision your life unfolding when you were younger?" I asked her.

"I always imagined that I would be a career woman. I wanted to have my own business. I assumed that I would have a few kids and a loving husband. I expected with all this that I would be happy." Tracy swallowed. "Technically, I have everything on my list except for the happiness. I just never expected this juggle to be so hard. I thought the super-mom fantasy was actually something that I could pull off."

By all accounts, Tracy was pulling off a lot of what she set out to do in life. Her husband was very encouraging of her time away from the office to be with the kids and was as equal a partner as he could be. He unloaded the dishwasher, he did homework with the kids, and he cooked dinner once a week, but there was always more to be done in their house. And Tracy felt like the additional chores always fell on her to be completed. I knew that if there was going to be a serious shift in Tracy's life, that would have to come from Tracy with the support of her husband. I set out to be a guide on her journey to help her create a life centered more around what she *wanted* to do rather than what she felt she *needed* to do. I knew that Tracy would feel better if she could find more of a balance between her work, her kids, and time for herself.

By the end of December, Tracy was dragging herself to the office and falling asleep at her desk in the evenings. She was surviving on coffee by day and sweets by night. Tracy noticed that she had started snapping at their nanny. "I think I'm jealous of this twenty-four-year-old woman. She gets all of these moments with my kids. She gets their hugs. She gets their 'firsts.'" Tracy looked down. "I used to say she was like their second mother, but lately it feels like I am the second mother."

Tracy was struggling with the complicated nanny relationship that many working moms navigate. Typically, when moms are feeling insecure, it's not really because the nanny is getting too close to the kids. It's because the mom feels that she is spending too much time away from her kids and her guilt is eating away at her. I had over six truly amazing years with the same nanny. Emily was like a member of our family. When Tracy began talking about her nanny, I couldn't help but think of how, at times, I had envied Emily's job. She got to come into our home and really focus on the kids. She was also young and rested enough to cook dinner and do laundry and still be cheerful. Then, at 6:00 p.m., she got to leave. That looked like a great gig from my vantage point. But being a mom is different from being a nanny. I felt most guilty in the mornings, when I would leave my kids with Emily. But that feeling would fade while I was working, and I realized that Emily being with my kids allowed me to focus on my work and my clients. And I did recognize that I was fortunate enough to be able to have a nanny like Emily who gave me the freedom and peace of mind to do my work.

Tracy then went on to say that she noticed that her kids seemed to be getting needier and needier. When she walked in the door at night, the kids would all speak over one another, practically tripping over each other to get her attention. She felt like there was no way she could give them enough of what they needed. She'd thought that looking over their homework, signing permission slips, listening to them talk about their day, reading books, and kissing and cuddling would be enough. But there were always more stories from school, more bickering to referee between siblings, more events and birthday parties to plan for, plus extra cuddles to hand out. By the time the kids got settled in their beds, it was usually nearly nine thirty at night.

While Tracy would change out of her work clothes, she would find herself breathing deeply in her closet, often with tears in her eyes. *Brandon is worried about math. I should have done flash cards with him tonight. Jenna is still not talking to her best friend. I should have lain in bed with her and talked to her more about that. The little one was so excited that he could point to the letters in his name and wanted to show me over and over. I should have taken down the plastic magnets from the refrigerator and worked with him.* Every night, Tracy marched herself through another soul-crushing guilt trip.

A care.com survey reported that "one in four working moms cry alone at least once per week" because they are so overwhelmed by all their responsibilities. When Tracy walked into her house, she was exhausted, starving, and crashing from all the coffee she relied on to get through the day. Her own tank was nearing empty and she had her *own* needs. And on top of it all, her husband was in about the same place as she was, except the kids seemed to need different things from him. Her husband was also exhausted, was wound up from the day, and still had a lot on his mind most nights. The kids wanted all of Mom's attention when she walked in. They wanted hugs from her. They wanted to show her their school projects from the day. They literally just wanted her to themselves. When Dad walked in, they wanted to be active with him: throw a ball, have him watch a handstand, wrestle with them. The second that Tracy and her husband walked in the door, they both had to be "on" for their kids. The difference was that Tracy felt the need to meet her kids' demands and felt guilty when she couldn't. Her husband, on the other hand, didn't think twice about telling the kids to wait while he took a few minutes for himself or that he couldn't play with them at all on nights when he needed to get back to work before dinner. *Why doesn't he carry around the same guilt and shame that I do?* she thought.

When January came around, Tracy perked up. Jenna was working on some research for her school's science fair on how to use clouds to predict the weather, and she had asked Tracy to help her. "She wants us to work on it together." Tracy smiled and bounced her knees.

As the weeks went by, though, Tracy had to keep putting Jenna off. She had to prepare for court and several hearings. "I know I'm failing here," she told me. "I told her I would help her, and I can't. The nanny is going to work on it with her." Tracy dropped her head. "I promised her that I would at least make it to the fair to see her present her project."

The morning of the science fair, Jenna reminded Tracy one last time that the fair would start at ten o'clock and the award ceremony would be around ten thirty. "You'll be there, right?" Jenna asked as Tracy organized a file for a meeting later that afternoon.

"Yes, I will be there. I promise." Tracy gave her daughter a big hug and a peck on the cheek. "I will also take a video and pictures to send to Daddy on his business trip."

Jenna smiled and went back to her Cheerios and milk.

At nine thirty, Tracy was still on a call with the attorney of her client's soon-to-be ex-husband. "I'm going to have to go in a minute," Tracy said. But the other attorney just kept right on talking about how they could set up the custody schedule. Tracy's heart was racing in her chest. The school was at least thirty minutes from her office.

Just before ten o'clock, Tracy was finally able to hang up from her call and she sprinted out to her car. She raced through the stop sign just beyond her office building and darted around cars on the highway. *Please let me get there in time. Please let me get there in time,* Tracy prayed as she swerved around the other cars on the road. She glanced down at the clock. It was ten twenty and Tracy still had one more exit to go on the highway. "Move, cars! Get out of my way!" she shouted.

At ten thirty-five, Tracy screeched into the parking lot and parked her car right in front of the "No Parking" sign in front of the school's entrance. As she rounded the corner of the gym where the science fair was being held, she saw Jenna standing on the podium wearing a blue sash. She had won for her grade. And Tracy had missed it. She noticed the nanny standing with her youngest and snapping pictures of Jenna. As she walked over to them, she felt her phone buzzing. *That's it. I can't do this anymore,* Tracy thought to herself. *I quit.*

Tracy quickly transitioned into a new life of sleeping until it was time to get the kids up for school. She wore her pajamas while getting her kids ready and would sit at the table and eat breakfast with them. She stopped wearing her contacts and blow-drying her hair straight. "This is the first time I have put on real clothes in a week," Tracy said, beaming and pointing to her jeans and blouse. "Life is so much more comfortable in yoga pants," she joked. Tracy watched *Good Morning America* while she cleaned the kitchen after her two older kids left for school. "Have you seen Michael Strahan lately?" she asked me one afternoon. "I can't decide if I think he's sexy or not."

Late morning, Tracy would run errands with her toddler. She made lunch plans with friends she'd never had time to see when she was working. She reveled in the time she could spend reading and playing with her youngest. "I just never had time like this with my other two. Kids are a lot of fun at this age." While her son napped, Tracy enjoyed being in the quiet of her house. And she enjoyed not seeing the nanny every day. She felt she had made the right decision.

During this time, I was seeing another client, Maggie, who also left her job to be home with her kids. Once she made the change, she couldn't believe how she had once left her son for her teaching job. She now shuddered at the thought of leaving him, of getting dressed and putting on makeup every day, of having emails to return all the time, and of basically being around other people's kids for a living. She felt like she was on the other side, looking at working moms and wondering why they do that to themselves. She felt free to have more kids if she wanted, and she no longer had to rely on an opening at a day care or a nanny showing up. Maggie embraced the change from working mom to at-home mom. But this is not the case for all women.

Within two months of her transition, Tracy began showing up to my office in sweats instead of the high-end business attire I used to see her in, or even her jeans and nice blouse. "Is it weird that I lounge around in yoga pants every day?" she asked, settling into her now relaxed position in the chair across from me. "I never wear makeup anymore. I throw my hair up in a messy bun all the time. Sometimes I even forget to brush my teeth until noon."

Tracy's kids got off from school at three o'clock, which used to be the midpoint of her workday. Once she got the two older kids out the door in the morning, Tracy had to walk the dog, run errands, feed her youngest snack and lunch, play, read him books, and put him down for his nap. While her son slept, she longed to crawl back into bed herself, but a little voice in her head would nag at her to take a shower, prep dinner, clean up, and fold laundry while she had time alone. By the time her son woke up, the other two kids were coming home from school and it was time for the drive around town for afternoon activities. After getting home from sports and music lessons it was time for homework, more toddler playtime, dinner, and the typical bedtime madness. "Why do moms put themselves through this?" she asked me. Tracy's tune had definitely changed from when she first made the switch.

I had one client with two young kids close in age, and the only thing she looked forward to during the week was when her little ones went to preschool. "It's only three hours twice a week, but they are the happiest six hours of my life right now," she told me. Many other at-home moms beat themselves up over "not contributing to their family or the world." To validate their existence, they stuff their schedules with volunteer work, overschedule their kids, and work out like fiends. "My kids are in school all day," one mom explained. "If I wasn't in shape, my friends would totally mommy-shame me."

Tracy started to drift off in thought over lunchtime conversations as her friends talked about kids, activities, and various projects. She longed for the more varied adult conversation she used to have—about work, litigation, politics, growing a business, and *Orange Is the New Black*. "I can really only handle these kinds of conversations once a week now," she said. "But that means that I don't have any other adults to talk to during the day."

At Tracy's house, even the kids' excitement over her being home began to wane. At first, they loved having their mom around more. But as the weeks went by, there were complaints about missing their old routines. "The nanny used to make homemade muffins for us when we got home from school," they would tell her as she opened granola bars. "The nanny let us watch television before we did our homework," they whined. It made Tracy nuts when they would barely touch their dinners. *They used to eat the nanny's dinners,* she thought. The kids would also run to their father—like they used to do with her—when he got home from the office. *At least they were happy to see me back then.*

Although Tracy understood how fortunate she was to be able to make this choice to stay home—she knew many moms whose income was necessary to cover the family's bills—she still felt like the happy image of motherhood she had been looking forward to had eluded her, and instead she had slipped into the role of cleaning lady, servant, and chauffeur. Her days revolved around laundry, unloading the dishwasher, loading the dishwasher, and picking toys up off the floor. She also realized that she hated cooking. She had assumed it would be a fun and creative outlet for her during the day, but it turned into just another chore on her to-do list. Tracy was convinced that her husband now thought she was less attractive. Ever since they stopped working together, she felt like they had nothing to talk about. "I swear he almost hung up on me when I called him the other day to ask which type of light bulb we use in the bathroom," she told me.

Tracy tried calling her sister for an emotional pep talk, but being in different time zones and with little kids made connecting a challenge. The most time they seemed to get on the phone with each other was ten minutes before one of them had to deal with a screaming child or run an errand. They had started texting more since Tracy left work, but that wasn't enough for Tracy to really unload what she was going through. She needed another at-home mom to talk to, someone who understood what her daily life was now like. At this point, most of Tracy's friends were also hard-charging working moms. She also felt a little silly that she had basically been telling her sister what an easy life she was leading at home with her kids, when now she was struggling under those same circumstances.

For the moms I have worked with who decide to stop working and stay at home to raise their children, there appears to be a honeymoon period after which they go from loving their new life to having a difficult time with the new routine. Just the other day, I had a mom in my office who recently left work to stay home with her kids and I asked her how the transition was going. "Lots of drop-offs and pickups!" she told me. These moms realize that their days are still full and that the feeling that they have no time still lingers.

They also struggle with shaping a new identity for themselves. Many women become extremely invested in their work identity— like, *who am I if I'm not a powerful attorney or consultant?* But letting go of our identity, whether it's professional or social (think Pinterest Queen), is often a tough adjustment. We are social beings. We gain a sense of security from identifying with a skill, talent, or profession. Changing that can make women feel unsure of their role or significance in the world. However, I have found that identities are more malleable than most of us realize. Smoother transitions occur when women look at themselves in total, rather than through the narrow lens of one set of talents and contributions. When we understand all that we offer, transitioning to a "new identity" feels more empowering.

Like Tracy, a countless number of moms have an unattainable standard of perfection that is affecting their health and the way their children view motherhood. Because a lot of moms today have so many opportunities—to work or not to work—they feel pressure to take advantage of all these opportunities. And social media fuels this pressure. Not long ago, I saw a post on Facebook that said, "I didn't want my daughter to grow up thinking that being a working mom is miserable!" There were other comments that questioned what our children are witnessing in us as we look frenzied and hurried most of the time. What we need to realize is that while there are a lot of opportunities today, we don't need to take advantage of them all. You're not a slacker if you don't sign up for every volunteer opportunity at school or if you don't work sixty hours a week.

The monotony of her days wore on Tracy. "I feel like time is standing still and the days simply blend into each other. I have nothing to look forward to anymore. I daydream about just sleeping for a whole day so I don't have to feel like this," she said. "I wasn't happy when I was working. And now I'm not happy because I'm home all day. I feel guilty even having these thoughts," she said. "I'm right back to where I started, feeling like a shitty, guilty mom. Why can't I just be happy?"

I thought that was an excellent question. Why do both at-home and working moms struggle to find their happiness? What women on either side of this fence don't often realize is that motherhood is larger than the work divide. Motherhood, as an experience, is very similar whether you work or not. Most moms feel guilty at some point. Most moms feel resentful of their kids at some point. Most moms, at some point, daydream about going on an extended vacation to a tropical island that does not allow children.

I straddle both worlds of motherhood. I took more control over my schedule when I resigned from my dream job as a clinical director over ten years ago. I look like the average mom at drop-offs and pickups, but in between the hours of 8:30 a.m. and 3:00 p.m., I'm working, either for my business or with stuff that needs

Bridging the Mom Divide

No matter what your employment status is, it's important to remember that we are all moms and in that regard, our job is the same. So, instead of focusing on what separates our experiences, let's come together and drop the assumptions that we make about each other. Here are some of the most **common misconceptions** between working and at-home moms:

- Working moms don't care about their careers more than their kids. They either have to work or find joy in their work.

- Not all at-home moms drink wine at noon and have mani-pedis every week.

- Working moms don't always love getting dressed up, wearing heels, and getting their roots touched up every four weeks. And some don't have the means to do any of that, despite working.

- Not all at-home moms love wearing yoga pants, sneakers, and ponytails and having snacks and diapers in their purses all the time.

The truth is that . . .

- At-home moms don't love their children more than working moms. We all love our children.

- Most moms rock out to music in their cars.

- Most moms want to lose baby weight.

- Most moms could use a date night, with someone.

- Most moms have issues.

- Most of us worry about money, finances, tuition, and bills.

- Most of us think we could be doing a better job.

- Most of us cry every week.

- Most of us could use some therapy.

- Lots of us have issues in our marriages.

- Most of us could use some help from someone in our village.

- ALL of us could use a hug, a kiss, and support from another mom.

to be done at the house. I go food shopping or write, film media segments, see clients, run a small business, work out, and make time for lunches or walks with friends. You name it, I am doing it in those school hours. At times, I find my balance and other times, I feel like I am drowning. I, too, daydream about going on a spa vacation with my girlfriends. I am also a work in progress. The difference between myself ten years ago and today is that I know better. I know I am in the good company of millions of other moms who feel the same way and that I am not alone. I also know when I am stressed or on the verge of burnout and now can prevent myself from going there.

When Tracy asked me why she couldn't find happiness, I knew that what she was really asking was whether she'd be happier at home or at work. But her question actually went much deeper than that.

"What do you believe is your meaning and purpose in life?" I asked her.

Tracy shifted in her seat and smiled. "I don't know."

I didn't expect her to have an answer, really. People have been searching for this for millions of years. As humans, we have an existential need to know why we are here. Some people believe life has no inherent meaning and that you must create it for yourself. Others feel that life is about the search—and that the meaning already exists. Either way, the quest for *your* meaning is inevitable.

When you become a mother, this search intensifies. When your baby is young, you are keenly aware of how dependent the baby is on you for his or her needs. Perhaps this gives you a deep sense of purpose. Perhaps you start to think more about your own mortality. *Who would raise my baby if something happened to me?*

For many moms, after that first year or so, those feelings shift. As your baby weans from breastfeeding or transitions from bottle to solid foods, you may find your connection to your child changes. The child no longer relies on you for every aspect of survival. You may have started to wonder, *Is this what motherhood is really about?* These feelings come as you juggle all the demands that raising children bring, and if you work outside the home, the difficulty of juggling that career with motherhood intensifies those feelings. Perhaps you still ask yourself these questions, even if your child is a teenager.

I often recommend the book *Man's Search for Meaning* by Viktor Frankl to my clients. The message of this book is that we don't stumble upon the meaning of our lives one day in a remarkable moment of epiphany. Our lives are full of meaning each and every day—but to glean that meaning you must have awareness. To be aware, you must be present in the moments of your life. This can be hard for mothers, as so much of the day-to-day of our lives is challenging. The inability to remain present is one of the greatest obstacles mothers today are up against. No wonder so many women feel their life has no purpose.

We are constantly running to-do lists in our minds. We are perpetually distracted by technology. We multitask without even realizing it. We research the best high chair or bicycle until well after midnight when we should be getting much-needed rest. We put everyone else's needs above our own. These things distract us and wear us down and make it that much harder to arrive at our purpose. Whether you are reading to your kids, grocery shopping, or giving a presentation at work, endeavor to be present and find the meaning in what you are doing in the moment.

As the weight of this mothering experience continued to bear down on Tracy, she reached out for adult interaction by calling her husband at work. "We should think about painting the outside of the house. It could use a little sprucing up," she told him one morning while she was cleaning the oatmeal off her little one's chin.

"Remind me later," her husband said into the phone before he politely hung up.

Later that afternoon, she called to inform him that their five-year-old had gotten sick at school and she had to go pick him up. "Okay," her husband said as he typed away at his computer. "Give him a kiss for me. I'll be home late tonight."

Tracy called two more times that afternoon, and by the fifth call her husband was losing his patience. "Why don't you go to the museum," he suggested. "Brandon is sick, remember?" Tracy snapped back at him. "And I went there yesterday." Tracy's freedom from work had morphed into isolation at her house.

She started shoving toys into closets instead of putting them into bins at night. She let her kids go to school in clothes that were "just a little dirty" so she could cut down on the amount of laundry she was doing. In the depth of her boredom, Tracy decided to have a garage sale and sell the extra toys and clothes they had at the house. "Take everything to Goodwill," her husband told her over the phone. "At a garage sale you'll get a few hundred bucks in the end and it will take you a full week to organize everything. It's not worth your time for that amount of money. It's not enough."

Tracy choked back her tears. "Yeah, well, folding the laundry all day is not enough for me either."

"My heart tells me that staying home with my kids is the right thing to do." Tracy patted tears from the corners of her eyes. "But when I'm with my kids, my mind tells me that I'm not contributing to the family. That I'll never be able to go back to work when they get older, that I'll lose my edge." Tracy shook her head. "I just don't know what to do." Tracy knew that the firm she built with her husband would still be around, but like many professional women, she felt that taking a break would take her out of the game—that clients and other lawyers would forget about her and that she would not be as confident when she returned. Women feel like they can be at a disadvantage having had a break for a while. These are all common fears among working moms, whether it's after maternity leave or just an extended leave to raise children.

"What would it be like if you approached being an at-home mom like your career?" I asked her.

Tracy sat back in her chair and thought about this for a moment. "I would be the best mom I could be, just as I approached being an attorney. I would go to music and gym and art classes and the park with my youngest and connect with other moms while I was there." She laughed a little to herself. "And I would enjoy all of it."

"What else?" I nudged her.

"I guess in my ideal world, I would take a few cooking classes and feed my kids healthy meals and snacks instead of the shitty packaged foods like the Goldfish I keep stashed in my car for them. I would be patient with my kids while we work together on their homework. I guess I would be my very own version of a super-mom. One that is specific to my kids and my family."

With these visions in mind, Tracy slowly went about becoming a career at-home mom. She started waking up earlier—like she did when she was working—to shower and really get dressed and do her hair before she made a healthy breakfast for herself and the kids. She would pack their lunches the night before to save time. She took a cooking class with her toddler. Tracy also started going on field trips with her two older kids and joined a local mommy group with her youngest. "I lost out on so many experiences with my two older kids," she explained. "I'm going to take the opportunity now to actually spend time with my children." Over the next few weeks, the sense of excitement and energy she felt when she first left her law firm started to return. She was more present and more engaged. "I can't believe that even though I'm waking up earlier I have more energy," Tracy told me. "I only needed one cup of coffee yesterday."

About six months into her new "mom career," Tracy reached out to some old friends from work. She had been wary of doing so before, because they used to scoff at the idea of staying home with their children. "We joked that we would go insane if we had to stay home with our kids every day," she admitted. But her friends were happy to hear from her. They were meeting for happy hour that night, so she asked her mom to babysit so she could meet them.

As Tracy sat with these women and listened to their stories about juggling work and kids, she remembered the constant strain she used to feel. One of the women shared a story about how just that morning, she had gotten a call from her son's school that she needed to pick him up because her husband told the teacher that the son had a fever the night before. "I was livid at my husband," Tracy's friend said while everyone else at the table shook their heads. "It's common knowledge that your kid must be fever-free for twenty-four hours to go to school. After I explained to the school that it was only a low-grade fever and that he woke up fine that morning, I called my husband and went off on him." The other moms around the table laughed. "I can't just leave my office at will," she said. "I had a presentation this morning. Not to mention that the school is going to think I'm a shitty mom now because I send my sick kid to school despite their policy."

"Did your husband get it?" Tracy asked.

"I don't know if he understood my concern over what the teacher now thinks of me, but he definitely understands the fever policy." She grinned. "Either way, I don't think he'll be chatting with the teacher when he drops our son off anymore."

Another woman shared her funny stories about coming back to the workforce. She had just joined the firm as Tracy was leaving. As the women all laughed and shared, Tracy realized that she wasn't so different from these working moms. "We all have moments of resentment and guilt," she told me later. Tracy also realized that she could certainly go back to work if that was something she wanted to do later. And, she still had a valuable network of friends.

As the night wound down, Tracy made a comment that they shouldn't let another six months pass before seeing each other again. The other women were shocked that it had been that long. Tracy joked that she felt like it had been years.

"I guess time slows down when you are home with your kids," Tracy told them.

"Well, you look great," another friend said. "You look happy."

Make Peace with Your Purpose

Stay present. Slowing down and focusing on the people and the experience in front of you will give you more energy and enjoyment. Stop what you are doing and listen to your kids when they talk to you. Look them in the eye and give them your full attention. Maybe even set alarms on your phone to prompt you to be present.

Be a career mom. Whether you work out of the home or not, find meaning in the time you spend with your kids and approach these experiences as you would your dream job. If you would like to offer your kids more nutritious meals (that they will eat), call up some friends and see if they have any recipes for you or take a healthy cooking class. If you want to spend more time together as a family, take a few minutes each week to brainstorm some fun things that you can all do together, whether it's playing a board game, visiting the zoo, or discussing a book you have all read. As you would hold weekly staff meetings in a place of employment, hold weekly family meetings that are intended to check in with everyone about how the week went and what is coming up. This is a good way not only to get activities organized but to get input from everyone on what they would like to do and how they are feeling.

Stop overthinking and look for the cues that already exist in your life. You probably are closer to your purpose than you think. Start listening to your gut or intuition. And if you are like many moms who say they can't figure out how to do that, find five minutes alone every day to quiet your mind so that you can hear what your intuition is telling you.

Start seeing everything that happens to you as part of your personal story line. Even painful experiences are opportunities to start living your purpose. I find a great way to accomplish this is through journaling. When you take the time to write your day's story down, it affords you the time for not only reflection but also introspection and the opportunity to learn and rewrite the next day. This can be done online or with paper and pen—whatever feels most comfortable for you.

BONUS EXERCISE

Imagine that your life is a movie and write out the story line you want for the main character (which is you!). Think about what this main character's purpose in life is and figure out how she will live that out in the movie.

Chapter 8

I Just Can't Get It All Done . . .

The First Step in Fighting Mommy Burnout—Ban "Busy"
as a Badge of Honor

Sound Familiar?

Busy has become a way of life today, but it's not healthy. And it can easily lead to mommy burnout. Here are a few red flags that you might be too busy.

- You feel like you never have any help even though there are people around you. You feel like you are on your own to get all the chores done and to figure out what needs to be accomplished (for everyone in the family) each day.

- Your days feel out of control. You feel like you no longer control your own schedule and your days are spent managing everyone else's problems that arise.

- Running around all day gives you a sense of self-worth. You feel important and needed by tending to everyone else's needs.

- You are consistently overwhelmed with what needs to be accomplished on any given day. You feel like you just can't get ahead.

- You aim to please people, all the time. Even people who aren't close to you. You go out of your way to bake homemade treats for your kids, beautifully hand-wrap gifts for birthdays, and sign up for every volunteer opportunity at the school.

- You often experience shame and guilt that you aren't meeting expectations. You fret over saying no to hosting your child's holiday party in his classroom, or that you haven't signed your kids up for enough extra lessons or activities and feel like they are at a disadvantage because of it.

- You prioritize work over self-care and relationships. You check your child's homework for a second time instead of taking a shower, or you check work emails late into the night instead of going to sleep.

Carmen was fifty-six years old and married, with two kids. Her son was fifteen years old and her daughter was seventeen. Carmen worked from home as a management consultant. She and her husband, a financial planner, had been married for twenty years. They had what most would consider rather traditional roles in their household, where she took care of most things in the house and with the kids and he worked all day out of an office nearby. The couple had established early on in their marriage that Carmen would be the primary caregiver to the kids and she was happy with that idea. She grew up in a similar household and had always looked forward to raising her kids. Before having children, Carmen worked in marketing at a company, but she left her job when she got pregnant.

Twelve years ago, Carmen called me to set up an initial appointment. "It's like I just can't keep my head on straight," Carmen explained to me on the phone. She would lose her keys daily, miss important calls for work, and even forget to stop by the grocery store while she was out running errands. She initially went to her primary care physician to see what was wrong. But after a battery of tests came back normal, her doctor—whom I knew professionally—referred her to me.

Though I hadn't yet identified mommy burnout when I met Carmen, I could recognize that her high stress levels were the source of her memory issues. Stress can impact many areas of your body, including how your brain functions. It can lead to distorted thinking, memory issues, and confusion. *But why was Carmen so stressed?* What I surmised was that her "busyness" was sending her stress levels soaring.

Now, I have come to realize that "busy" moms are especially vulnerable to mommy burnout. "Busy" is a way of life for many moms. It's almost worn as a badge these days, but it's not healthy. Moms are constantly doing several tasks at once. They are running from one errand to the next. They barely even sit down to eat. While moms are seeking greater efficiency, they are really making themselves less productive. Our brains were built to focus on one task at a time. And when we don't allow our brains to function the way they are supposed to, we slow ourselves down and spike our anxiety levels upward.

When Carmen walked me through her typical day during our first session, I nearly fell off my chair. By the time she got to her afternoon schedule, I could practically feel the overwhelm oozing from her pores. I'm pretty sure I saw her left eye twitching a tiny bit as she waded further into the story of her daily routine.

"Around three o'clock, the kids' bus pulled up outside the house and I immediately started scrambling to finish my work because I knew that I wouldn't get back to my computer until ten o'clock that night." Carmen took a pause to sip from her Diet Coke. "The front door opened and my kids made a beeline to the refrigerator." Carmen thought, *Oh shit! I forgot . . .*

"You didn't go to the grocery store?" Her fifteen-year-old son stared into the nearly empty fridge.

"I think we have some leftovers," Carmen offered.

"That meat loaf looks gross." Her daughter scrunched up her face.

Is it a problem that my seventeen-year-old daughter wears more makeup than I do? Carmen thought to herself.

"There's nothing to eat in this house." Her son closed the fridge.

"I'll make you some eggs." Carmen walked over next to her kids.

They looked at her blankly.

"Okay, how about a packet of instant oatmeal?" Carmen turned from the pantry to see her kids sitting at the kitchen island scrolling through their phones, completely ignoring her and eating a sleeve of Oreos.

"I'm just gonna make you guys PB&J sandwiches and throw a frozen pizza into the oven for you to eat for dinner on the way home."

The kids barely looked up from their phones. As Carmen placed all the food onto the kitchen counter, the dog started whining in front of his empty water bowl. She turned again to her kids, who were now even more sucked into their phones, took a deep breath, and filled the bowl with cool water before returning to the sandwiches and pizza.

She set a sandwich in front of her son and daughter and asked if they had any homework to do before they left. Her daughter had soccer practice that afternoon and her son had a basketball game. "We only have about forty-five more minutes before we have to be in the car," she reminded them.

Both kids started on their homework while nibbling on their sandwiches. Carmen tidied up the kitchen while checking her phone for work emails. "Of course, I lost track of time and didn't remind the kids to get their uniforms on, so I went from calm to screaming through the house like a crazy person in like three seconds," she told me. "I soon realized that I'd never washed my son's basketball socks and we couldn't find my daughter's jersey. I was trying to keep it together, but I felt like I was going to have a heart attack."

Twenty minutes later, they all piled into the minivan and Carmen opened all the windows in her attempt to escape the stench of her son's dirty socks. It didn't work. She thought, *I know that playing college basketball is his dream, but this travel team is killing me. All the kids are scattered everywhere so no one carpools, and they have practices or games six days a week.* Carmen was nearing the end of her neighborhood and was deep into her own internal pity party when she slammed on the breaks. "The pizza!" she yelled. Her kids rolled their eyes as she turned the car around and sped back to their house.

Carmen ran back inside, which now reeked of burned pizza, turned off the oven, and threw the pizza dough on the stove to cool off. *I'll deal with that later.* She grabbed the last Diet Coke from the fridge, ran back outside, and hurled herself into her car. As Carmen raced across town to get her son to his game, she snapped at her kids for stealing her sodas. They ignored her. She had just dropped her son off and was heading back across town to her daughter's last soccer practice for the season when she remembered that she was supposed to buy the coach a gift on behalf of the team. Just as she was figuring out in her head the closest store for her to get the gift, her daughter started crying over some fight she had with her best friend that afternoon. Carmen asked her daughter about the fight as she pulled into the store's parking lot, but then told her daughter to "hold that thought" as she dashed inside the store. Unfortunately for Carmen, the woman in front of her in line was also getting a present wrapped. Carmen tapped her foot and sighed loudly while she waited. *I wonder how high my blood pressure can spike before I have a stroke,* she thought.

Finally, she pulled into the school parking lot for the practice. Carmen patted down her spiky, gray hair and ran her palms over her slightly wrinkled blouse. *Maybe I should have changed clothes,* she thought. Her daughter disappeared from her side the moment they stepped onto the field. Carmen found a seat by herself on the side of the bleachers and pulled her phone out to check emails.

"Hi there! How are you?" A perky blond mom popped up in front of her.

Carmen jumped a little and gave the woman a half smile. She wanted to tell the woman that she was totally overwhelmed and ready to jump out of her skin. Instead, she just nodded politely and told her that she was doing fine.

"I can't believe the season is over," the perky blonde pressed on.

Carmen put her phone on her lap and politely shook her head in agreement. *I wonder if this mom is losing sleep over her daughter's social life or her son's insane sports schedule.*

"Don't sit over here all by yourself." The blonde motioned for Carmen to follow her over to where the other moms were seated. "Come sit with the rest of us."

Carmen slid her phone into her pocket and reluctantly followed her. She really needed to get some emails out, but she didn't want to come off as a bitch. She politely listened to the idle chit-chat from the other moms while reshuffling her to-do list for the evening in her brain. As soon as the practice ended, she handed the coach the gift and grabbed her daughter. She hissed at her daughter to hurry up as they crossed the parking lot. They were already late to pick up her son.

By the time she pulled up to get her son, he was waiting for her and pointing at his watch. She yelled for him to get into the car through the closed window. "What's for dinner?" he asked as he buckled his seat belt.

"Do you realize that you *only* ask me about food? We talk about nothing else," Carmen pointed out to her son, but his headphones were already on.

As she pulled up to the McDonald's drive-thru window, her daughter smirked and said she had been looking forward to the pizza from earlier. Carmen ignored her.

Finally, at seven o'clock, Carmen pulled into her driveway. Her husband greeted her with a peck on the cheek and, "What's for dinner?"

I wish that Carmen were the only mom I knew with afternoons like this. But, in truth, many of my clients run through their days muttering to-do list items and circling back for errands they forgot. "There's just not enough time to get everything done," they tell me. Carmen, for example, worked while the kids were at school. She schlepped them around in the afternoon. The groceries she bought on Saturday were gone by Thursday. "When do I have time to think?" Carmen asked me. "And I'm lucky, because I can stop working when the kids get off the bus. I know that I can pick back up again at ten o'clock. Other moms I know don't even walk in the door until six o'clock, but they seem fine.

Why am I the only one who can't seem to catch my breath?" The reality is that when you are constantly in "go-go-go mode," your stress response is going to settle into a steady idle.

By that point, Carmen had been in "go-go-go mode" for years. Even when her kids were younger and she was at home with them and not working, she was constantly running around. She signed the kids up for every class that she could. She volunteered at their preschool. She did tons of craft projects, which required lots of shopping. She cooked with her kids. She baked with them. She set up playdates. They were always busy, but Carmen enjoyed the time with her kids. She didn't want them to miss out on anything.

As her kids got older, Carmen wanted to maintain control of their schedules as she had when they were younger. But as kids grow more independent, most moms realize that their own schedules fall to the whims of their children. "It just seemed easier when I was arranging everything," she explained. "At some point, the kids took control over my schedule. Or I gave them the control. I don't know which it was, but, either way, I'm no longer in control of my own days. And this doesn't feel good."

As busy as moms are today, it's a necessary evil to "have control" over their family's master schedule. They aren't only in charge of their own schedules, but, often, the schedules for each family member. They must keep track of multiple kids' extracurriculars as well as their social calendar with their spouse and then their own days as well. The need for control is a coping mechanism to handle the stress that this creates. Without "control," moms never know where they should be or where their family members are.

Carmen continued with her story about the previous day. As dusk faded to darkness outside her windows, Carmen was red-eyed from fatigue and starving because she hadn't wanted to eat fast food again for dinner. Other nights, Carmen would feel guilty about feeding her family fast food and not sitting down to a home-cooked meal, but on this night, she was just too tired to even care. While her kids and husband had eaten together at the table, Carmen returned an urgent work email and answered a call from a client. Finally, at 7:45 p.m., she found time to eat dinner. *It's not that bad,* she said to herself as she picked around the burned edges of the pizza from earlier that afternoon. As she loaded the dishwasher, she realized that she hadn't heard the shower running yet. Carmen's jaw clenched and her heartbeat quickened. *It's eight o'clock. What are those kids doing up there?*

She stormed into her daughter's bedroom and immediately started yelling at her to hurry up with her homework so she could get into the shower and go to bed. Just as she was finishing her tirade, Carmen saw a small image of herself on her daughter's computer screen, waving around her burned piece of pizza and with her hair shooting up every which way. Her daughter's best friend looked back at her on the screen with *fear.* Carmen looked at her daughter and slunk out of the room.

She took a deep breath and then went over to her son's room to yell at him, but first made sure to check his computer for any friends lurking on a video chat. He had headphones on and she needed to scream just to get his attention.

The kids eventually showered, she got back to work and, finally, she collapsed into bed at eleven o'clock. Her husband had fallen asleep in bed at some point watching the news. She turned off the television and let her limbs release the tension from the day. She settled into a deep and steady rhythm of breath. *Ahhh* . . . Sleep was just within her grasp when her eyes popped open. She had forgotten to walk the dog.

Carmen had expected her work-from-home gig to be perfect. She figured she would work from nine to three and then be around for her kids after school. But she couldn't get all her work done in that time frame, especially when she had to make appointments and run errands for the family, so she also worked from nine to eleven at night. What seemed like a dream freelance career turned into a time-crunch nightmare when something unexpected popped up with the kids. She worked nights and weekends, and never got to sleep at a decent time.

Carmen blamed work for her running around, but at-home moms are just as frazzled. These clients often tell me about their "night shift." After their kids go to bed, they return a slew of emails, make lunches for the next day, and check that their kids have turned off their screens and are asleep. "It's like I'm closing up shop just to wake up and do it all over again," one such mom told me. They stay up late checking the kids' schedules for the next day and logging on to the parent portal to make sure their kids turned in their assignments. "This household just would not run without me," one mom said. "It takes me at least an hour every night to literally check all the boxes on my to-do list before I can get into my pajamas." For me, 8:30 p.m. starts my "night shift," which means that's when I return emails and phone calls, clean up the house, clean out my kids' lunch boxes from the day, and try to have a conversation with my husband.

As Carmen attempted to beat the time trap during the day, she would usually try to complete two or three tasks at a time. On the nights when she did cook dinner, she would check emails, stir her sauce, and step outside to throw a ball to the dog while helping her kids with their homework—all at once. She always checked work emails while watching her kids' games and practices. She grazed on snacks and junk food while on work calls and scheduled various appointments while waiting in line to pay at Target. Carmen could see that her lifestyle was probably causing her to feel stressed, but she didn't see any other way. She also didn't understand why nothing ever seemed to get done—even though she was doing so much all the time.

I consider multitasking, or over-tasking as I see it, one of the biggest time drains on moms today. Moms never allow themselves to focus on any one task. We search for coupons on our phone while walking the mall. We pay our bills while helping our little ones with a puzzle. And we bring our laptops to do work while watching our kid's swim meet. We are constantly, incessantly, switching our attention from one item to the next and then back again in the name of efficiency, but our brains were simply not built to continuously bounce our attention between tasks. Every time we switch from one task to another, we lose time as our brains figure out and execute on what needs to be done. In an article summarizing the research on multitasking, the American Psychological Association states, "Although switch costs may be relatively small, sometimes just a few tenths of a second per switch, they can add up to large amounts when people switch repeatedly back and forth between tasks . . . even brief mental blocks created by shifting between tasks can cost as much as 40 percent of someone's productive time."

Over-tasking makes us late. And rushed. And forgetful. I remember one time when I forgot to order the pizza for my daughter's birthday party because I was so busy managing every single other detail by myself. I had a client who was making pancakes one morning while feeding her baby in a high chair and trying to talk to her husband before he left for work. And so, she dumped cumin instead of cinnamon into the batter and ruined the whole batch. See? Time drain.

I realize that most moms wear their over-tasking badges with honor, but I see it as a cry for help. I see smart, competent women who confuse what time they need to pick their kids up from baseball practice or who perpetually arrive everywhere at least fifteen minutes late. They pay the wrong amounts on their bills. They burn dinner. They lose things. They are driving themselves into the ground because they are trying to accomplish four things at the same time, and their brains won't let them.

Time Management Tips for Busy Moms

- Prioritize your to-do list by making buckets around when tasks need to get done. Create "today," "later this week," and "someday" buckets.

- Focus on only one task at a time. You will save time by not having to refocus when you shift between tasks, or redo things that get ruined because you made a mistake.

- Have dedicated phone-free, kid-free, and even computer-free blocks of time during the day to complete tasks that require your complete, focused attention. Shoot for forty-five minutes in the morning so that you start your day feeling accomplished.

- Get a good night's sleep—at least eight hours. You will be more efficient the next day if you are rested.

- Limit the amount of "stuff" you have in your home, like clothes, toys, books, CDs, and magazines. These things clutter your house and your mind.

- Plan meals for the week so you can shop and cook more efficiently. Make it a Sunday afternoon tradition to set the menu for the week with the whole family so everyone has a say in the week's lunches and dinners, and then go to the grocery store. Maybe even make shopping a family activity if you have older children.

- Online grocery shopping is a huge time saver if it is available in your area. The little extra that it costs can usually be justified by the time it allows you to do other things, like hang out with your kids or meet a friend for coffee.

- When cooking, make a double portion and freeze half for a future meal.

- Keep a family calendar in a central place so that everyone can see it. This puts the responsibility of planning for and keeping appointments on each family member. It saves you from running through the house searching for the lost soccer socks in the last moments before a game.

- Set up organization systems at home. Your kids need to have a place to put their things, especially sports equipment, so make sure it's easily accessible.

Carmen was clearly running herself ragged. Her mommy burnout manifested in her emotional and physical exhaustion. "If I could attach myself to an IV with a steady drip of Diet Coke, I would," she told me. I understood that she was addicted to her Diet Coke because her energy tank was so low, but caffeine can make you feel worse because it spikes your energy and then you plummet. I suggested to Carmen that she reduce her cola intake, but I could tell when she just shrugged her shoulders that she wasn't yet ready to make this change. I knew from other clients, though, that there would be a time when she would be more open to this suggestion.

She was snapping at her kids at night to hurry up and get to bed so she could get back to her work. She was frustrated because her son barely spoke to her anymore and she was growing tired of her daughter's ups and downs, which she always took personally. She still saw her friends during the week, but she had started to notice that she was becoming the Debbie Downer of the group because she was constantly bitching and complaining about her family. She forced herself to find upbeat stories in fear that her friends would stop inviting her out.

Carmen's kids also felt her frantic energy. They never felt like they could talk to her because she was always rushed and running around. They were also exhausted. They never got to bed before ten thirty and they were buckling under their school workloads piled on top of their extracurricular schedules and socializing. Both kids followed their mom's multitasking lead and did their homework while Snapchatting with their friends. Eventually, her daughter started to get test anxiety and her son's grades slipped. When Carmen's kids brought up their concerns to her, she just told them, "These activities will look great on your college applications."

Soon after, Carmen brought her daughter in to see me for a few sessions for her test anxiety, and that's when I learned more about how her busyness was impacting her kids. "My mom doesn't even know what's going on with me or my brother anymore," her daughter told me. "She's just always running around and worried about everything, but she's the one that needs help." What Carmen's daughter didn't know was that I had been seeing her mother for months and I knew that Carmen was simply moving along the recovery process, where she would get worse before getting better.

In another session, Carmen explained that she felt like she was running around with a brick tied to her back. Still, she felt like it was worth it so her kids could thrive. She felt that she was just doing what any "good mother" would.

I prodded her around how she defined a "good mother." Carmen explained that a good mother protects her kids. A good mother knows what's going on in her kids' lives so she can help guide them through the rough patches. A good mother gives her kids every opportunity possible so they can achieve their dreams. Carmen justified driving all over the place for her son's travel basketball team because his coaches thought he might be good enough to play in college.

I hear the "good mom" excuse often. While we moms can model values, we can only take a child so far. Sometimes, we do have to let our kids fail. It's important for them to see us fail, too. It's valuable for our kids to see that we are human rather than perfect. That we are balanced. Some days we eat healthy and some days we have burgers, fries, and dessert. If we are trying to be super-mom, they will try to be super-kids and will ultimately end up with our super-stress. The "good mom badge" isn't good for anyone in the family.

We moms were raised in families that told us that we could do anything—and we believed it. What we didn't learn was how to capture balance in our quest to be everything to everyone. We have no models of women who have successfully forged this path for us, so we are still figuring out what's possible. Now, we have multiple generations of mothers who feel overwhelmed, but, really, we're just still figuring out how to create this "do-it-all mom" and still stay sane.

I had one family who re-mortgaged their house so that their kids could both play on travel baseball and lacrosse teams. All their time and money went to their kids. "I would do anything to support my kids and their talents," the mom told me. I knew another mom who felt it was important to role-model a healthy lifestyle for her kids. She would go for a walk outside by herself even when it was 20 degrees out and would also take them to the gym with her. While she worked out almost to the point of hyperventilating, her kids sat by the welcome desk and watched reruns of *The Real Housewives of . . .* somewhere. These moms were both doing what they thought was best for their kids, but they were only running down their own personal resources.

What moms don't realize is that most kids will find a way to get where they need to go in life. Children still find ways to be healthy and to make it onto sports teams without their parents getting so overly involved if that's something they want for themselves. The same goes for kids who go to great universities. And that mom who was exercising to exhaustion to prove a point? Her kids still don't exercise. There is no guarantee that your kids will achieve the results you are striving for.

One of the biggest challenges today's moms face is letting their kids fail. We think our kids' failures mean that we have failed as a mom. I tell clients all the time that it's great to tell your kids to dream big and to understand the value of hard work to achieve great things. But kids must learn flexibility. They need to know how to fall along their path and get back up. I used to work with a client whose daughter was an amazing skier. When she got into an elite ski academy, her parents scraped together every last cent they had to purchase a second home near the academy. After one season, their daughter broke her leg. She spent the next few months struggling to find her identity outside of "ski star." Her parents struggled to rebuild their finances. And what moms don't realize is that while they are running around like mad, trying to jump through self-imposed "good mom" hoops, they are damaging themselves and their kids. The hoops are false and of their own making.

A few weeks later, it was practically a blizzard outside when Carmen came into my office windblown and covered in snow. "I forgot my hat," she muttered as she sat down.

After some small talk, I asked her what she wanted to focus on that day.

"I'm a little embarrassed to tell you this." Carmen dropped her chin so she was looking down at her brown and now waterlogged leather clogs.

"I'm listening," I said softly.

"I have this fantasy sometimes." She looked up at me. Her cheeks were pink.

I waited for her to go on. Carmen shook her head, but I remained silent.

"Sometimes I fantasize about getting really sick or needing a minor surgery so I can go into the hospital and have others wait on me while I rest. No one would expect anything of me. They may even feel sorry for me. And I wouldn't have to do anything for a while." Carmen pulled her glasses off her face, tugged her shirtsleeve down a little over her palm, and wiped her lenses. Without her glasses, the bags under her eyes looked like bruises. "I wish that I could just press pause. That I could get a break from all the running around."

Carmen was not the first client to share this kind of fantasy with me. I have had women who fantasized about running away, extending business trips without their spouses knowing that their conference ended a day earlier, and sleeping in hotels close to their homes just to have a peaceful eighteen hours. Even I can confess that while writing this book, I had to go to the emergency room for what turned out to be kidney stones. I was given an IV with meds that made me feel just the right mix of groggy and pain-free, but still alert enough to watch Sunday night football alone in my room. While I waited around for blood work and tests to see if I needed surgery, I did consider what it would be like to spend the next few days in the hospital for a forced and much-needed break. In the end, I didn't need surgery and was sent home to pass the stones. The next morning, I got up, made breakfast and lunches for the kids, and went on with my life, but I must admit that I was a little disappointed that I didn't get "a night off" at the hospital.

When women tell me that they want to run away or get injured so they will be taken care of for a change, I hear chronic stress that has turned into mommy burnout ringing through. When moms share these secret thoughts, I urge them to take a hard look at how they can carve out alone time for themselves. In many cases, this means being vulnerable enough to ask for help. When clients or even my friends make these kinds of comments to me, I hold them accountable for getting their needs met in whatever way possible because I know the consequences if they don't.

"You're so overwhelmed that you feel like you need to be hospitalized to make it all stop? Like you have no control otherwise?" I asked Carmen that day.

"Yes, and I don't know how to make it stop. There is no end in sight. If I literally could not do anything, it would all have to end." Carmen squinted and slid her glasses back on.

I nodded.

"I'm just so busy," Carmen said to me. "How do I make it stop?"

I hear this "busy" excuse almost daily. We've come to a place in our society where "busy" has become the wall that moms bang their heads against when they consider sitting down for five minutes so they can catch their breath, or to take a break for lunch or to reach out to a friend. "Busy" keeps moms separated from one another just when they need each other most. "Busy" keeps moms alone. "Busy" keeps moms burned out and reeling. So, let's take a look at this. Are you *really* too busy? What's eating up your time and energy?

According to the American Time Use Survey, women spend an average of two hours and fifteen minutes every day on household chores, such as preparing food, washing and folding laundry, and cleaning the house. If you're like many of the moms I know, a good chunk of your time is also spent checking off items on your to-do list. You pick up new ballet tights for your daughter. You schedule your son's annual checkup. You run to the pharmacy, the grocery store, and the cleaners. You research and then register your kids for their after-school activities and then special camps for vacation and summertime.

You're probably also going overboard on at least one project that is not necessary. Do you need to bake the cupcakes your kid takes to school from scratch? Do you need a professional photo shoot for your holiday card? How much time do you spend coordinating your kids' outfits (even your son's with your daughter's) and keeping your house decorated according to the latest trends? Do you have to take off from work and meet with your child's teacher in person when a phone call or email is acceptable? Do you need personalized gifts with special gift wrap for your kids' teachers at the end of the year? I knew a mom who spent a whole afternoon roasting nuts—with all the accompanying spices— for her daughter's teachers. Yes, it was a nice gesture. But I don't think the teachers would have thought poorly of her for a gift that ate up less of her time. Chances are, you could save at least two hours a day—most days—if you didn't need to reach for what you consider to be super-mom status.

Although Carmen did maintain her friendships, even if she wasn't so honest in her sharing, many moms hide behind the "busy" excuse to isolate themselves. Which is a shame, because often, spending time with a good girlfriend will energize you and deflate some of your stress. If you really can't get out of some of your obligations, consider how you can include your friends. Maybe you can invite a friend to join you while you shop for a new coffee table for the living room or bake cookies for your daughter's playdate that afternoon.

Of course, friendships *are* a two-way street. Clients often tell me that they feel like their friends are too busy for them, saying things like, "I would just be a burden if I called another mom to complain about work or if I asked a friend to grab a cup of coffee or meet me for lunch." So, what's going on here? Are our friends too busy for us? The answer is *sometimes*.

Sometimes our friends are suffering from mommy burnout, too. But many times, we project our own busy schedules onto our friends and assume they are just as overwhelmed. We assume that our friends can't add anything to their days, so we don't ask for help. And in saying nothing to each other, both women remain alone and in crisis.

The other side of "busy" are those who seem to revel in how packed their schedules are. Yes, they probably do have a lot going on, but more likely, speaking about their "busy-ness" helps them maintain a perception of significance. They want to be relevant in today's world, and the perception these days is that if you're not "busy," then you must not be doing anything meaningful with your life. Moreover, if you're not busy with your kids, then you're just not doing enough as a mother.

Three weeks after Carmen shared her hospital fantasy with me, she sat down in my office again and told me that she had been taken to the emergency room two nights before. I noticed that her tan shorts appeared loose on her. Her cheekbones were a bit more prominent.

"Are you okay?"

"I got a call from my dream client about a project I had been pitching for the last five months and they were finally ready to get started. On the one hand, I was thrilled. I mean, this project will take my freelancing business to a whole new level. But then I realized that I am already struggling to complete my smaller projects. When am I supposed to do this work?"

I sat back in my chair and listened.

"I told my husband the news when he got home and he was happy for me, but he was also concerned about how I would find the time to get it done and how the added stress would impact me. Even though he had the same initial reaction as I did, his hesitation made me even more anxious." Carmen explained that she realized she would have the money and enough work to hire an assistant for this project, so she quickly set out to find help.

That process proved time consuming, but after two weeks of sifting through résumés and interviewing candidates, Carmen was convinced that she had found the perfect assistant. She sent the woman she had chosen an email with her offer first thing in the morning . . . and then waited. Every hour that the woman didn't respond, the muscles in Carmen's neck twisted a little tighter. She kept going back to check her emails and by lunch the woman still had not responded. Carmen considered sending her the offer again, thinking that maybe she hadn't received it for some reason. Then, just before three o'clock, Carmen got an email from the candidate explaining that she had decided to go with another job. Carmen could hear the bus pulling up just as she was reading the email, so she had to set that disappointment aside and deal with the usual afternoon chaos.

That night, Carmen told her husband what had happened, and he gave her a hug and told her that he would come back to help her after he finished a few things in his office. "After he left my office, the only thing I could think to do was to sort through résumés again. As I was reading through my stack, my heart started to pound so hard that I could almost hear it in my ears. Then, I got dizzy and I felt like I couldn't breathe. A searing pain exploded in my chest. I thought I was having a heart attack, but then I decided it was just stress." Carmen's husband came back into her office to tell her that he was going to bed. When he saw how pale her face was, he became concerned.

"'I just need to lie down and catch my breath,' I told him. But the look on his face freaked me out, and then I thought that maybe I was actually having a heart attack." When Carmen's husband suggested that he should take her to the emergency room to get checked out, she let him. "The hospital ran a bunch of tests and it turns out that I had had a panic attack."

I shook my head.

"I've never had a panic attack. Why would this happen now? Out of nowhere?"

Mommy burnout moms are more vulnerable to panic and anxiety because of their prolonged stress. Panic attacks are usually not triggered by one specific stressor, but rather a combination of stressors. When moms hit a wall of hopelessness, like Carmen reached with her search for an assistant for her big project, anxiety or panic attacks can strike.

In Carmen's case, her panic attack occurred because she was constantly running and trying to juggle multiple tasks at one time. And even though the news of this project was good for her, it was the final tipping point of her stress threshold. She had stepped outside of her window of tolerance, as I like to call it. Her fearful thoughts pushed her body to prepare for either fight or flight, which caused a surge of adrenaline. Her body was reacting naturally, as it should. However, her mind knew that there was no real danger to her life, so she froze.

"I am sure you were not able to move or speak at first, right?"

"That's right," admitted Carmen. "But why now?"

"Panic attacks don't always have a clear trigger—and often can occur months after a significant stressful incident. Even the medical field isn't quite certain why panic attacks occur. In my experience, fears that people have not truly dealt with can manifest in a panic attack."

"So, what do I have to do to never have this happen again? It was one of the scariest experiences of my life."

I shared with Carmen several things that some of my other clients, both adolescents and adults, have done to protect against panic attacks. First, sleep is particularly important in preventing panic attacks, so I encourage adults to aim for eight hours of good-quality sleep and for adolescents to aim for ten hours a night. Also, regular exercise helps to manage and prevent panic attacks by releasing mood-boosting hormones called endorphins, relaxing your muscles and easing tension in your body, and helping you to fall asleep easier and stay asleep, all of which decrease anxiety levels. Educate yourself around understanding stress and know what your triggers are. Know what your stress style (fight, flight, or freeze) is so you can identify when the stress is building, making you anxious, and use some de-stressing strategies early on to prevent a panic attack from happening.

Are You Too Busy?

Many moms today are over-tasking and racing through their days and it's pushing their stress response into overdrive. If you answer "yes" to three or more of the following questions, you may want to consider taking some tasks off your daily to-do list.

1. Do you miss dinner with your family or eat standing up three or more days a week?

2. After a conversation, do you sometimes realize that you didn't hear more than half of what was said?

3. Do you find yourself saying things like, "I can't catch my breath" or "I feel like I am drowning" several times a week?

4. Do you feel like a failure or that you are "half-assing" most of your responsibilities?

5. Do you joke that you feel like you have ADD? Do you struggle to focus for more than ten minutes at a time?

6. Do you have a to-do list that never seems to end? Do you have unfinished projects and things you want to get accomplished that have been lingering for months or years?

7. Do you have a hard time saying no to favors, committees, or volunteer opportunities?

8. Do you miss appointments or forget special days (like your child's pajama party day at school)?

9. Do you sometimes forget or skip going to the bathroom because you can't find time in your day?

10. Do you want to get your nails done, your roots colored, or your brows waxed, but cannot find the time?

11. Have you not scheduled your mammogram or annual visit to your gynecologist because you don't have any breaks in your schedule?

12. Do you need new prescription glasses, but this task just never hits the top of your priority list?

13. Do you need to buy new clothes, but don't feel like that's important enough to take time out of your day to do?

After we tackled strategies to keep future panic attacks at bay, we needed to address Carmen's chaotic schedule and near constant multitasking. The first thing we talked about was her work schedule and all the interruptions that were slowing her down. Like most moms who work on a computer all day, she was often interrupted by news alerts, pop-ups, and social media posts. "I didn't even consider this multitasking because I just go from reading one thing back to reading something else," Carmen told me. She agreed to turn off all alerts during her work hours. She also set special rings on her phone for important calls so she could let all other calls go to voicemail to handle later in the day, both of which cut down on interruptions and gave her back focused time to get her work done. She later told me that managing her phone distractions was like giving herself the gift of time. I hear about these phone interruptions a lot, both with moms who work at home and in an office.

I felt like this was a good time to bring up Carmen's caffeine usage again because she was now ready to make real changes. I suggested that Carmen substitute half of her Diet Cokes with water to keep her energy levels more consistent rather than get the intermittent jolts from the caffeine. "What about my two o'clock slump?" Carmen asked. "I'll fall asleep at my desk unless I get some caffeine or sugar."

"Stand up and do a few jumping jacks or go for a quick walk around your neighborhood," I told her. "Even if you feel like you can't step away from your desk for a minute, getting your blood flowing and giving your brain a break will actually refresh you and make you more productive than when you try and force yourself through your work."

"I didn't realize how much junk food I was eating throughout the day," Carmen said in the next session. "All of the cookies and candy that I thought I was buying for my kids, I realized I was eating most of it." Carmen decided to take time out to eat breakfast and lunch rather than graze on high-sugar foods throughout the day. "I really do feel better actually," she told me. "I'm not bleary-eyed by two o'clock now."

I also prodded Carmen around all that she was doing for her kids, who were teenagers. I pointed out that giving her kids opportunities to do things for themselves would give them a sense of responsibility and that they could take care of themselves, both of which are important for self-esteem and independence. "They are fifteen and seventeen years old," she said with a big smile. "That's old enough to find yourself a snack and to get yourself ready for practice or a game." This bought Carmen back a full hour of work time before she had to drive her kids wherever they needed to go before dinner.

Once Carmen settled into this new routine, she also reached out to other moms to set up a carpool. "Even the travel team moms were into it. We live in different areas around our town, but just dedicating one or two nights to driving rather than six is so much better." This bought Carmen back even more time to work and/or cook dinners for her family.

Carmen and I also discussed the traditional roles she and her husband played in their home, and she came to understand that the "traditional model" that she grew up in wasn't working for their family. She noted, "My mom wasn't shuttling me and my siblings around to different activities every night." I suggested that Carmen explain to her husband that she needed help at the house, and it turned out he was open to the idea. He didn't want to see her struggling. Carmen ultimately assigned her kids and husband chores after dinner so she wasn't stuck in the kitchen for over an hour every night cleaning up. "I can even read or watch a little television with my husband to relax before bed now," she told me. "And I'm on track to finish my big project on time, without an assistant."

Mommy Burnout Prescription Plan

Ban the Word "Busy"

Schedule time for yourself on your calendar. You need time to decompress and reenergize by reading a book, taking a walk outside, or even meeting up with friends for lunch.

Check out meal or grocery delivery services for busy nights. Find ways to cut down on your to-do list. Grocery services, if they are available by you, are a huge time-saver.

Practice asking for and receiving help. All moms need help. It's not weak to admit that. If you have a partner, ask him to get the kids dressed in the morning while you make breakfast. Ask another mom to carpool with you for some of your kids' activities.

Say yes only to things you absolutely need or want to do. You're not being rude if you decline invitations that don't work for you or your schedule. You need to guard your time wisely.

Turn off your reminder alerts on your phone and computer. Make it easy for yourself to stay focused on one task at a time.

Monitor your television binge-fests to make sure you are watching for entertainment and not distraction. Television can be relaxing, as long as you're not using it to "flight" a stressful situation.

BONUS EXERCISE

Ask everyone in your house to pitch in! Even small children can help in some way. Your younger kids can put their toys away. Your partner can help with the bedtime routine. Your teenagers can do the laundry. Don't take everything on yourself.

Chapter 9

I'm Sick and Tired, All the Time.

How Mommy Burnout Makes Us Sick

Sound Familiar?

It's not uncommon for stress to manifest as physical pain. If you have any of the following physical ailments and cannot find the root cause, you can likely self-diagnose mommy burnout:

- Trouble falling or staying asleep

- Chronic diarrhea or constipation

- Stomachaches or nausea

- Lack of appetite or frequent overeating

- Neck pain

- Lower back pain

- Chronic fatigue

- Chest pain, pounding heart

- Headaches

- Frequent colds or sniffles

- Hives or skin rashes

- Random aches and pains in a joint (your jaw, for instance)

- Memory problems

Karen was forty-seven years old and married, but functioned as a single mom because her husband traveled all the time as an airline pilot. She had been married for twenty-five years. She had a fifteen-year-old daughter and two sons, twelve and seventeen years old. Karen had been a social worker, but left work when she had her second child.

I originally met Karen when her twelve-year-old's school had recommended that he see me. He was angry a lot and sad, and was often complaining of stomachaches. After a family session, though, I understood better that Karen was also having health issues and that they might, in part, stem from emotional strain. She began seeing me alone shortly thereafter.

Many moms who suffer mommy burnout experience physical symptoms as well. Stress can hurt physically. This is not to say that moms' physical pain is not real. It is! But if no medical source of the pain can be found, exploring emotional connections to the pain can be helpful. The vast majority of the moms I see who are burned out experience both emotional and physical symptoms.

Karen was one mom who had everyone fooled. Maybe even herself, for a while. She was upbeat, always on time, and pretty laid back. She had sparkling green eyes that lit up her whole face every time she told a joke, which was often. We laughed all through her sessions.

To any outsider, Karen looked healthy and happy. She was responsive to her kids. Even when she was telling me about a problem she was having, it was easy to miss the significance because her charm and humor pervaded her stories. I remember one story from an early session that I think of as classic Karen.

"So, I'm sitting there with all these pale, runny-nosed folks. I have a clipboard holding the doctor's questionnaire balanced atop my leaving-the-house leggings and I'm reading through this laundry list of symptoms." Karen flashed me her trademark smile. Her green eyes glinted against her fair skin and dark bangs.

"Fatigue. *Check.*

Headaches. *Check.*

Back pain. *Check.*

Sleep issues. *Check.*

Scattered thoughts. *Check.*

Gut discomfort. *Check.*"

Karen mimed how she was going through the doctor's questionnaire. "I'm just sitting there checking off almost every box. I had no idea that I was so sick." She smirked. "A knot popped up in my neck. I could feel my shoulders inching themselves toward my ears as I neared the bottom of the page." Karen started to laugh. "And then I realized that there was a back to this form also. I had a whole other side to keep my anxiety simmering while waiting to see the doctor."

Inside his office, the doctor noted that Karen had checked off a lot of the boxes on his questionnaire. He did a quick physical exam and then asked how she was feeling.

"'From the face of your form, I'm a walking disease,' I said to him. Then, I asked if he thought something was actually wrong." The doctor suggested that Karen have some blood work done. "'If there is anything going on with you, we'll find it,' he told me."

"Did the blood work find anything?" I asked her.

"Oh, I haven't gone yet." Karen sat back in her chair. "I picked up the prescription for the tests from the nurse on my way out, and then promptly tucked it into my purse and forgot about it until just now." Karen gave me a crooked smile.

"How long ago did you say you went to the doctor?"

Karen thought for a moment. "Hmm, maybe about a month ago."

I just looked at her.

"I'm sure I'm fine," she told me. "I'm still walking and talking. I'm not eating much anymore, but that's not so bad. I've been getting compliments on my weight since my stomach has been acting up. I call it the 'how to avoid getting diarrhea diet.'"

I remained silent.

"Okay, okay," she said. "I'll run over to the lab after I leave here."

The first few times I spoke with Karen, though, our conversations centered around her twelve-year-old son, Jordan. "He is pretty hard to handle," she told me on the phone before our first session. "I guess it won't hurt to have him checked out. My brother went through something similar when he was younger, also."

Karen went on to tell me that at home, her youngest son seemed angry all the time. "He's irritable. We just never know what will set him off. One morning I made pancakes and he was happy. And the next day, I made the same thing and he got mad at me." She went on. "He's also a total downer. He'll make a tiny mistake, like spilling juice or forgetting a book at home, and it sends him into this abyss of self-pity. He'll go on and on about how stupid he is or how he'll never be able to do things right." Jordan would also do things that he knew would bother everyone else in the family. He would steal his sister's hair clips and purposefully leave the kitchen counter a mess after his snack. "I'm just always yelling at him," Karen told me. On the rare occasions that Karen found him crying, he slammed the door in her face.

At school, Jordan was in the nurse's office at least twice a week complaining of a stomachache and he would often throw his lunch out without eating anything. He was quiet and a bit withdrawn. He would also melt down if he answered a question wrong or didn't ace a quiz. "I'm so stupid. Nobody likes me," he would say to his teacher.

For a few weeks, I met with Jordan alone for thirty minutes and then brought Karen in at the end of the session. One afternoon, she mentioned that her husband, who spent several nights a week traveling for work, would be home the following week. I suggested that the whole family come in to see me.

Although I thought the session would be centered around her son and how his moods were impacting the rest of the family, Karen's husband quickly turned the spotlight on her. "These issues with Jordan are not just his own," Karen's husband started. "They impact Karen a lot as well. The kids really are her world. And Jordan's issues are hitting her hard."

I looked at Karen, who was shaking her head. She crossed her arms and legs.

"Has she told you about the migraines she gets at least twice a week? Or the neck pain that keeps her in bed every few weeks?"

"Jordan's issues are my fault," Karen said. "They are from my side of the family. These are my messed-up genes."

"She feels so guilty," her husband said to me. "But I don't blame her. I know that she has a lot on her plate with me gone most of the time, so I try to make her rest when I am home. I tell her to get a massage or to take a nap. She just needs to rest."

The children all shifted in their seats and glanced around at each other.

"Did you know that she was diagnosed with irritable bowel syndrome?"

"The medicine is helping with that," Karen said, waving off her husband. "And I'm seeing a chiropractor now for my neck. I'll be good as new is no time." Karen flashed a big smile. "Now, can we please talk about Jordan?"

I was a bit taken aback by how adamant her husband was. Karen had never mentioned any of her specific medical issues to me. I made a note to ask her more about her health in a later session. As this session was wrapping up, I suggested that Karen schedule two appointments for her and Jordan. I wanted to meet with Jordan first, and then follow up with Karen on parenting strategies she could implement with her son.

Over the next few weeks, Karen shared more about her history as a mom and her struggles with Jordan. "I was such a happy mom with my first two," Karen told me. "I stopped working as a social worker to be with them. I loved working with people, but I never regretted staying home when my kids were little." Karen took the kids to every toddler class in the area; she set up play-dates and looked forward to her days. She felt strong. And she felt happy.

Karen and her husband were so happy with their family that they wanted a third child. But Jordan was difficult from the start. Other moms told her, "From one to two kids is a big transition. But from two to three kids is nothing." But that's just not how things went for Karen. Suddenly, she and her husband were out-numbered. When Jordan came along, her other kids were already out of diapers and able to feed themselves. Yet the diaper changes and feeding felt like a lot more work with Jordan. She was more tired with him. And it didn't help that he was fussier than her other two children. And he never slept well.

About a month after that first family session, Karen came into the office wearing sunglasses. "Are you okay?" I asked her.

"Yeah," she said and gingerly lowered herself into the chair. "I'm just at the tail end of a migraine and I know that any bright lights will trigger it to start again." She paused. "And I'm also testing out what it feels like to be a celebrity. I'm in therapy *and* wearing sunglasses!"

"I love your sense of humor but, I'm concerned about your health," I told her.

"Me? I'll be fine. I'm here for Jordan. He's the one you should be worried about. I know you think he has depression, so . . ."

"Families are systems. If one person is sick, it impacts everyone else."

Karen nodded her head, but stayed silent.

I went on. "Over the last few weeks, you've mentioned quite a few doctor visits, but all of your blood work and other tests have come back normal. I think it's possible that some of your physical issues might stem from stress. I think that our sessions together should start to focus more on you and your health."

"I think I just need to find the right doctor."

"You might need another doctor. And I know that you feel like all the medications you are taking are helping. But I think you need a therapist on your team as well."

Karen, like so many women who are experiencing physical pain, don't always think to check their mental health. They become so focused on the pain, discomfort, or remedies that they fail to think about our mind/body connection. I remember that when I began my doctoral program, I started suffering from excruciating stomach pain that would double me over. I went to the student health center and when none of the tests revealed the source of my pain, I started to put together that the new level of stress I was piling on myself with school was impacting my physical health. At this point in our therapy, I knew that to some degree Jordan and Karen's health were connected and that they needed to continue their journeys separately, but with both working toward the goal of physical and mental health.

Over the next several months, Karen missed more than one session because she didn't feel well. She continued to lose weight. Her lower back started to bother her in addition to her neck. With tears in her eyes, she told me during an appointment, "I just feel like if it's not one thing, it's another. There is always something wrong with me." She saw one doctor after another but wasn't getting much guidance, only more appointments for more tests.

"A nurse from another doctor's office called me yesterday," she told me. She was slouched in her chair. "All of my initial test results came back normal." Karen shook her head. "Then, the nurse gave me a message from the doctor. Dr. Smith wants me to remember to drink enough water, which I do. Eating is my issue. He wants me to get enough sleep." Karen rolled her eyes. "And he wants me to stay away from caffeine, even though I would literally fall asleep at the wheel without it. Oh, and he wants me to get some exercise, even though my joints hurt so much that even the thought of jogging makes me cringe."

"Did you tell the nurse these things?" I asked.

"Of course not. I told her thank you and hung up. She can't help me. I'm starting to think that no one can help me. I feel like shit and there is nothing anyone can do."

At home, Karen had started snapping at her kids while helping them with their homework. Some nights, she was too tired to cook dinner, so her two oldest pitched in. They also now helped with the laundry. Everyone knew that they had to be quiet for Karen, so the kids started spending more time over at their friends' houses. Karen started seeing her friends only sporadically. She just didn't want to do anything anymore, but she found a Karen way to spin this to me: "It's like I'm taking a vacation from my own life."

Karen's kids were impacted by the change in their mom. In another family session, they admitted that they were confused that their mother seemed more tired and not like herself. They were also frustrated that she never wanted to talk about this with them. "Is she hiding something from us?" her oldest asked. They also seemed to resent her a little for their increased responsibility. While their friends always seemed free to hang out at the mall or play video games, they sometimes had to stay home to do chores around the house. They would tell me, "I don't know anyone else who cooks meals, vacuums, and drives their brothers and sisters to school and sports." Jordan grew more withdrawn and started lashing out at his older brother and sister, who now treated him more like the kid they had to babysit than their sibling.

Although Karen's symptoms were primarily physical, chronic stress can lead to psychological issues as well. Substance abuse, which is sometimes triggered by chronic stress, is a growing epidemic in this country, and moms are not immune to its grip and devastation. The World Health Organization reports that one in twelve women will become dependent on alcohol at some point in their life. A 2015 survey from the Substance Abuse Mental Health Services Administration revealed that in the United States, 3.6 million women over the age of twenty-six struggled with alcohol in 2015; 5.6 million women over the age of twenty-six misused prescription pain relievers, sedatives, stimulants, or tranquilizers that same year.

Like moms who laugh at humorous mommy blogs like *Scary Mommy* and movies about mommy burnout like *Bad Moms,* the misuse of alcohol, painkillers, sedatives, and sleeping medications has become a part of the mommy culture, and it's unhealthy. "I need my nightly cocktail of a sleeping pill and two glasses of wine to fall asleep," clients tell me. And because their friends are doing the same, they consider such behavior normal during this phase of their lives, but it can quickly become dangerous for their health. Substance abuse has become so normalized in our society that many moms don't realize when they have slid into dangerous territory.

When it comes to drinking, I believe that if the moms were downing tequila or beer as much as they drink wine, red flags would go up a lot sooner. There is something sophisticated about wine. Maybe the bottle, the European roots, the higher price point, and the culture around it that makes wine acceptable at almost any time. Women bond around wine. I've heard of moms drinking wine at playdates at eleven thirty in the morning, or needing three glasses of wine to relax enough to fall asleep at night—neither of which is healthy.

I remember one client who was shocked when she realized that her drinking had moved to what I felt was unhealthy territory.

"I'll have a glass with dinner," she told me. "And then I'll pour a glass for after the kids go to sleep. It's like my reward at the end of the day." If she was particularly wound up, she would pour herself a third. "It helps me unwind," she explained.

"Why do you think you're having a drink or two or three every night?" I asked her.

"My girlfriends do the same thing. I'm just sharing a drink with my husband and then relaxing at the end of the day."

"How would you feel if you didn't drink any alcohol for the next week?" I asked her.

She thought for a moment and then realized that she couldn't do it. "I would never get to sleep," she pushed back.

This is not an uncommon conversation. What many moms don't know is that substance abuse can sneak up slowly over time. One glass of wine with dinner, one sleeping pill a few nights a week, or a few painkillers to relieve your cramps each month can eventually escalate. Women slowly become dependent on these substances to manage their stress, wind down, fall asleep, and escape their pain. Before they know it, they have jumped from use to abuse to addiction. Their mommy burnout surges and their lives spin out of control. It is frightening for everyone involved.

A few years ago, I had a good friend who invited me and my family over for dinner on a Saturday night. When we were sitting down to eat, she offered me a glass of wine and told me she would not be having one. She shared that she had been drinking and wanted to cut down. She said she knew it was too much (and was a little embarrassed) when her husband and two children commented on her slurring and the empty wine bottles in the garbage. She realized then that she had been using the alcohol to deal with her stress and wanted to stop before it became a bigger issue.

Whether you feel persistently overwhelmed, suffer from insomnia, or deal with consistent discomfort—either emotionally, physically, or both—your pain is real. Be honest with yourself and your doctors so you can find the relief you need in a healthy way for both you *and* your family.

Is Your Wind-Down Unhealthy?

It's not uncommon for moms to use various substances to de-stress and unwind. And this can lead to substance abuse and dependence. Read through the following questions. If you answer "yes" to three or more questions, you may want to consider reevaluating your de-stressing strategies.

1. Do you consume more than seven drinks in a week?

2. Do you ever consume more than three drinks in one night?

3. If you have been prescribed anti-anxiety medication, painkillers, or sleeping pills, do you ever take more than your doctor prescribed?

4. Do you ever mix alcohol with your prescription medication to relax or fall asleep?

5. Do you ever feel the need to hide that you are taking prescription medicine?

6. Have you ever tried abstaining from alcohol and found it too difficult?

7. Have you ever gone a few days without drinking and found that you were on edge and irritable?

8. Has anyone in your life ever commented on your substance use?

9. Do you find yourself looking forward to your nightly drink during the day?

10. Do you plan your social activities around being able to drink alcohol?

11. Have you used alcohol to relax for more than two weeks?

Over time, it became clear to me that mommy burnout played a role in Karen's issues. As I came to understand Karen and her family, I could see that issues with her son Jordan, coupled with the regular, everyday stressors of juggling multiple responsibilities with her family, as well as her husband's frequent absences because of his job as an airline pilot, had persisted for so long that they were driving her physical ailments. I came to better understand that her blood work could come back as normal only because there is no formal blood test for mommy burnout.

This is not to say that Karen's pain was just in her head. Her pain was real. She did need certain medications. I will always remember Karen for being one of my first clients, but not my last, whose stress was so significant that it manifested as physical pain in multiple places in her body. Just as the renowned trauma expert Bessel van der Kolk states in his book of the same name, "the body keeps the score," meaning that trauma and/or chronic stress literally alters the brain and body.

The Mayo Clinic explains that persistent stress can lead to a variety of health-related ailments, including "anxiety, depression, digestive problems, headaches, heart disease, sleep problems, weight gain, and memory and concentration impairment." In my earlier days of private practice, a middle-aged mom named Sarah came to see me because she was going through a drawn-out, high-conflict divorce and was very concerned about her two children. When she came in for our initial session, I noticed that she took two puffs from her inhaler while we were talking. She casually mentioned that she sometimes suffered from asthma. While I didn't think much of this during our first session, the next time I saw her she had a "terrible cold." As we moved through the winter, her health ailments bounced between asthma attacks, bronchitis, and eventually anxiety attacks. When she started experiencing severe anxiety and insomnia, I finally made the connection that her symptoms were triggered by the stress of her divorce and the court hearings. Her health would always deteriorate during the weeks that she had to be in court or mediation with her ex-husband.

Whenever I nudged Karen a little to look at her own stress, especially regarding her health, she would change the conversation and talk about Jordan. As she continued to power forward, her emotional and physical health continued to fail. "I'm just so tired of everything," she told me in one session. "My body always hurts. My son is depressed. I know my other kids are taking on a lot of my slack. I just feel like I'm in a bad situation that has no exit door."

"Karen," I said. "If you put all your symptoms together and look at all your test results that have come back normal, I would consider the diagnosis to be burned out."

"Burned out on what? My kids?"

"Your kids are one of the many stressors that are burning you out. It's your kids. It's your husband being gone a lot. It's you not seeing your friends as much. It's your worry over how you are going to pay for your kids' college in a few years. It's everything that you experience as overwhelming, all at once."

It was no big surprise to me that Karen's medical issues spiraled in the way they did. The women I see divide into two main camps. The first are those who go to their doctor and are told that they are anxious and/or depressed. They are usually given a prescription and referred to a therapist. The second camp are those whose doctors cannot figure out why they don't feel well, and start sending them through a revolving door of specialists in the hope that another doctor will find the source. After these moms have seen numerous specialists and undergone a substantial number of tests, I find that either they seek out therapy or a friend or spouse suggests that they contact a therapist. I often wish that more doctors were like this one OB/GYN I know who will not renew a prescription for a mental health medication without first making sure that the patient went to see a therapist. She really does right by her patients by following through with the standard treatment protocol.

It is my belief that primary care doctors are missing the mommy burnout issue because, first and foremost, there is no formal medical diagnosis or test for this. When a patient walks into their office complaining of chronic physical and/or emotional issues, doctors will listen for symptoms of more common ailments, such as hormonal imbalances related to estrogen or thyroid dysfunction. Once these physical causes are ruled out, they might suggest seeing a therapist.

Most therapists will initially listen for signs of anxiety and/or depression. However, I meet many moms who are functioning, but they just "don't feel right." Perhaps they often feel a little down or jumpy. They forget dates and appointments. Maybe snap at their kids. Still, they do experience moments of joy and happiness. They can turn their worries off. These moms might not meet the criteria for clinical depression or anxiety, but that doesn't mean that they don't need help to feel better. And, perhaps more importantly, it doesn't mean that they shouldn't get help before they slide into full-blown depression.

Another area that therapists will consider is acute stress disorder or post-traumatic stress disorder. Within these two diagnoses, the triggers are a traumatic event like the death of a loved one or being physically attacked—and can last from one day all the way through a woman's life. What we are missing from this conversation is the in-between stress, the chronic mid-grade–level stress that comes from consistent multitasking, constantly comparing yourself and your kids to others, perpetual lack of sleep, and running yourself ragged while trying to be a good mom. These are the stressors that can go on for years, and are exactly what plague women everywhere. These are the stressors that few doctors know how to treat, even as women continue to function with their health and well-being at risk and often in decline.

At some point, moms, we need to accept that the super-mom cape (as we have envisioned it) just doesn't fit. We need to ask for help. Because even though mommy burnout is not a formal diagnosis, it is real. And, it's even more important to know how to advocate for yourself and to talk about your issues with your doctor to ensure that you get the care you need. Your life depends on it.

Be Your Own Advocate

Doctors today are not listening for your mommy burnout symptoms. They also don't have much time to spend with you. It's important to be prepared so you can present useful information to get the help you need.

- Know your family's medical history. Some of these conversations can be uncomfortable, but doctors do need a complete picture. Did anyone in your family suffer from depression or anxiety? Have there been any suicides in your family? Did anyone have heart disease or chronic fatigue? Gather this information before you see your physician.

- Keep a symptom record. It is common to forget just how often your headaches may come and go without writing them down before seeing your doctor.

- Ask to complete the medical history forms ahead of time. Make sure that you have plenty of time and are under no pressure when you complete your forms. You want to make sure they are accurate.

- Keep a document of your health history and medications on your home computer and add to it as details change. Print out a copy and take it with you to appointments, lowering your chances of forgetting details in your doctor's office.

- You are the only one who can be fully honest and open about what has been going on with you. So, topics like sex, alcohol, drugs, depression, suicidal thoughts, sleep, and fatigue should be areas that you come in ready to discuss openly.

Once Karen had spoken to her other doctors, it was time to tackle her mommy burnout head-on. Because her husband was away so much, I felt that community support would be the fastest way to get her back on track. She needed to talk to other people about her stressors and ask for help with some of her daily logistics.

I explained to Karen that a sense of belonging was essential to human functioning. That by her connecting with others in her neighborhood, kids' school, sports teams, and organizations, she would naturally come to see that she was not alone in her experience. While the connection between stress and health is clear, both are also affected by social and emotional support. Research has shown that people who have strong emotional support—specifically, that they have someone they can ask for and lean on when they need emotional support, such as family and friends—fare better, emotionally and physically, than those who do not. With her husband gone so often, Karen really needed to create this emotional net for herself. "You have to build your own village," I told her.

"Do I get to name my village?" she joked.

"You need to talk to others about Jordan's depression, because the weight of his diagnosis and managing him alone for most of the week is killing you," I told her. "Opening up will give you relief. You can also find some moms to carpool with and some neighbors who will take your two older kids for a few hours if Jordan is having a particularly rough day. You can even find some neighborhood kids to shovel your driveway when it snows. You have been doing everything by yourself for years. And it's hurting your body."

Karen did eventually take my advice and reached out to a few friends for help and conversation. Two of these moms grew to be a tremendous support system for her over time. They would switch off taking Jordan for playdates with their kids after school a few nights a week and would offer to take her older kids to practices or to friends' houses if they were already going out.

Karen realized that on top of the actual time she got back to focus on herself, simply knowing that she could rely on these women in an emergency (or just when she needed a break) served as a huge emotional boon for her. In return, Karen's husband was able to use his discounted flight benefits to send the three women on weekend getaways every few months. And, in time and as Karen's aches and pains started to fade and her energy levels moved upwards, she returned the favors.

"I was so ashamed to ask for help," Karen told me. "But, really, it's these small asks that make a world of difference. I feel much better." Her green eyes glinted and she flashed her classic smile. "So, can we finally talk about Jordan now?"

Regain Your Health

Be your own health advocate. Know your medical history and how to discuss your issues with your doctors. Keep a running list of any medical conditions you have and medications you take that you can bring with you to doctor's appointments. Also, keep track in your calendar of when you need to make your annual doctor's appointments and schedule your mammogram. Notice any changes in your hair, skin, or nails to mention to your doctor at your next visit.

Build your village. You can't mother all by yourself. We all need help. Start small to build up to a village of your own. Join a local sports league for running or even soccer for adults, get involved in planning your neighborhood block party, or attend a mom's night out at your child's school.

Reconnect with your girlfriends. They are good for your health. Talk on the phone, plan playdates with other families, go on a girls' weekend away, or attend a book club event.

Unplug from technology. Give your brain a rest and tune into yourself. Take time to meditate, catch up on your reading, or just leave time with nothing planned and see what happens.

Be consistent with your exercise, diet, and hydration. Don't forget to be good to your body. Find an exercise buddy to work out with or attend group classes to make these activities more social. You can even plan for a different kind of exercise each day to keep your workouts exciting.

Mommy Burnout Prescription Plan

BONUS EXERCISE

Put your oxygen mask on first! For the next week, every time you go to do something for your kids—whether it's grabbing another snack for your toddler or driving your tween to her piano lesson—see if you can take even a minute or two first for yourself. Quick mom-break ideas can be spritzing yourself with a sweet-smelling facial mist, making sure you have your water bottle iced and filled before you leave the house, and grabbing a snack for yourself.

Chapter 10

Are My Kids Burned Out, Too?

Sound Familiar?

Do you know what mommy burnout looks like now? Can you identify it in your kids?

- Do you go to bed late when you are stressed? Does your child do the same?

- Do you over- or under-eat when you are stressed? Does your child do the same?

- Do you isolate yourself when you are stressed? Does your child do the same?

- Do you binge on social media and/or television when you are stressed? Does your child do the same?

- Do you snap at those around you when you are stressed? Does your child do the same?

- Are you forgetful when you are stressed? Is your child the same?

- Have you stopped participating in hobbies that you enjoyed because you are stressed? Has your child done the same?

Ashley was twelve years old and in the sixth grade. Her mother, Sarah, was thirty-eight years old and was a real estate agent. Ashley's father was a physician.

Sarah initially brought Ashley to see me because she felt like she was a perfectionist. I soon picked up on Ashley's anxious tendencies . . . and her mother's. Sarah was experiencing mommy burnout and as the months moved on, I noted a mirror effect between mother and daughter. As Sarah fell deeper in mommy burnout, Ashley's emotional health also tumbled.

One of the biggest reasons to intervene with mommy burnout is because it impacts our kids. When moms suffer, the kids suffer as well. Kids will report headaches, stomachaches, excessive worry, and prolonged sadness. As we've mentioned before in this book, when one family member suffers, the whole family suffers. Healthy families require healthy moms.

I remember my first session with Ashley quite clearly. "This was my mom's idea," Ashley told me matter-of-factly. "I have no idea why I'm here." At twelve, Ashley had the poise and appearance of a fourteen-year-old.

I sat up a little straighter in my chair and smiled. "Well, we have some time. While you're here, why don't you tell me about yourself."

"I'm in sixth grade," Ashley started, absentmindedly pulling her long, blond hair over her shoulder and braiding it while she spoke. "I play basketball on the school team. So far, I'm the top scorer this year. My best friend, Bella, is on the team with me. I'm a pretty good student. I'm in some honors classes. I'm actually third in my class, but I still have a few more months to get to number one. Umm . . . what else would you like to know?"

"Sounds like you have many talents."

Ashley shrugged and continued to braid her hair.

"With all that you have going on, tell me about your typical day."

"I set the alarm on my phone so I get up by myself. Not like my older brother, who sleeps until my mom starts yelling that we'll all be late if he doesn't get out of bed and pulls the comforter off him." She giggled. "Then, I go to school. I really like school, even though that sounds totally dorky. Then I have practice three afternoons a week. After practice, I have dinner with my family. Although my mom's idea of family dinner is her standing at the counter while the rest of us eat at the table because she eats and cleans the kitchen at the same time. That's weird, right? She says she's just being . . . what's that word? Efficient. She always has something she has to do. After dinner, I have about four hours of homework every night."

"That's a lot."

"Yeah, but it's always been that way for me. And, it's not so bad because my mom sits with me and does her own work. She says that she has a lot of important work to do too, and so this works for us. My parents always say that it's important to be the smartest and the best. I guess I agree with them." She paused. "My mom says that this setup saves her time because she can help me with my work while she does her own. We have this thing where we both chew on our pens while we're thinking." She smiled at me. "We just noticed that the other day."

"Why is it important to be the smartest and the best?" I asked her.

Ashley shrugged her shoulders. "If you want to get anywhere in life, you have to be the best. My dad is a super-successful doctor and I want to be just like him, so I have to get good grades."

I made a mental note of that. "So, what else are you into?"

"I love fashion and beauty. I am in love with Kylie Jenner's nail polish line." She held out her hands to show me her mint-green nails. "I have my own collection. And I've been trying to convince my mom to let me get ombre highlights in my hair. Maybe you could help me with that. The other girls at school would be so jealous. And I also want her to get me some new eye shadows that I saw in Sephora the other week."

"Well, it looks like your mom already lets you wear some makeup."

"Yeah, I have mascara and bronzer and lip gloss on, but these eye shadows would totally complete my look." She untangled her braid and flipped her hair back over her shoulder. "I'm trying to win best eyes for the yearbook this year and I know those eye shadows totally make the blue in my eyes pop." She paused for a moment. "My dad hates that I'm wearing makeup, but he just doesn't get it."

I thought back to when I was Ashley's age. I wasn't wearing makeup or thinking about getting highlights. I played with my friends, talked on the phone, and practiced feathering my hair. Girls just grow up faster today. A few months ago, a fifteen-year-old girl came over to babysit for a few hours while I ran some errands. I explained to her that my boys were really wound up and that they probably needed to go to the park to get out their energy. She replied, "Oh yeah, I know boy energy. I'll pack a bag of snacks and bring them to the park and they'll be fine."

"What else are you interested in?" I asked Ashley.

"I've been researching a skin-care line to try out. I would love to start an Instagram or YouTube channel about all the different beauty products I test."

I remained silent, but in my head, I thought, *I've never met a sixth grader like this kid.*

"My skin is clear now, but I'm sure the zits are coming," she continued. "And I have to get new Uggs, because my feet stink suddenly and I ruined the pair I got for Christmas last month, which totally sucks."

This pleasant back-and-forth went on like this for about twenty more minutes. Ashley was easy to talk to and had a nice energy about her. I could see why she had so many friends.

Ashley was very articulate and mature. She just seemed wise beyond her years. She seemed more grounded than other girls her age and tried to avoid drama in her social relationships. She was clearly very goal-oriented. I had a sense that these qualities that made her special could also make it difficult for her to handle failure or times when she felt like she wasn't performing at her best.

After a half hour, I asked her mother to join us. The first thing I noticed was how put together Sarah was. She had on a beautiful fuchsia silk scarf that made her blue eyes shine.

"I've had such a nice time talking to Ashley today."

Sarah chuckled.

"Ashley doesn't know why she's here," I said. "Why do you feel like she needed to come see me?"

"Yeah, Mom," Ashley chimed in. "Why did you want me to come here?"

"She just seems like a bit of a perfectionist." Sarah settled more into her chair and crossed her arms over her chest. "I guess she is getting older. Maybe it's all hormonal?"

"Why do you think that Ashley is a perfectionist?"

I soon learned that Ashley was getting up at five o'clock in the morning when she didn't have to leave for school until seven. She would make her bed perfectly, then shower and get ready. "It takes her an hour to do her hair and makeup," Sarah said. "She's twelve years old. What could be taking that long?" She would also try on several outfits before settling on one and check her backpack three times to make sure her homework was packed before heading down to the kitchen. There, she would eat the same breakfast of yogurt and banana every morning before hovering over her mom while she made her lunch to make sure Sarah packed only the foods that she liked. "She's very into healthy foods, which is great," Sarah said. "But she literally reads the label of everything I put in her lunch bag. It takes forever to get through the morning."

Sarah inched up toward the edge of her chair. "And she has to get everywhere early or she freaks out. We have to leave for school fifteen minutes early every day."

"That's only because you're always late." Ashley turned to look at her mom. "Dad's not late all the time."

"We weren't late coming here," Sarah snapped back at her daughter.

"Actually, we walked in right at four o'clock. Our appointment was supposed to start at four o'clock. I was sitting in the car in the driveway for fifteen minutes, waiting for you to come out of the house."

Sarah rubbed her temples and looked at me. "This is what I mean."

Over the next several months, I learned more about Ashley. She wasn't only perfectionistic; she was also anxious. She stopped eating in restaurants when she was eight years old. "She needs to know everything that goes into her food and who made it," Sarah explained.

"Bella's mom read some book about what *actually* goes into our food and it's totally gross. There could be rat poop in there. *Yech.*" Ashley cringed in her chair.

Sarah rolled her eyes.

Ashley also asked Sarah to get her teacher's assignment list early so she could have extra time to work on big projects. Everything she turned in had to be just right. "She checks every assignment at least four times before handing it in," Sarah explained.

"Kind of like how you go over your housewish lists for clients a hundred times," Ashley shot back.

"That's work," Sarah snapped. "It's different.

"She also seems to be getting harder and harder on herself as she gets older. It's not enough for her to get an 'A.' She needs the 'A plus.' It's not enough for her to start on the basketball team. She needs to be the lead scorer. It just seems like a lot of self-imposed pressure for a kid her age."

It was clear to me that Ashley was a child with anxiety. I would love to say that she was the only anxious child I ever saw, but that's far from true. I had one young girl who changed all the clocks in her house so she wouldn't be late. Another client melted down because her parents bought the wrong shade of blue poster board for a school project.

One of my kids shows some of these anxious traits as well. My child gets stressed out when we are late, is highly sensitive about being embarrassed and doesn't like when their personal belongings are moved without asking. I try techniques like showing them the time on the kitchen clock and reminding them to breathe, but it doesn't always help. I understand how challenging it is to be the parent of a child who can be anxious at times.

The National Institute of Mental Health (NIMH) found that 25 percent of thirteen- to eighteen-year-old kids have an anxiety disorder. This is considered an epidemic in our country. I know from my own practice that this is so prevalent that we talk about how we could change our name to the Childhood Anxiety Center. Symptoms of anxiety are often physical, so kids can have heart palpitations, trouble breathing, and upset stomach. They also suffer with racing thoughts and constant worry. The psychological community believes that there are a variety of factors that can cause anxiety in kids, including poor sleep, over-scheduling, and genetic factors.

Back in my office, Sarah and Ashley continued their mother-daughter banter. "She doesn't shower often enough," Sarah told me during one session. She yawned and rubbed her eyes.

"How often does Ashley shower?" I asked.

"Once a day." Sarah leaned over and pulled a candy bar from her bag. "Sorry," she said. "I just need a little energy today."

I shifted in my chair.

"That's normal, Mom! None of my friends shower the second they get home from school," Ashley said, defensively. "Most people don't shower twice a day like you do."

For her real estate business, Sarah spent a lot of her days rushing around between different showings and closings and then some evenings meeting with clients in their homes. Her husband was helpful when he was home, but he commuted an hour each way to his office. "If one of the kids gets sick, or something unexpected pops up," Sarah explained, "it's all on me. He said that he would talk to his partner about cutting down on his office hours, but I just don't think that's necessary."

Sarah also volunteered to help decorate her kids' school for dances and for special holidays, so every few weeks she had to cram in planning and shopping for the school into her schedule. And she made it a point to be at all of Ashley's basketball practices and games as well as her son's hockey games. "I don't remember a time when my mom wasn't rushing," Ashley told me. "She's always yelling at me and my brother that she's going to be late for something." At this, Sarah chuckled and nodded her head in agreement.

Sarah was also very protective of her kids. She never let Ashley have any social media. "Who knows who she could be talking to out there," Sarah told me in one session. "There are so many crazies in the world today."

"She has never trusted me," Ashley shot back. "It's so annoying. All my friends are on Instagram and Snapchat and all I have is texting. No one really texts anymore." Ashley shook her head. "I don't understand why I can't snap when she's on Facebook all the time."

"When you're thirty-eight years old, you can look at all the social media you want," Sarah snapped at her. She took a deep breath and looked back at me. "I can't handle the stress of this Internet stuff either. I'm not around all the time to monitor what she's looking at and doing on there. And my husband has his patients to take care of. Neither of us can watch over her while she's on the Internet, so we decided together that she's not allowed to use the home computer unless one of us is with her. End of story."

I hear these complaints from both parents and kids around social media usage in almost every session—regardless of what issue brought the client in to see me. There are always disagreements over how many hours the children can be on social media, what time at night they need to turn off their phone, and at what age they should get their own social media account. Most parents feel lost navigating this new world of social media for their kids. They don't know yet what is safe and what's not. I hear a lot about parents signing their kids up for Cyber Civics classes at their kids' school. Whether their kids are trustworthy or not, most parents are more concerned with the people that their children might come to interact with online. There's just no way of knowing who these people really are.

Sarah would also call home to remind the kids to lock the front door if she and her husband were out, and she made them lock their doors as soon as they got into the car. "Our car doors lock automatically, but Mom makes us lock them ourselves anyway," Ashley told me. "She is super wound up."

"All the women are like this in my family. We're just nervous nellies." Sarah shifted in her chair. "I remember my mom not even leaving her bed for three months when I was sixteen." Sarah waved her hand as if to blow off the significance of that last comment. "I guess I got a little worse after I had my son. And then I dipped again after Ashley. It's just stressful to work and to have two kids. But I guess other moms are this way too . . ." She trailed off, shaking her head.

Sarah stayed up late cleaning the kitchen and bathrooms. "I'm a night owl," she explained. "What else should I do while I'm up? Watch some silly television show? At least cleaning is productive." She paused. "I keep a very clean house, but I'm hardly sick, so I'm doing something right." Ashley rolled her eyes. She didn't know that her mom relied on Ambien every night to fall asleep after she was done cleaning.

This is not as uncommon a story as you might think. One time, while I was away for a women's retreat, one of the women in the group shared that she spent many nights awake with racing thoughts. She would sometimes clean her house and arrange her closets and clothes because she didn't know what else to do with her time.

As Ashley settled into her first year of middle school, she had a lot of adjustments with the increased and harder schoolwork in addition to her entering puberty, which set her moods on a kind of emotional roller coaster. Also, friends who used to be predictable would now snub her for no apparent reason. Ashley struggled to understand why some girls would be friends with her one day and not the next, which is normal social behavior for this age. Because Ashley was predisposed to anxiety, though—which I had learned about through her childhood worries and need to be perfect—she was now triggered even more.

Over the next few months, Ashley's tween perfectionist mode took a turn—as if she hit a wall and was now sliding backwards. She started complaining of headaches and didn't want to get out of bed in the morning. Sarah now had to pull the comforter off Ashley, too. "I'm just tired," Ashley explained in our sessions. She also started falling asleep while doing her homework at night.

She would cry almost every morning while trying to pick out her outfit. "I just can't decide anymore," she told me. Sarah started laying clothes out for her the night before to ease the morning chaos. At school, Ashley would cry before tests and quizzes, and Sarah had to ask the teachers to give her more time. "They must think I'm a complete nut," she told me. "I ask for the assignment list each month and now for extra time during tests. What's wrong with me?" Ashley's grades started to slip, but she didn't seem to care. "She didn't try out for the volleyball team because she didn't think she'd make it." Sarah shook her head. "With a kid this tall, how could she not play volleyball?"

As Ashley started to slide, I noticed Sarah struggling as well. "I had a total meltdown in the Nordstrom shoe department last night," she told me. "I had twenty minutes to get a new pair of sandals before I had to pick Ashley up from school and I just started crying. I was like some unhinged Desperate Housewife." She also told me that she had forgotten to show up at her client's closing and completely forgot her husband's birthday. She had visible bags under her eyes and yawned throughout our sessions. "She hides Red Bull in her car," Ashley told me. "What is she trying to be, sixteen again or something?"

"She barely sees her friends anymore," Sarah said about Ashley. "She used to go to the mall all the time with a ton of girls from her class."

"Bella and I text all the time," Ashley shot back at her mom.

"Do you still see your friends?" I asked Sarah.

Sarah chuckled. "I don't have time for friends. No one has time these days. It's not just me. I barely even see my husband and we live in the same house."

Ashley and Sarah were both clearly buckling under emotional strain. What was most startling to me was the mother-daughter connection. This is a pattern I am seeing more and more. I have met with other mothers and daughters who were both depressed, both had difficulty making or connecting with friends, and both had low self-esteem. I've even seen sons who were quitting sports teams and whose grades were suffering who were burned out, just like their moms. One client even declared she was having a midlife crisis at the exact same time her daughter told me she was having a teen-life crisis after a particularly busy school year that included membership in several sports teams and honors classes.

Unfortunately, the number of people impacted by mental health issues in our country is growing. According to the National Institute of Mental Health, just over 20 percent of kids between the ages of thirteen and eighteen have experienced or are currently suffering from a significant mental health illness. The Centers for Disease Control and Prevention found that between 1999 and 2014, suicide rates among girls ages ten to fourteen years old tripled. This age group experienced the biggest rate increase in suicides, rising from .5 to 1.5 per 100,000 people over this period.

In 2015, the NIMH also reported that nearly 18 percent of adults in the United States had suffered from mental illness in the past year. The World Health Organization predicts that unipolar depression will be "the second leading cause of global disability burden by 2020." Research has also surfaced that anxiety and depression are twice as common in women than in men. And, of course, mommy burnout is unique to women.

One of the things I hear a lot from women who are experiencing symptoms of anxiety, depression, and mommy burnout is that well-meaning friends and family tell them to "just go out more" or to "take a vacation." But depression, anxiety, and mommy burnout are not conditions that you snap out of. Let me make something very clear—sadness, worry, and feeling "stressed out" and tired from time to time are all normal. They become problems when they endure, when they can't be turned off no matter what is going on in your life. They become problems when they interfere with daily existence, impacting sleep, mood, fatigue, concentration, and even physical pain. Depression is not a bout of the weekend blues. An anxiety disorder is not transient worry. Mommy burnout is not a single stressful event or feeling sluggish one afternoon.

I also want to stress that depression, anxiety, and mommy burnout are all different. Depression and anxiety are commonly recognized mood disorders that are acknowledged in the *DSM-V*. Mommy burnout, on the other hand, is not a disorder commonly recognized by the psychological community. Mommy burnout also differs from these issues because depression and anxiety often have genetic factors (in addition to environmental components). Some people are just wired for depression or anxiety. Mommy burnout stems only from environmental factors and it can be reversed with lifestyle changes alone, such as increased social supports and more self-care. There is no pill for mommy burnout, whereas depression and anxiety may require medication in addition to therapy.

We know that mommy burnout is unique to women because of the way our bodies respond to oxytocin, nudging us to "tend and befriend." Mommy burnout surfaces when this natural response gets thwarted and we misdirect our natural tendency to take care of our kids and to reach out to other women for social support, and thus our stress levels continue to climb. But why are depression and anxiety, which can often be intertwined with mommy burnout, more common in women? The answer lies in psychological, hormonal, and social factors.

As women move through different phases in their life—from puberty to pregnancy and then menopause—their hormones fluctuate. These hormone shifts can cause fatigue, headaches, and cramps and can even be the culprit for depressive and anxious symptoms. And while these symptoms may sound common, you should not ignore them. It's important to ask your primary care physician, gynecologist, or therapist for help. The CDC reports that depression occurs most frequently in women ages forty to fifty-nine, which is interesting as this is the age window when women are well into their child-rearing and (perhaps) work obligations, in addition to experiencing hormonal fluctuations with the earliest stages of menopause.

Psychological factors are also at play. We women tend to ruminate on what's distressing us rather than what we can do about it, meaning that we incessantly spin these negative thoughts through our heads repeatedly, which feeds depression and anxiety symptoms. When a woman does not have anyone to talk to, she loses the advantages gained from her natural instincts to talk about her worries, which perpetuates ruminations.

We are also prone to carry the emotional burdens of our family, work, and relationships. We tend to think about and worry about our children and careers in ways that are different from men's. Men seem to be able to distract themselves and turn these thoughts off. We just cannot. The key is knowing what you are experiencing—when your stress has become burnout, and the difference between feelings of burnout and actual depression and anxiety. Not every mom who is burned out is depressed or suffering from anxiety, but so many times, this is the diagnosis our doctors give us. If you really have slipped into depression or are suffering from anxiety disorder, medication may be the only way to stabilize your moods. But burnout can't be fixed with medication—it requires a shift in thinking and lifestyle.

When to Seek Professional Help

Yes, some women can alleviate their mommy burnout by rebuilding a community of friends and confidants and taking more time for self-care, but sometimes mommy burnout stretches into clinical depression or anxiety, requiring medical attention.

Many times, doctors diagnose an issue and prescribe medication. But pills are only 50 percent of the treatment plan, in my opinion. Today, the medical community is getting better at taking a 360-degree approach to treatment, suggesting talk therapy in addition to other positive activities.

First, however, it is paramount that you identify your symptoms—and seek professional care if you need it.

Are You Stressed or Are You Depressed?

- When thinking about friends and activities that you enjoy, if you feel that you are simply "too busy" to keep up with your social life, but that you still have a desire to connect and participate, you are probably *stressed*.

- If you find yourself consistently blowing off invitations that you have historically enjoyed, or leaving phone texts or emails unanswered, you could be *depressed*.

- Do you feel frustrated about certain issues in your life, such as wanting to lose those last ten pounds, but keep trying? Do you try different strategies, knowing that persistence will get you to your goal? If so, you are probably *stressed*.

- Do you no longer care about working toward your goals because you don't believe that you'll ever achieve them? Do you think or say, "I hate the way I look but I just don't care about my weight," or "The way I look doesn't matter to anyone, anyway"? Do you abandon your goals completely? You could be *depressed*.

- If you have a hard time falling asleep, or you wake up in the middle of the night with your mind racing about some specific stressor, then you are probably *stressed*.

- If you feel generally fried or tired, you're *stressed*.

- If you have become accustomed to your lack of sleep and energy as your normal state, or you say things like

"I just never sleep" because you can't remember the last time you felt energized or well-rested, then you are likely *depressed*.

- If your sleep and/or energy levels have been negatively affected for more than two weeks, you might be *depressed*.

- Do you feel tired much of the day? Do you struggle to get out of bed in the morning? Do you fantasize about being able to sleep all the time? Do you spend your day looking for windows when you can get back into bed? If so, you might be *depressed*.

- Can you compartmentalize your issues? Can you put aside your stresses for periods throughout the day and enjoy what you are doing? If so, you are probably *stressed*.

- If you can pinpoint the source of your irritability, such as an upcoming public speaking engagement, you are most likely *stressed*.

- If you find yourself easily agitated and snapping at people, you have close to zero patience for your kids or your spouse, and everything seems to bother you, you are most likely *depressed*.

- Are the people in your life walking on eggshells around you, for fear of upsetting you? If so, you are probably *depressed*.

- Do you over- or under-eat for a short period of time, with no real change in your weight, clothing size, or health? These are symptoms of feeling *stressed*.

- Are you consistently over- or under-eating, causing you to gain or lose a significant amount of weight? These are symptoms of feeling *depressed*.

Other Signs of Depression

- You are particularly hard on yourself.

- You engage in reckless behavior, such as drinking heavily or doing recreational drugs. You may seek to escape your family and responsibilities.

- You seek out a new social group as you prefer to be around people who don't know your issues, so you can pretend to be someone else.

- You experience problems with your attention and concentration. You can no longer track topics in a meeting or focus on single activities.

- You experience headaches and stomachaches, suicidal thoughts or fantasies of "disappearing" permanently (versus just running away for the weekend). You find yourself thinking about what would happen if you died, such as who would take care of your kids or whether your husband would remarry, and maybe even make arrangements for your finances.

Worry versus Anxiety

- If in the last six months you have been concerned about one thing, but only occasionally, that is *worry*.

- If in the last six months you have been preoccupied with something most days of the week, most hours of the day, that may be *anxiety*.

- If you are concerned with mainly one event/life circumstance, that may be *worry*.

- If you are concerned with several events/life circumstances at the same time, that is more likely *anxiety*.

- If you experience occasional forgetfulness or irritability, that is likely *worry*.

- If you experience at least three of the following symptoms related to your concerns: trouble sitting still, fatigue, trouble concentrating, easily agitated, tight or sore muscles, or difficulty falling or staying asleep, difficulty turning off your brain, it may be *anxiety*.

- If your concern over something only mildly affects you and you can go about your days without issue, that is *worry*.

- If your worry causes you significant distress and/or interferes with your daily life, it may be *anxiety*.

- If you can find the root cause of your stress, you are most likely *worried*.

- If you can no longer pinpoint why you are worried or just can't articulate the reason, or you sometimes wake up feeling worried or feel like your worries spring up out of nowhere, then you may have *anxiety*.

Other Red Flags of Anxiety Disorder

- There is a family history of this mental illness.

- You find that you experience extreme concerns about your kids' safety that do not abate as they get older. For example, you may have been very frightened of SIDS and now you are completely preoccupied with baby-proofing your entire house.

- You find that several people in your life, from your spouse, to your friends, to your child's pediatrician, to your own doctor, frequently tell you things like, "You need to relax," "Calm down," "There's nothing to worry about," and "Everything will be fine."

Important Connection

Anxiety and depression often occur at the same time, working hand in hand, so you may find that you experience symptoms of both.

Sarah's eyes grew serious and she inched up in her chair. "It was like any other Tuesday night at our house," she started. "We were working side by side, as we always do. It's getting a little stuffy in the house now that it's spring, so Ashley pulled off her sweatshirt and took a sip of her water." Sarah paused to swallow.

I remained silent.

"'What's that on your arm?' I shouted at her." Sarah tipped her head in Ashley's direction. Ashley looked down at her lap. "I mean I knew what it was. I had read magazine articles about this. And some of my friends' daughters did the same thing. But I was just so taken aback. She's just so young." Sarah was breathing quickly as she recounted the story to me. "Isn't she too young to be cutting herself?"

I looked at Ashley.

"That was the first time." Ashley wrapped her cardigan tighter around her body.

"How often do you cut yourself now?" I asked as a fire engine roared by the window of my office.

Ashley raised her voice a little over the siren. "Not that much. It's only when I'm *really* stressed. And it kind of makes me feel better. Lots of other girls at school do this. I saw some girl doing it on a YouTube video, so I tried it too."

Sarah's mouth fell open. "When were you watching YouTube?" She looked at me with wide eyes. "This is why I never wanted her on the computer!"

"It's not like I'm trying to kill myself. It's just something I do that sometimes makes me feel better." Ashley looked at me.

"Why can't you see that this is a big problem?" Sarah's voice was getting louder.

"My mom is totally overreacting. She told my dad and now he asks to see my arms all the time. She also told the school, so now my teachers look at me weird and I have to see the school counselor and they want me to tell them who else is doing this."

"I understand that this is a hard position for you to be in, but those girls are in just as much pain as you are," I told her.

"I hate that she checks my body every day." Ashley started to cry in my office. "It's so embarrassing." She looked at her mother next to her. "Why can't you ever trust me?"

Sarah sat back in her chair and shook her head no.

It was clear to me that both mother and daughter were suffering. For years, I have observed a group of very specific symptoms that had no clear diagnosis. Sure, there were elements of depression. There were also elements of anxiety. But these moms—and sometimes their daughters—didn't fall squarely into those buckets. Much like Betty Friedan's *Feminine Mystique* from all those years ago, I found myself treating a condition that had no name. Now, I know it's mommy burnout, and that their daughters are feeling the effects of their mother's pain.

What has become a familiar pattern for me is one of complete over-exhaustion. These moms (and sometimes their kids) talk about forgetting things. They have lost their enthusiasm for activities that were once significant to them. "I used to love running in marathons," one mom told me. "Now I don't even have enough energy or will to walk around the track a few times." Other moms fall into a puddle of their own tears because they can't keep up with the reading for their monthly book club. They will have fun and laugh at the occasional girls' night out or a date night with their husband, but then they return home and become shells of themselves. Their physical and emotional exhaustion holds them hostage. "I just don't see a way out," they tell me. "It's not like the bills are going to stop coming in or life is going to get any easier. If anything, the older my kids get, the harder it is."

"I want the best for my kid," "I want my kid to be happy." These are two sentences I hear all the time from burned-out moms. And, on the surface, they seem so heartfelt. But, to make kids happy, a lot of things need to happen. Kids need to learn how to handle adversity. They need to know their limits and boundaries. They need to hear the word "no." They need their parents to guide them through their challenges, not fix their challenges for them to make their lives "easier."

But today, these things aren't always happening. Instead, moms are over-tending to their children. They are calling me to schedule a therapy appointment for their children about their divorce before they even tell them. I often tell these moms to first see how their kids react to the news. Not every child whose parents get a divorce needs therapy. Other moms call me because they are concerned that their kids have no friends. But when I ask if *they* are in touch with their friends, they tell me that they have no time. They call me because their toddler is hyper and unfocused. Yet when we talk about their kid's stage of development, they realize that their expectations were unrealistic.

I had one mom who brought her three-year-old in to see me because she wasn't completing her worksheets correctly in preschool. She was putting squares around the answers instead of circles. At first, this mother was convinced that something was horribly wrong with her child. She was almost in tears when she called me to make the appointment. After we all met, she realized that her daughter was just being three.

I feel like some very well-intentioned moms are looking for an issue so that they can solve their kids' problem before it even manifests. As moms continue to "do it all for their kids" and unravel in the process, what happens to their kids? As you've seen from the client stories in this book, kids assume that they aren't their mom's priority because they are constantly told to hold on and wait. They are anxious about their mom showing up late, forgetting things, or even bursting into tears because she is so overwhelmed. Kids even feel like they need to manage their mothers. Our kids learn unhealthy ways to cope with stress, either by over- or under-eating, snapping at people, or over-consuming the empty calories of social media. Moms can't give their kids something that they don't have themselves. When mothers learn more effective ways to manage their stress, they can then pass these strategies along to their kids.

I see burned-out kids who follow their mom's lead and over-schedule themselves. They ensconce themselves in their screens, either to connect to other people, disconnect from those around them, or calm themselves down. They are losing their natural stress relievers of free and messy play because moms today don't see the value in it. "That's not stimulating enough for my kid," moms tell me while cramming math camp and fencing lessons in after school. And that's just in one afternoon! I tell clients all the time to stop trying to be, do, or buy "the best" for their kids. Just be present with them. *You* are what they need. You are enough.

Is Your Child Showing Signs of Burnout??

If Your Daughter...

- Doesn't want to go to school

- Is exhausted most mornings

- Cries over doing homework

- Says things like, "I just can't do this" or "I just don't get it"

- Takes everything personally, shows signs of low self-esteem

- Faces competition by wanting to quit rather than try harder

- Fears making mistakes and so avoids risk

- Has a hard time relaxing

- Reaches for unhealthy food, maybe even sneaks it

- Stays up late studying or on social media

- Often complains of headaches and stomachaches

- Recently had a decline in her grades

- Has trouble sleeping

- Changed her eating habits

- Shows excessive crankiness or mood shifts

- Has problems with friends (Even though "drama" is often associated with female friendships, avoid using that term, as it minimizes the social stress that many girls experience.)

If Your Son . . .

- Says things like school is stupid or boring

- Gets angry at his favorite sports team when it loses

- Is drawn to video games or television as an outlet for stress

- Fears making mistakes, so avoids risk

- Is reckless to the point of self-sabotage

- Reaches for unhealthy food, maybe even sneaks it

- Stays up late studying or on social media

- Often complains of headaches and stomachaches

- Recently had a decline in his grades

- Has trouble sleeping

- Changed his eating habits

- Shows excessive crankiness or mood shifts

- Has problems with friends, often around rejection and not fitting in

- Has trouble prioritizing his work and chores

I requested a one-on-one with Sarah after we discovered that Ashley was cutting. Sarah was already crying when she sat down.

"Ashley looks up to you," I began. "You are the most influential person in her life. Can't you see that she is mirroring a lot of your angst?" I paused. "The angst of a twelve-year-old looks different in practice from that of a thirty-eight-year-old, but you are both suffering."

"So, are you saying that Ashley's cutting is *my* fault?"

"I am saying that Ashley has learned some unhealthy ways of managing her feelings of overwhelm. She puts a lot of pressure on herself and is also very sensitive to the pressure around her— from coaches and teachers and even you and your husband. You are all well-intentioned, but all this pressure is driving her to succeed at any cost. And, clearly, the cost is now dangerous for her." I paused.

Cutting is something that I see quite often in my office. A 2012 study published in *Child and Adolescent Psychiatry and Mental Health* on non-suicidal self-injury (NSSI)—a category in which cutting is included—reported prevalence rates between 7.5 percent and 23 percent among preadolescents and adolescents. It's become an almost socially acceptable way among kids—both boys and girls—to express pain and emotion. This is something that I'm also seeing in younger and younger kids—I have seen children as young as ten years old who are cutting. There is also a high correlation between cutting and eating disorders, which can sometimes overlap with depression and anxiety.

"She's also picking up on some of the ways that you deal with stress. When you get overwhelmed, you can take a drive. Or work more. Or have a drink. Or take your Ambien at night. She can't do any of those things, so cutting has become a desperate option for her."

Sarah nodded.

"And this issue will most likely impact Ashley's own kids in the future, much like your mother's issues did for you all those years ago. If you begin to change the way you deal with stress, Ashley will try to find new strategies."

"So now what?"

"You are both living in a chronic state of stress. We should focus on reducing your baseline stress by looking at the expectations that you have for yourselves, and readjusting them. Right now, Ashley is living with the belief that she needs to be the best. And we must stop fueling that. There are belief systems that you will have to stop fueling also to make room for healthier ideas."

Sarah nodded her head in agreement.

"If you value your family first. If you want your life filled with supportive friends. If you want health to be important to your kids, then your own actions need to support those priorities." I paused. "So, how do you do that? You need to ask for help from your community. You need to talk to your girlfriends on the phone and in person. You need to let your husband help you. You need to be vulnerable with the people in your life and admit that life isn't the beautiful picture you have worked so hard to portray. And you need to stop telling yourself that you're too *busy* for all of this." I paused again. "You need to slow down and stop multitasking. You need to get off your screen. You need to stop 'flighting' from your stress by cleaning for two hours every night before you pop an Ambien. Instead of striving to be the best mom, strive to be the mom that your child needs. And know that sometimes life will be messy. And that's okay."

As I was talking to Sarah, I remembered a moment from the week before with my own daughter. I had watched a video online that taught how to make a clean and tight bun. When I tried out what I learned the next day for my daughter's gymnastics meet, I totally nailed it. This bun was perfect.

As I was patting myself on the back, my daughter said, "Wow, you actually did it. This looks good."

"You don't think I can do anything, do you?" I laughed and gave her a little pinch.

"Not really," she said, laughing.

I was so happy with her answer. She knows I love her. And she knows that I make mistakes. Lots of them. Remember when I forgot to order pizza for her birthday party?

One of the things that helps guide me as a therapist and as a parent is remembering the legacy that I want to leave for my kids. Part of the legacy that I'm leaving for my children is to show them that mistakes are a part of life. And that after I fail at something, I just try again. That I learn from my mistakes. And can laugh at most of them.

I sat forward in my chair and waited a moment for Sarah to absorb what I had said. "How would you like your kids to remember you?" I asked her. "What do you want your kids to say about you after you're gone?"

Sarah's eyes brightened.

"What is the legacy that you want to leave for *your* child?"

Mommy Burnout Prescription Plan

Create a Healthy Vision for Your Family

Cut down on activities, obligations, and commitments. Prioritize your plans with your family and those closest to you. You don't need to accept every invitation, only those that you are truly excited about.

Have family downtime in addition to "mandated" individual alone time for yourself. Plan enough time for yourself and your family **that doesn't involve screens.** Encourage family dinners, family movie nights, and different seasonal activities that you can do together, like apple picking in the fall, ice skating in the winter, visiting a local garden in the spring, and enjoying an afternoon at the local pool club in the summer. Also, carve out time for yourself to take walks and naps, listen to music, and write in a journal.

Laugh. Laughter is good for your health, especially when shared with someone else. Watch silly videos as a family, read funny books and discuss your favorite parts, and go to comedy shows together.

Contribute to your community. Giving feels good. Volunteer at your local food drive, bring toys to a children's hospital, and participate in marathons that raise money for different causes.

Set healthy boundaries at home and work. Do your work at work and be with your family at home. If you really need to blend the two, set time limits. Take ninety minutes to work each day on the weekends and forty-five minutes a day at work to make appointments for family members or sign your kids up online for activities.

Stop multitasking and monotask. Don't allow yourself to slip back into doing multiple things at once. Before you go grocery shopping, take fifteen minutes to clip your coupons so that when you get to the store, you can focus on moving through the aisles and getting what you need. When you are doing your work, turn off alerts on your phone and put your phone on silent so you are not tempted to check it every time you hear a ding. Your brain will be much happier and you will be more productive.

Put your oxygen mask on first. Get at least eight hours of sleep, find at least five minutes (hopefully more!) every day to break away and just be by yourself in silence, practice deep breathing when you feel your stress levels rising, and maintain a healthy exercise regimen. If you don't bring your stress levels down, your kids will suffer for it.

Ban the word "busy." Set boundaries around your time so you only accept social invitations that bring you joy and that are healthy for you and your family. Look at your calendar every week and find at least one hour to do something just for you, whether that's getting your nails done or going on a nature walk by yourself. You are not too busy to take care of yourself.

Leave room and space for boredom and unstructured time in your life and your kids' lives. Enjoy the creativity that this will bring to the surface. You may be surprised at the art projects, baking ideas, and new games that you all come up with. Free play is healthy for everyone.

BONUS EXERCISE

Plan your family legacy. Sit down with your family and discuss what all of you would like your family legacy to be. What would you like your family to be known for and what steps can you take to make that happen?

#momlife for a New Age

Mommy burnout is not new. Moms have been burned out for generations. We've laughed about tired, harried moms for decades. Comic strips, sitcoms, blogs, Internet memes, and even movies give women the opportunity to bond, through laughter, over the difficulties around the motherhood experience. What has changed in recent years is that with the advent of social media, more research on exhaustion and stress, and an increase in mental health diagnoses, it is not enough to laugh. Sure, all the depictions in popular culture give light to our situation, but as the situation has changed, and become more extreme, the time has come to act. Laughing feels good, but it doesn't give moms the tools they need to STOP and learn how to feel better. And it is important to stop mommy burnout—for ourselves, our partners, our children, our whole families, and families in the future.

The good news is that we *can* do something. We can put an end to the sense of isolation and being overwhelmed that we feel, that our mothers felt and their mothers felt before them. The cure to mommy burnout isn't medication, or even therapy (though, in some instances, therapy can be helpful). The cure, in the most basic sense, is us. We moms must come together. We must understand that we *all* love our kids. We *all* want the best for our families. And, to some degree, we are *all* also suffering. And mostly in silence. So, let's change this picture. Let's get talking!!!

In addition to the book club meetings and glasses of wine you feel guilty about grabbing with your gals, pull together a few mommy friends and carve out Mommy Burnout moments where you do something together and just for yourselves. Create monthly Mommy Movement forums to discuss your struggles in motherhood, or grab a few colleagues and open a new dialogue at your workplace around flexible scheduling. Make a pact with other moms in your social circle to be more conscious about your social media posts. Print up "No More Mommy Burnout" and "Let's Be Mom Friends" T-shirts. Tag your social media with #mommyburnoutmoment (for those "real" family moments when your kids are freaking out or you are looking at a sink full of dishes at 10:00 p.m.), #banbusyasabadgeofhonor, #mommyburnoutmovement, and #buildingmyvillagemommyburnout. Let's use the technology and social media that can make us feel "less than" to make us feel part of one big mommy army. United, we can make real change.

Reach out to the moms you know and ask them how they are doing, *really*. Use the tools you've learned in this book to ask for help—and *do not* feel bad about it. Dig deep and find that extra ounce of energy to join your girlfriends for a girls' night out when you are invited. You'll come home more energized than when you left, trust me. And make some time for yourself, whether that's creating an hour every day when you are truly "unplugged," connecting with an old girlfriend, or being fully present with your kids—because all these things feel good.

I've been treating mommy burnout for years, and one thing I know for sure is that it can get better, and even get gone!

#momlife can mean happiness for you, and everyone.

Acknowledgments

It seems impossible to think that I could thank every person who had a hand in making this dream of writing a book a reality.

My cowriter, Emily Klein, has been my better half on this book. You and I were meant to work with each other and you were meant to help give birth to the words on every page. You are the closest thing to a superhuman that I have ever known, and I am in awe of you. Working with you on this project has felt like a blessed partnership in which I have gotten to witness your intelligence, strength, and resiliency. Thank you for your tireless commitment.

My agent, Yfat Reiss Gendell, at Foundry Literary + Media, saw the potential in what I had written and for that I am grateful. The proposal that you received needed work, and instead of turning me away or simply saying it wasn't ready, you said yes. You have been by my side every step of the way, you took a chance on me and you were the mastermind in identifying that what I was talking about was mommy burnout. The day I signed with you, I knew that this book was actually going to happen, and I am incredibly thankful.

My editor, Carrie Thornton, understood this project right away. You took a risk on an idea and have given me creative freedom, unconditional support, and encouragement for which I don't actually know how to thank you. I am profoundly grateful for your vision, commitment, and passion. You have treated me with enormous kindness in multiple ways and I pinch myself every day that I get to work with you.

My book coach, Melanie Gorman, has been with me from the creation of the proposal right here to the finish line in many roles. You have been a coach, a mentor, and are one of the smartest women in my life. Thank you for making everything I gave you even better. There were many times where your ability to articulate what I was saying gave me the encouragement to keep improving. Thank you for the work you do in empowering others to achieve their goals.

To the incredible team at Dey Street including Lynn Grady, Liate Stehlik, Sean Newcott, Kelly Rudolph, Kaitlyn Kennedy, Ben Steinberg, Kell Wilson, Imani Gary, and Jeanne Reina. Thank you for all that you did behind the scenes to make this book come to life.

And thank you to Jessica Felleman, Sara DeNobrega, Kirsten Neuhaus, Richie Kern, Colette Grecco, Heidi Gall, and Molly Gendell at Foundry, as well as Deirdre Smerillo, Hayley Burdett, and Melissa Moorehead at Smerillo Associates. I have a newfound appreciation for all that is involved in getting a book published. Thank you for all you've done to make this happen.

My friend and attorney, David Ratner, thank you for your wise advice and looking out for me on this and multiple projects together.

My forum experience with Entrepreneur Organization (EO) opened up my mind as well as doors for me. To all my previous spousal forum mates, thank you for believing in me and being great listening ears. To Colin Collard, you had an unrelenting belief in me that I did not even see at the time, and which has stuck with me all these years. After years in EO, it was ultimately Laura Love, a rockstar mother and leader in her own right, who suggested that I speak with her friend, international bestselling author Rebecca Rosen, who introduced me to her agent, Yfat. To this day, I have never met Rebecca in person, but when I do I will surely give her a big hug. Laura and Rebecca are both great models of women supporting other women and for that I owe you both a debt of gratitude.

My friends, some of whom I have known for more than thirty years, have brought me so much comfort throughout this time. The question "How's the book coming along?" is one that I have been asked many times. Kirsten, Allison, and Laura you have listened to my motherhood stories and have shared your mothering journeys with me for a very long time. I would be lost without each of you and I love you. And for the friends in Colorado who have supported me in many ways, you have all had a hand in this project and I thank you.

My clients—I've dedicated this book to you because without you I could never have authentically written this collection of stories. You have each helped me be a better therapist, an awakened human being, and a better mother. You have provided me the gift of your true selves so that I could help other women, and for that I am humbled. More times than you will ever know you have been wiser, braver, and more vulnerable than I could ever be.

My mother, who told me that I could do anything, be anyone, and go anywhere, thank you for never placing limits on my dreams. And to my grandparents, Mima and Papa, thank you for being role models of living the American Dream. I wish that Papa were still here. I know he would be proud.

My husband, Steve, you have given me the ultimate gift of becoming a mother and that is the greatest privilege of my life. You have been my biggest supporter, and I know that without you this road would look very different. Thank you for dreaming bigger than me and for the countless hours that you put into keeping our family afloat, so I could do my work. I am forever grateful, and I love you.

My three children, Isabella, Hazen, and Hudson, are my greatest teachers. Every day you challenge me, surprise me, and inspire me to be a better mother. Without you, I would have no idea that I could love so much. I would also have never known the other side of motherhood, the one that has me staying up late nights, worrying, exhausted, and reflecting if I did right by you. I hope more times than not, I have. I love you each very much.

Notes

Chapter 1: Why Am I So Overwhelmed? What Mommy Burnout Looks Like

13   **a UCLA study that was published in 2000:** Shelley E. Taylor et al., "Biobehavioral Responses to Stress in Females: Tend-and-Befriend, Not Fight-or-Flight," *Psychological Review* 107, no. 3 (2000): 411–429, DOI: 10.1037//0033-295X.107.3.411.

14   **You feel the effects of oxytocin:** Navneet Magon and Sanjay Kalra, "The Orgasmic History of Oxytocin: Love, Lust, and Labor," *Indian Journal of Endocrinology and Metabolism* 15, no. 7 (2011): 156–161, published online September 13, 2011, DOI: 10.4103/2230-8210.8485; Maureen Salamon, "11 Interesting Effects of Oxytocin," *Live Science*, December 3, 2010, http://www.livescience.com/35219-11-effects-of-oxytocin.html.

14   **"When it is operating during times of low stress, oxytocin":** Tori DeAngelis, "The Two Faces of Oxytocin: Why Does the 'Tend and Befriend' Hormone Come Into Play at the Best and Worst of Times?" *Monitor on Psychology* 39, no. 2 (2008): 30, http://www.apa.org/monitor/feb08/oxytocin.aspx.

19   **Acute stress, which is the stress:** "Stress," University of Maryland Medical Center, last reviewed on January 30, 2013, http://umm.edu/health/medical/reports/articles/stress.

20   **If you're a fighter:** Leon F. Seltzer, PhD, "Trauma and the Freeze Response: Good, Bad or Both?" *Psychology Today,* July 8, 2015, https://www.psychologytoday.com/blog/evolution-the-self /201507/trauma-and-the-freeze-response-good-bad-or-both.

20   **A cascade of hormones:** "Stress Management," The Mayo Clinic, April 21, 2016, http://www.mayoclinic.org/healthy-life style/stress-management/in-depth/stress/art-20046037.

20   **heart rate increases, you get a sudden burst of energy:** "Understanding the Stress Response," Harvard Health Publishing, last updated March 18, 2016, http://www.health.harvard.edu /staying-healthy/understanding-the-stress-response.

20   **or you may even vomit:** Jim Folk and Marilyn Folk, BScN, "Nausea, Vomiting Anxiety Symptoms," *anxietycentre.com,* updated September 10, 2017, http://www.anxietycentre.com /anxiety-symptoms/nausea-vomiting.shtml.

20   **the parasympathetic nervous system:** "Understanding the Stress Response."

20   **slow your heart rate and gets your gut moving normally again:** Ibid.

20   **when this same stress response is triggered:** "Stress Management."

24   **Chronic stress is typically associated:** "Stress."

24   **Your hippocampus will shrink:** Mohammed Mostafizur Rahman et al., "Early Hippocampal Volume Loss as a Marker of Eventual Memory Deficits Caused by Repeated Stress," *Scientific Reports* 6, no. 29127 (2016), DOI:10.1038/srep29127.

25   **lead to memory problems, difficulty learning new things, and even more poor stress control:** Madhumita Murgia, "How Stress Affects Your Brain," YouTube video, 4:15, published by Ted-Ed, November 9, 2015, https://www.youtube

.com/watch?v=WuyPuH9ojCE[EK1]; L. Mah, C. Szabuniewicz, and A.J. Fiocco, "Can Anxiety Damage the Brain?" *Current Opinion in Psychiatry* 29, no. 1 (2016): 56–63, DOI: 10.1097/YCO.0000000000000223.

25 **Your prefrontal cortex may also get smaller:** Bruce S. McEwen et al., "Mechanisms of Stress in the Brain," *Nature Neuroscience* 18, no. 10 (2015): 1353–1363, DOI:10.1038/nn.4086.

25 **Has your judgment:** Murgia.

25 **Do you have trouble:** Amy F.T. Amsten, "Stress Signaling Pathways That Impair Prefrontal Cortex Structure and Function," *Nature Reviews Neuroscience* 10, no. 6 (2009): 410–422, DOI:10.1038/nrn2648.

25 **flips your amygdala into overdrive:** Murgia.

25 **Like Stacy, you may feel anxious:** J. Amiel Rosenkranz, Emily R. Venheim, and Mallika Padival, "Chronic Stress Causes Amygdala Hyperexcitability in Rodents," *Biological Psychiatry* 67, no. 2 (2010): 1128–1136, DOI: http://dx.doi.org/10.1016/j.biopsych.2010.02.008.

27 **I now use an informal set of criteria:** Christina Maslach, Michael Leither, and Susan E. Jackson, *The Maslach Burnout Inventory Manual: Third Edition* (Palo Alto, Calif.: Consulting Psychologists Press, 1996), file:///Users/emilyklein/Downloads/MBIchapter.97.pdf.

Chapter 2: Didn't I Used to Have Friends? The Connection Between Mommy Burnout and Isolation

39 **A 2011 study:** Matthew E. Brashears, "Small Networks and High Isolation? An Examination of American Discussion Networks," *Social Networks* 33, no. 4 (2011): 331–341, DOI: 10.1016/j.socnet.2011.10.003.

39 **"we should be less concerned about social isolation":** Jeanna Bryner, "Friends Less Common Today, Study Finds," *Live Science*, November 4, 2011, https://www.livescience.com/16879 -close-friends-decrease-today.html.

41 **A 2015 study published in *Human Nature*:** Sam B.G. Roberts and R.I.M. Dunbar, "Managing Relationship Decay: Network, Gender, and Contextual Effects," *Human Nature* 26, no. 4 (2015): 426–450, doi:10.1007/s12110-015-9242-7.

42 **It's called pagophagia:** M.S. Bhatia and Nirmaljit Kaur, "Pagophagia: A Common but Rarely Reported Form of Pica," *Journal of Clinical & Diagnostic Research* 8, no. 1 (2014): 195–196, https://www.ncbi.nlm.nih.gov/pmc/articles/PMC3939500/.

43 ***Lean In*, which talks about the gender gap in leadership roles:** Sheryl Sandberg, *Lean In: Women, Work, and the Will to Lead* (New York: Alfred A. Knopf, 2013).

56 **Keeping secrets like this:** Michael L. Slepian, Jinseok S. Chun, and Malia F. Mason, "The Experience of Secrecy," *Journal of Personality and Social Psychology* 113, no. 1 (2017): 27–28, DOI: 10.1037/pspa0000085.

56 ***The Power of Vulnerability:*** Dr. Brené Brown, *The Power of Vulnerability*, video, 20:19, *TedxHouston*, filmed June 2010, https://www.ted.com/talks/brene_brown_on_vulnerability.

56 ***Listening to Shame:*** Dr. Brené Brown, *Listening to Shame*, video, 20:38, *TED2012*, filmed March 2012, https://www.ted .com/talks/brene_brown_listening_to_shame.

57 **"For women," she said in her 2012 presentation, "shame is do it all":** Ibid.

57 **You must be vulnerable:** Ibid.

Chapter 3: I Know My Mom Is Just Trying to Help: The Difficulties of Creating a Support Network

69   **"In 2014–15, the number of children":** "Children and Youth with Disabilities," National Center for Education Statistics, last updated May 2017, https://nces.ed.gov/programs/coe/indi cator_cgg.asp.

74   **support from parents can sometimes create:** Karen L. Fingerman et al., "Help with 'Strings Attached': Offspring Perceptions that Middle Aged Parents Offer Conflicted Support," *The Journals of Gerontology: Series B* 68, no. 6 (2013): 902–911, DOI: 10.1093/geronb/gbt032.

75   **In 2012, the Clark University Poll of Emerging Adults:** Jeffrey Jensen Arnett, PhD, and Joseph Schwab, "The Clark University Poll of Emerging Adults," Clark University, December 2012, http://www2.clarku.edu/clark-poll-emerging-adults/pdfs/clark -university-poll-emerging-adults-findings.pdf.

75   **Social trends like:** Karen Fingerman, "The Ascension of Parent-Offspring Ties," *The Psychologist* 29 (February 2016): 114–117, https://thepsychologist.bps.org.uk/volume-29/february /ascension-parent-offspring-ties.

75   **boom of text, and Skype:** Ibid.

77   **A comprehensive review paper published in *ISRN*:** Harold G. Koenig, "Religion, Spirituality, and Health: The Research and Clinical Implications," *ISRN Psychiatry* 2012, no. 278730 (2012): 33 pages, DOI:10.5402/2012/278730.

84   **Since the late 1800s, studies have linked weak social ties:** S. Leonard Syme and Miranda L. Ritterman, "The Importance of Community Development for Health and Well-Being," *Community Development Investment Review* 5, no. 3 (2009): 1, 9, http://www.frbsf.org/community-development/files/cdre

view_issue3_09.pdf; Maija Reblin, MA, and Bert N. Uchino, PhD, "Social and Emotional Support and Its Implication for Health," *Current Opinion in Psychiatry* 21, no. 2 (March 2008): 201–205, DOI: 10.1097/YCO.0b013e3282f3ad89; Sidney Cobb, MD, "Social Support as a Moderator of Life Stress," *Psychosomatic Medicine* 38, no. 5 (September–October 1976): 300–314, https://campus.fsu.edu/bbcswebdav/institution/aca demic/social_sciences/sociology/Reading%20Lists/Mental%20 Health%20Readings/Cobb-PsychosomaticMed-1976.pdf.; John Cassel, "The Contribution of the Social Environment to Host Resistance," *American Journal of Epidemiology* 104, no. 2 (1976): 110, http://citeseerx.ist.psu.edu/viewdoc/download?doi =10.1.1.454.1555&rep=rep1&type=pdf.; Emile Durkheim, *Suicide, A Study in Sociology*, trans. John A. Spaulding and George Simpson, ed. George Simpson (Glencoe, Ill.: Free Press, 1951), 5, http://www.bahaistudies.net/asma/suicide-durkheim.pdf.

Chapter 4: How Many "Likes" Did I Get Today? The Social Media Mommy Trap

100 **children who have ADHD are more likely:** Margaret D. Weiss et al., "The Screens Culture: Impact on ADHD," *ADHD Attention Deficit and Hyperactivity Disorders* 3, no. 4 (December 2011): 327–334, DOI: 10.1007/s12402-011-0065-z.

101 **mothers are more likely than fathers to find parenting information:** Maeve Duggan, Amanda Lenhart, Cliff Lampe, and Nicole B. Ellison, "Parents and Social Media," Pew Research Center (July 2015): 20, file:///Users/emilyklein/Downloads /Parents-and-Social-Media-FIN-DRAFT-071515%20(1).pdf.

101 **support from their social media network:** Ibid., 17.

101 **for parenting-related issues:** Ibid., 21.

102 **you get a dopamine rush:** Aaron Mamiit, "Blame it on Do-pamine: Here's Why People Text and Drive Despite Knowing the Risks Involved," *TechTimes,* November 8, 2014, http://www .techtimes.com/articles/19689/20141108/blame-it-on-dopa mine-heres-why-people-text-and-drive-despite-being-aware -of-risks-involved.htm; Simon Sinek, interview by Tom Bilyeu, YouTube video, 14:57, *Inside Quest,* accessed October 22, 2017, https://www.youtube.com/watch?v=hER0Qp6QJNU&sns=em.

103 **A study published in the** *CSCW '16*: Moira Burke and Mike Develin, "Once More with Feeling: Supportive Responses to Social Sharing on Facebook," in *CSCW '16 Proceedings of the 19th ACM Conference on Computer-Supported Cooperative Work & Social Computing* (San Francisco: ACM, 2016) 1460–1472, DOI: org/10.1145/2818048.2835199.

109 **2009** *Psychiatry* **article:** Ronald Pies, "Should DSM-V Des-ignate 'Internet Addiction' a Mental Disorder?" *Psychiatry* 6, no. 2 (February 2009): 31–37, https://www.ncbi.nlm.nih.gov /pmc/articles/PMC2719452/.

Chapter 5: I Just Want What's Best for My Children:
How the Need to Achieve Perfection for Our Kids Adds to
Mommy Burnout

123 **there were over three thousand four-year colleges:** "Digest of Education Statistics, table 105.50," National Center for Educa-tion Statistics, 2014, https://nces.ed.gov/programs/digest/d14/ tables/dt14_105.50.asp.

126 **researchers looked at 401(k) participation:** Sheena Sethi-Iyengar, Gur Huberman, and Wei Jiang, "How Much Choice Is Too Much? Contributions to 401(k) Retirement Plans," in *Pension Design and Structure: New Lessons from Behavioral Finance,* ed. Olivia S. Mitchell and Stephen P. Utkus (Ox-

ford: Oxford University Press, 2004), 88–91, DOI: 10.1093 /0199273391.003.0005.

126 **products, like jams and chocolates**: Sheena Iyengar and Mark R. Lepper, "When Choice Is Demotivating: Can One Desire Too Much of a Good Thing?" *Journal of Personality and Social Psychology* 79, no. 6 (December 2000): 995–1006, DOI: http://dx.doi.org/10.1037/0022-3514.79.6.995.

127 **207 public schools:** "DPS by the Numbers," *Denver Public Schools,* accessed November 16, 2017, https://www.dpsk12.org /about-dps/facts-figures/.

127 **82 private schools:** "Denver County Private Schools," *Private School Review,* accessed November 16, 2017, https://www.pri vateschoolreview.com/colorado/denver-county.

127 **44.7-square-mile radius:** "Denver—the City," *hometodenver .com,* accessed October 22, 2017, http://www.hometodenver .com/stats_denver.htm.

127 **the more options people have, the greater their expectations rise:** Barry Schwartz, *The Paradox of Choice,* video, 19:34, TEDGlobal 2005, filmed 2005, https://www.ted.com/talks /barry_schwartz_on_the_paradox_of_choice?language=en.

127 **pulls up close to 400,000 diaper options:** "diapers," amazon.com, accessed November 16, 2017, https://www.amazon .com/s/ref=nb_sb_noss?url=search-alias%3Daps&field -keywords=diapers.

127 **five pages worth of chocolate chip cookies:** "chocolate chip cookies," accessed October 22, 2017, https://shop.shoprite.com /store/F442733#/search/chocolate chip cookies/3?queries=sort %3DRelevance.

128 **top-tier schools, including Harvard, endorse gap years:** William Fitzsimmons, Marlyn E. McGrath, and Charles Ducey,

"Time Out of Burn Out for the Next Generation," Harvard University, updated 2017, https://college.harvard.edu/admissions/preparing-college/should-i-take-time.

130 **our search for the best kicks into high gear:** Cassie Mogilner, Baba Shiv, and Sheena S. Iyengar, "Eternal Quest for the Best: Sequential (vs. Simultaneous) Option Presentation Undermines Choice Commitment," *Journal of Consumer Research* 39, no. 6 (April 2013): 1300–1312, DOI: 10.1086/668534.

134 **There's an opportunity cost to every choice we make:** Schwartz, "The Paradox of Choice."

Chapter 6: He Just Doesn't Get It: How Burnout Puts Our Marriages in Jeopardy

146 **fathers have more than doubled their time spent doing household chores and nearly tripled:** Kim Parker and Gretchen Livingston, "6 Facts About American Fathers," Pew Research, June 15, 2017, http://www.pewresearch.org/fact-tank/2017/06/15/fathers-day-facts/.

146 **42 percent of women reported as being the primary or sole breadwinner in their family:** Sarah Jane Glynn, "Breadwinning Mothers Are Increasingly the U.S. Norm," Center for American Progress, December 19, 2016, https://www.americanprogress.org/issues/women/reports/2016/12/19/295203/breadwinning-mothers-are-increasingly-the-u-s-norm/.

148 **mothers are more likely to acknowledge their helicopter tendencies:** "Parenting in America," Pew Research Center (December 17, 2015): 8, file:///Users/emilyklein/Downloads/2015-12-17_parenting-in-america_FINAL.pdf.

149 **Men tend to feel stress:** Laura R. Stroud, Peter Salovey, and Elissa S. Epel, "Sex Differences in Stress Responses: Social

Rejection Versus Achievement Stress," *Biological Psychiatry* 52, no. 4 (August 2002): 318–327, DOI: 10.1016/S0006-3223 (02)01333-1.

149 **We experience stress with relationships:** Ibid.

154 **recent study published in *Nature Neuroscience*:** Elseline Hoekzema et al., "Pregnancy Leads to Long-Lasting Changes in Human Brain Structure," *Nature Neuroscience* 20, no. 2 (December 2016): 287–296, DOI:10.1038/nn.4458.

154 **Teens go through a similar process:** Linda Patia Spear, PhD, "Adolescent Neurodevelopment," *Journal of Adolescent Health* 52, no. 2 (February 2013), S7–S13, DOI: http://dx.doi .org/10.1016/j.jadohealth.2012.05.006.

154 **The prevalent idea here is that this pruning:** Daniel J. Siegel, MD, "Pruning, Myelination, and the Remodeling Adolescent Brain," PsychologyToday.com, February 4, 2014, https:// www.psychologytoday.com/blog/inspire-rewire/201402 /pruning-myelination-and-the-remodeling-adolescent -brain; Clara Moskowitz, "Teen Brains Clear Out Childhood Thoughts," LiveScience.com, March 23, 2009, https://www.live science.com/3435-teen-brains-clear-childhood-thoughts .html; Hoekzema et al., 8.

154 **helping moms transition:** Hoekzema et al., 2.

Chapter 7: What the Hell Am I Doing with My Life? The Working Mom's Dilemma

174 **a family's socioeconomic status and structure play a role in how children fare:** Rachel G. Lucas-Thompson, Wendy A. Goldberg, and JoAnn Prause, "Maternal Work Early in the Lives of Children and Its Distal Associations with Achievement and Behavior Problems: A Meta-Analysis," *Psychological*

Bulletin 136, no. 6 (November 2010): 915–942, DOI: 10.1037/ a0020875.

179 **A care.com survey reported:** "Care.com Survey Finds One in Four Working Moms Cry Alone At Least Once a Week," care .com, October 23, 2014, https://www.care.com/press-release -carecom-finds-1-in-4-moms-cry-alone-once-a-week-p1186 -q49877680.html.

189 **I often recommend the book** *Man's Search for Meaning*: V. Frankl, *Man's Search for Meaning* (Boston: Beacon Press, 2006).

Chapter 8: I Just Can't Get It All Done . . . The First Step in Fighting Mommy Burnout—Ban "Busy" as a Badge of Honor

207 **"Although switch costs may be relatively small":** "Multitask-ing: Switching costs," APA.org, March 20, 2006, http://www .apa.org/research/action/multitask.aspx.

215 **According to the American Time Use Survey:** "American Time Use Survey," *United States Department of Labor,* last updated December 16, 2016, https://www.bls.gov/tus/charts /household.htm.

219 **Even the medical field isn't quite certain:** "Panic Attacks and Panic Disorder," Mayo Clinic, May 19, 2015, https://www .mayoclinic.org/diseases-conditions/panic-attacks/basics /causes/con-20020825.

219 **all of which decrease anxiety levels:** "Exercise for Stress and Anxiety," Anxiety and Depression Association of America, July 2014, https://adaa.org/living-with-anxiety/managing-anxiety /exercise-stress-and-anxiety.

Chapter 9: I'm Sick and Tired, All the Time. How Mommy Burnout Makes Us Sick

233 **Substance abuse, which is sometimes triggered by chronic stress, is a growing epidemic:** "Alcohol: A Women's Health Issue," The Office of Research on Women's Health, Office of the Director, and the National Institute on Alcohol Abuse and Alcoholism (two components of the NIH) 4956, no. 15 (updated 2015): 2, https://pubs.niaaa.nih.gov/publications/brochurewomen/Woman_English.pdf; Jen Simon, "I'm a Stay-at-Home Mom. I'm an Addict," WashingtonPost .com, June 6, 2016, https://www.washingtonpost.com/news /parenting/wp/2016/06/06/im-a-stay-at-home-mom-im-an -addict/?utm_term=.483f2a4098e3.

233 **The World Health Organization reports that:** "Gender and Women's Mental Health," World Health Organization, accessed October 23, 2016, http://www.who.int/mental_health /prevention/genderwomen/en/.

233 **A 2015 survey from the Substance Abuse Mental Health Services:** "Results from the 2015 National Survey on Drug Use and Health: Detailed Tables: Table 5.8a," Substance Abuse and Mental Health Services, Administration Center for Behavioral Health Statistics and Quality, U.S. Department of Health and Human Services, accessed October 23, 2017, https://www .samhsa.gov/data/sites/default/files/NSDUH-DetTabs-2015 /NSDUH-DetTabs-2015/NSDUH-DetTabs-2015.htm#tab5-8a.

233 **5.6 million women over the age of twenty-six misused:** Ibid., table 1-67a.

237 **renowned trauma expert Bessel van der Kolk states:** "About Dr. Bessel van der Kolk," Trauma Center and Justice Resource Institute, accessed October 23, 2017, http://www.traumacenter.org /about/about_bessel.php.

237 **The Mayo Clinic explains that persistent stress can lead to:** "Chronic Stress Puts Your Health at Risk," Mayo Clinic, April 21, 2016, https://www.mayoclinic.org/healthy-lifestyle/stress-management/in-depth/stress/art-20046037.

239 **hormonal imbalances related to estrogen:** "What Is Estrogen," Hormone Health Network, accessed October 23, 2017, http://www.hormone.org/hormones-and-health/hormones/estrogen.

239 **thyroid dysfunction:** Colin M. Dayan and Vijay Panicker, "Hypothyroidism and Depression," *European Thyroid Journal* 3, no. 2 (September 2013): 168, DOI: 10.1159/000353777; "When Depression Starts in the Neck," Harvard Health Publishing, July 2011, https://www.health.harvard.edu/newsletter_article/when-depression-starts-in-the-neck.

241 **connection between stress and health:** Kendall Powell, "Can Stress Really Make Us Sick?" WashingtonPost.com, May 5, 2014, https://www.washingtonpost.com/national/health-science/can-stress-really-make-us-sick/2014/05/05/a1af9dd2-d074-11e3-937f-d3026234b51c_story.html?utm_term=.f8dae6c26d6a.

242 **also affected by social and emotional support:** Peggy A. Thoits, "Mechanisms Linking Social Ties and Support to Physical and Mental Health," *Journal of Health and Social Behavior* 52, no. 2 (June 2011): 145–161, DOI: 10.1177/0022146510395592.

242 **people who have strong emotional support:** "Stress in America: Paying with Our Health," American Psychological Association (February 4, 2015): 7, https://www.apa.org/news/press/releases/stress/2014/stress-report.pdf; Julianne Holt-Lunstad, Timothy B. Smith, and J. Bradley Layton, "Social Relationships and Mortality Risk: A Meta-Analytic Review," *PLOS Medicine* 7, no. 7 (July 27, 2010), DOI: 10.1371/journal.pmed.1000316.

Chapter 10: Are My Kids Burned Out, Too?

253 **25 percent of thirteen- to eighteen-year-old kids have an anxiety disorder:** "Any Anxiety Disorder Among Children," National Institute of Mental Health, accessed October 23, 2017, https://www.nimh.nih.gov/health/statistics/prevalence/any -anxiety-disorder-among-children.shtml.

258 **suicide rates among girls ages ten to fourteen years old tripled:** "Data Brief 241: Increase in suicide in the United States, 1999– 2014," The Centers for Disease Control, accessed October 23, 2017, https://www.cdc.gov/nchs/data/databriefs/db241_table .pdf#2; Rae Ellen Bichell, "Suicide Rates Climb in the U.S., Especially Among Adolescent Girls," NPR.org, April 22, 2016, http:// www.npr.org/sections/health-shots/2016/04/22/474888854 /suicide-rates-climb-in-u-s-especially-among-adolescent-girls.

259 **nearly 18 percent of adults in the United States had suffered from mental illness:** Jonaki Bose et al., "Key Substance Use and Mental Health Indicators in the United States: Results from the 2015 National Survey on Drug Use and Health," Center for Behavioral Health Statistics and Quality, HHS Publication No. SMA 16-4984, NSDUH Series H-51 (2016), https://www .samhsa.gov/data/sites/default/files/NSDUH-FFR1-2015/NS DUH-FFR1-2015/NSDUH-FFR1-2015.htm#mhi01.

259 **unipolar depression will be "the second leading cause of global disability burden":** "Gender and Women's Health," World Health Organization, accessed October 23, 2017, http:// www.who.int/mental_health/prevention/genderwomen/en/.

259 **Research has also surfaced that anxiety:** "Generalized Anxiety Disorder," Anxiety and Depression Association of America, accessed October 23, 2017, https://adaa.org/understanding -anxiety/generalized-anxiety-disorder-gad.

259 **depression are twice as common:** Daniel E. Ford, MD, PMH, and Thomas P. Erlinger, MD, PMH, "Depression and C-Reactive Protein in US Adults: Data from the Third National Health and Nutrition Examination Survey," *Archives of Internal Medicine* 164, no. 9 (May 2014): 1010–1014, DOI: 10.1001/archinte.164.9.1010.

259 **Depression is not a bout of:** Sharon Toker et al., "The Association Between Burnout, Depression, Anxiety, and Inflammation Biomarkers: C-Reactive Protein and Fibrinogen in Men and Women," *Journal of Occupational Health Psychology* 10, no. 4 (2005): 356, DOI: 10.1037/1076-8998.10.4.344.

260 **As women move through different phases in their life:** Paul R. Albert, PhD, "Why Is Depression More Prevalent in Women?" *Journal of Psychiatry and Neuroscience* 40, no. 4 (July 2015): 219, DOI: 10.1503/jpn.150205.

260 **These hormone shifts can cause:** "Depression in Women," National Institute of Mental Health, no. TR 16-4779, accessed October 23, 2017, https://www.nimh.nih.gov/health/publications/depression-in-women/tr-16-4779_153310.pdf.

260 **depression occurs most frequently in women ages forty to fifty-nine:** Laura A. Pratt, PhD, and Debra J. Brody, MPH, "Depression in the U.S. Household Population—2009–2012," National Center for Health Statistics, no. 172 (December 2014): 1, https://www.cdc.gov/nchs/data/databriefs/db172.pdf.

260 **We women tend to ruminate:** "Women and Depression," Harvard Health Publishing, May 2011, https://www.health.harvard.edu/womens-health/women-and-depression.

268 **Much like Betty Friedan's** *Feminine Mystique***:** Betty Friedan, *The Feminine Mystique* (New York: W.W. Norton, 1963).

272 **A 2012 study published in** *Child and Adolescent Psychiatry and Mental Health*: Jason J. Washburn et al., "Psychothera-*Child and Adolescent Psychiatry and Mental Health* 6, no. 14 (March 30, 2012), DOI: 10.1186/1753-2000-6-14.

Index

About the Author

Dr. Sheryl Ziegler is a Doctor of Psychology and Licensed Professional Counselor in the state of Colorado and a member of the Colorado Association for Play Therapy and American Psychological Association. She lives in Denver with her husband and three children.